PROFESSIONAL SWIFT™

PROFESSIONAL

Swift™

PROFESSIONAL

Swift™

Michael Dippery

wrox™

A Wiley Brand

Professional Swift™

Published by
John Wiley & Sons, Inc.
10475 Crosspoint Boulevard
Indianapolis, IN 46256
www.wiley.com

Copyright © 2015 by John Wiley & Sons, Inc., Indianapolis, Indiana

Published simultaneously in Canada

ISBN: 978-1-119-01677-9

ISBN: 978-1-119-14872-2 (ebk)

ISBN: 978-1-119-14871-5 (ebk)

Manufactured in the United States of America

10 9 8 7 6 5 4 3 2 1

For general information on our other products and services please contact our Customer Care Department within the United States at (877) 762-2974, outside the United States at (317) 572-3993 or fax (317) 572-4002.

Wiley publishes in a variety of print and electronic formats and by print-on-demand. Some material included with standard print versions of this book may not be included in e-books or in print-on-demand. If this book refers to media such as a CD or DVD that is not included in the version you purchased, you may download this material at http://booksupport.wiley.com. For more information about Wiley products, visit www.wiley.com.

Library of Congress Control Number: 2015937849

To Jean Gold, for encouraging me to put pen to paper in the first place.

ABOUT THE AUTHOR

MICHAEL DIPPERY is a software developer for Industrial Light & Magic in San Francisco, CA. A graduate of Bucknell University's computer science program, he has also worked for SocialCode in San Francisco and *The New York Review of Books* in New York. While most of his day is spent writing Python code, he has long been fond of Objective-C. He has contributed to both the Adium and Colloquy projects on OS X and has written and released numerous open source libraries for Objective-C. When he's not working in Objective-C, Michael is just crazy enough to enjoy writing code in Haskell and Erlang. He looks forward to the potential for Swift to improve software development on iOS and OS X. Outside of programming, Michael enjoys reading, writing fiction, and taking photographs with one of his many cameras.

CREDITS

ACQUISITIONS EDITOR
Aaron Black

PROJECT EDITOR
Maureen Tullis

TECHNICAL EDITOR
Chaim Krause

PRODUCTION EDITOR
Dassi Zeidel

COPY EDITOR
Nancy Rapoport

**MANAGER OF CONTENT DEVELOPMENT
& ASSEMBLY**
Mary Beth Wakefield

MARKETING DIRECTOR
David Mayhew

MARKETING MANAGER
Carrie Sherrill

**PROFESSIONAL TECHNOLOGY & STRATEGY
DIRECTOR**
Barry Pruett

BUSINESS MANAGER
Amy Knies

ASSOCIATE PUBLISHER
Jim Minatel

PROJECT COORDINATOR, COVER
Brent Savage

PROOFREADER
Rebecca Rider

INDEXER
Johnna VanHoose Dinse

COVER DESIGNER
Wiley

COVER IMAGE
©iStock.com/OJO_Images

ACKNOWLEDGMENTS

THANKS TO MY PARENTS, STEVEN AND KIM, for never wavering in their support of my education and career, even though they've never fully understood what it is I do.

Liza Veloz, for giving me my first opportunities as both a technical writer and a programmer.

Professor Luiz Felipe Perrone, for taking me under his wing and providing valuable mentoring and friendship over the last ten years.

Mary James, for inviting me to write a book in the first place.

CONTENTS

INTRODUCTION

THE POPULARITY OF IOS has drawn many programmers to Apple's platforms. Software on both OS X and iOS has long been written in Objective-C, a language first developed in the 1980s that is best described as an amalgamation of C and Smalltalk. Objective-C lacks many features that modern programmers expect to find in a programming language. Over the last ten years, Apple has adapted and improved Objective-C, but many programmers still find it to be an alien language.

Enter Swift. Swift is a modern programming language, built with knowledge gained in the last 30 years of programming language research. Developed by the same researchers who developed clang, the modern compiler toolchain used by Apple to build OS X and iOS software, Swift incorporates many features that are expected of a modern programming language. It sports a strong type system to prevent many of the mistakes prevalent in both C and Objective-C programming. It has a refined class system complete with static and computable properties. It supports closures and treats functions as first-class objects, allowing them to easily be saved as variables or passed to functions and methods as parameters. As you read this book, you'll find many more advanced features that are present in Swift as well.

Swift has been designed from the ground up to be a modern programming language suitable for both systems and application development on Apple's platforms. Apple has already thrown a lot of support behind Swift, and the language is constantly being improved. Swift represents the future of software development on iOS and OS X, and programmers working on that platform should expect Swift to occupy an increasingly dominant position on those systems.

WHO THIS BOOK IS FOR

This book is aimed at software developers with experience writing Objective-C applications on OS X or iOS. Some knowledge and experience with Swift are recommended but are by no means necessary to understand the material presented in this book. The book introduces the key concepts of Swift that may be new even to advanced iOS and OS X programmers. Over the course of the book, several small projects are used to illustrate the concepts as they are introduced. The text also makes extensive use of playgrounds, a new feature of Xcode that allows you to write and interact with Swift code without the overhead of an entire Xcode project.

The first chapter is an overview of Swift's syntax and semantics but does not cover any advanced features of the language. The second chapter covers the use of Xcode, including playgrounds. If you already have some familiarity with Swift and Xcode, you may want to skip the first and second chapters and get started immediately with Chapter 3.

WHAT THIS BOOK COVERS

This book first offers a primer to the Swift programming language, released by Apple in June 2014. It quickly moves on to more advanced Swift programming topics, including the new playgrounds feature in Xcode; classes, structs, and enums; concurrent programming; and advanced features of Swift's type system. It also covers practical topics that you will deal with on a regular basis as a Swift programmer, including interfacing with web services using JSON, Core Data, and using C and Objective-C code in your Swift project. It shows some of the advanced features of Xcode, including the use of the debugger built in to Xcode, and discusses the lower-level details of the Swift and Objective-C runtimes. And because it is impossible to completely avoid C when writing software on OS X and iOS, an index provides a quick overview of the C programming language.

Swift has been constantly evolving since its release in June 2014. This book covers version 1.1.

Because Swift is still changing, you may find some minor differences between the version discussed in this book and the latest released version. However, the vast majority of material presented in this book will still be valid for future versions of Swift.

HOW THIS BOOK IS STRUCTURED

This book is divided into two sections. The first section provides an introduction to the Swift programming language and covers many of the more practical topics you will encounter as a Swift programmer. The second section is a "deep dive" into the intricacies of Swift.

➤ **Chapter 1:** Reviews the syntax and semantics of the Swift programming language. It is useful for those programmers who are new to the language or want a quick refresher.

➤ **Chapter 2:** Covers the Swift-related changes to Xcode. It introduces Xcode's new feature, playgrounds, which provide a way to interactively work with Swift code.

➤ **Chapter 3:** Covers Swift's classes, structs, and enums in greater detail than Chapter 1, providing a solid foundation for object-oriented programming in Swift.

➤ **Chapter 4:** Discusses concurrent programming in the context of Swift and the Foundation framework on iOS and OS X.

➤ **Chapter 5:** Shows you how to communicate with remote web services using JSON.

➤ **Chapter 6:** Discusses how to use Core Data to store and search for information used by your program.

➤ **Chapter 7:** Shows you how to extend classes using protocols and class extensions.

➤ **Chapter 8:** Covers Swift's type system in fine detail and shows you how to take advantage of Swift's strong type system to write less error-prone code.

➤ **Chapter 9:** Shows you how you can mix C and Objective-C code in your Swift programs.

➤ **Chapter 10:** Introduces the debugger and shows you how you can track down and fix problems in your code.

➤ **Chapter 11:** Discusses the runtime architecture of both Swift and Objective-C and demonstrates how programs are loaded and executed on iOS and OS X.

➤ **Appendix:** Covers the features and concepts that the C programming language introduces.

If you are already familiar with Swift and Xcode, you may want to skip Chapters 1 and 2 and start right in on Chapter 3.

WHAT YOU NEED TO USE THIS BOOK

To run the samples in the book, you will need the following:

➤ A Mac running OS X 10.9 or later

➤ Xcode 6

➤ An iPhone, iPod Touch, or iPad if you want to run the examples on an actual device instead of the iOS simulator that ships with Xcode

The source code for the samples is available for download from the Wrox website at: `www.wrox.com/go/proswift`.

CONVENTIONS

To help you get the most from the text and keep track of what's happening, this book uses a number of conventions.

> **WARNING** *Warnings hold important, not-to-be-forgotten information that is directly relevant to the surrounding text.*

> **NOTE** *Notes indicate notes, tips, hints, tricks, or asides to the current discussion.*

As for styles in the text:

➤ We *highlight* new terms and important words when we introduce them.

➤ We show keyboard strokes like this: Ctrl+A.

➤　We show file names, URLs, and code within the text like so: `persistence.properties`.

We present code in two different ways:

```
We use a monofont type with no highlighting for most code examples.
```

We use bold to emphasize code that is particularly important in the present context or to show changes from a previous code snippet.

SOURCE CODE

As you work through the examples in this book, you may choose either to type in all the code manually or to use the source code files that accompany the book. All the source code used in this book is available for download at `www.wrox.com`. Specifically for this book, the code download is on the Download Code tab at `www.wrox.com/go/proswift`.

You can also search for the book at `www.wrox.com` by ISBN (the ISBN for this book is 978-1-119-01677-9) to find the code. And a complete list of code downloads for all current Wrox books is available at `www.wrox.com/dynamic/books/download.aspx`.

At the beginning of each chapter, we've provided a list of the major code files for the chapter. Throughout each chapter, you'll also find references to the names of code files as needed in listing titles and text.

Most of the code on `www.wrox.com` is compressed in a .ZIP, .RAR, or similar archive format appropriate to the platform. Once you download the code, just decompress it with an appropriate compression tool.

> **NOTE** *Because many books have similar titles, you may find it easiest to search by ISBN; this book's ISBN is 978-1-119-01677-9.*

Once you download the code, just decompress it with your favorite compression tool. Alternately, you can go to the main Wrox code download page at `www.wrox.com/dynamic/books/download.aspx` to see the code available for this book and all other Wrox books.

ERRATA

We make every effort to ensure that there are no errors in the text or in the code. However, no one is perfect, and mistakes do occur. If you find an error in one of our books, such as a spelling mistake or faulty piece of code, we would be very grateful for your feedback. By sending in errata, you may save another reader hours of frustration, and at the same time, you will be helping us provide even higher quality information.

To find the errata page for this book, go to `www.wrox.com/go/proswift`, and click the Errata link. On this page you can view all errata that has been submitted for this book and posted by Wrox editors.

If you don't spot "your" error on the Book Errata page, go to www.wrox.com/contact/ techsupport.shtml and complete the form there to send us the error you have found. We'll check the information and, if appropriate, post a message to the book's errata page and fix the problem in subsequent editions of the book.

P2P.WROX.COM

For author and peer discussion, join the P2P forums at http://p2p.wrox.com. The forums are a Web-based system to which you can post messages relating to Wrox books and related technologies and where you can interact with other readers and technology users. The forums offer a subscription feature to e-mail you topics of interest of your choosing when new posts are made to the forums. Wrox authors, editors, other industry experts, and your fellow readers are present on these forums.

At http://p2p.wrox.com, you will find a number of different forums that will help you, not only as you read this book, but also as you develop your own applications. To join the forums, just follow these steps:

1. Go to http://p2p.wrox.com and click the Register link.

2. Read the terms of use and click Agree.

3. Complete the required information to join, as well as any optional information you wish to provide, and click Submit.

4. You will receive an e-mail with information describing how to verify your account and complete the joining process.

> **NOTE** *You can read messages in the forums without joining P2P, but in order to post your own messages, you must join.*

Once you join, you can post new messages and respond to messages other users post. You can read messages at any time on the Web. If you would like to have new messages from a particular forum e-mailed to you, click the Subscribe to this Forum icon by the forum name in the forum listing.

For more information about how to use the Wrox P2P, be sure to read the P2P FAQs for answers to questions about how the forum software works, as well as many common questions specific to P2P and Wrox books. To read the FAQs, click the FAQ link on any P2P page.

PROFESSIONAL

Swift™

PART I
Building Applications with Swift

A Swift Primer

WHAT'S IN THIS CHAPTER?

➤ Understanding Swift

➤ Declaring constants and variables and working with Swift's data types

➤ Transforming values with operators

➤ Controlling code execution with conditional statements and loops

➤ Defining and using Swift's enumerated data types

➤ Understanding, declaring, and using functions, anonymous functions, and closures

This chapter introduces the key concepts featured in the Swift programming language and covers the language's new syntax and data types. It is not intended as an introductory guide to Swift, but rather, as a way for programmers who have already worked with Swift to refresh their knowledge of the language. Prior knowledge of C and Objective-C programming on iOS and OS X is also assumed, although the information presented in this chapter should still make sense to those with no experience in C and Objective-C.

If you are already familiar with the foundations of the Swift programming language, you may want to dive right in with Chapter 2. Chapter 2 also shows you how to use Xcode's new playgrounds feature, which allows you to experiment with the effects of Swift code as you write it. The examples in this chapter can be entered directly into a playground so you can see the results of your code immediately, without having to create an Xcode project and compile the code.

WHAT IS SWIFT?

Swift is a brand-new language, developed by Apple, that is meant to offer an alternative to Objective-C for iOS and OS X development. Although it is designed to interoperate seamlessly with Objective-C, as well as C and C++, Swift is not an evolution of Objective-C, but rather an entirely new language with a much different pedigree. It drops a number of classic Objective-C language features, while introducing a host of new ones designed to make development of iOS and OS X programs safer and faster, as well as to make the development process itself more expedient.

Swift is the product of several years of development, as well as the research and insight gained from many languages that came before it. Far from being a simple improvement over Objective-C, its feature set is inspired by programming languages as diverse as Haskell, C#, Ruby, Python, and Rust. Swift also incorporates many features of the Cocoa and Cocoa Touch frameworks, such as key-value observing, into the language itself. The Swift compiler draws on much of the research and experience gained in creating LLVM and the clang compiler for Objective-C.

Unlike Objective-C, Swift is not a dynamically typed language. Instead, it uses static typing to help ensure the integrity and safety of your programs. Swift also prevents many of the problems inherent to the C language (and, by extension, Objective-C), especially with regards to memory integrity. While experienced Objective-C developers may lament this supposed loss of flexibility in their program design and construct, Swift's new features make writing programs simpler and easier, while still allowing programmers a great deal of freedom. Apple intends Swift to be suitable for application development as well as systems programming, and the design of the language exemplifies both of these areas of development.

Fortunately, Apple has also taken great care to integrate Swift into its existing ecosystem. Swift seamlessly operates with existing Objective-C code, libraries, and frameworks, as well as code written in C and C++. Programs can even mix these languages with little extra effort from you. Swift code is also completely supported by Xcode, allowing you to continue to use the development tools, such as compilers and debuggers, that you were familiar with when developing in Objective-C.

In fact, the introduction of Swift has added a new tool to the Xcode ecosystem's arsenal: playgrounds. Playgrounds are an interactive development environment for Swift that give you instant feedback on what blocks of code will do when executed. Swift also supports a read-eval-print loop, or REPL, that allows you to test snippets of Swift code right in the console. You can read more about playgrounds in Chapter 2.

Swift represents a massive leap forward in iOS and OS X development. While Objective-C programs will continue to be supported for quite some time, Swift is the way forward for iOS and OS X developers, and it is crucial to master the new skills introduced by Swift. Luckily, most of what you know about iOS and OS X is still important, even if you are writing your programs entirely in Swift. Most of all, Swift's new features make writing iOS and OS X applications more exciting and fun than they have ever been.

Before diving into the finer details of Swift development, you should familiarize yourself with Swift's basic concepts. If you already have a firm grasp of these concepts, however, feel free to skip to Chapter 2.

WHY LEARN SWIFT?

A bigger question is: Why should you learn Swift instead of writing your iOS and OS X apps in Objective-C? The truth is that Objective-C is not going to disappear any time soon. Most of the frameworks included in iOS and OS X are written in Objective-C, along with a large selection of third-party libraries and frameworks, and most iOS and OS X development tutorials are written for Objective-C. A thorough knowledge of Objective-C is important for developers of both of these platforms. However, Apple has already thrown a lot of weight into the development of Swift, and it is clearly the way forward for iOS and OS X development. Apple designed Swift to be both an applications and systems programming language, and it is certain that many future operating system components, frameworks, and libraries will be written in Swift. Swift will become increasingly important in the future.

Moreover, Swift expands and improves upon a lot of concepts from Objective-C, while adding a number of advanced features, such as closures, as well as making existing features, such as enumerated types, much more rich. Swift's syntax is cleaner and easier to learn and use than Objective-C, and it adds a lot of flexibility to APIs. It also allows iOS and OS X developers to explore other paradigms than the object-oriented development model inherent to Objective-C, such as functional programming. Finally, Swift is fun and adds a new level of exploration to the Apple development landscape.

WORKING WITH CONSTANTS AND VARIABLES

Swift has all the data types you are familiar with from languages such as C and Objective-C: numerical types such as Int, Float, and Double; Boolean types such as Bool; and character types such as String and Char. It also adds support for more complex types such as Array and Dictionary at the language level, providing a neat syntax for declaring and working with these container types.

Swift uses names to refer to values. These names are called *variables*. In Swift, a new variable is introduced using the keyword var. As with C and Objective-C, the actual value referred to by a variable can change. In the example that follows, the variable x first refers to 10, and then to 31:

```
var x = 10
x = 31
```

Swift also includes support for variables whose values cannot change. In this context, "variable" is a misnomer; these identifiers are more correctly referred to as *constants*. Constants are introduced with the let keyword:

```
let x = 10
```

You cannot change the value of x after it is declared—doing so will result in a compiler error. The following bit of code is not allowed:

```
let x = 10
x = 31    // This line will generate an error
```

Because constants' values cannot change, it is much easier to reason about the state of a constant than a variable. In Swift, it is preferable to use constants whenever possible; you should only use a variable when you absolutely need a value to vary over a program's execution. Good Swift programs will make extensive use of constants and minimize the number of variables that they use.

> **NOTE** *Technically speaking, constants are not variables because their values do not vary. However, in the context of programming languages, the term* variable *often does not adhere to the strict mathematical definition of the term; instead it indicates a name used to refer to a variable in a program's code. In this book, the term* variable *is often used when talking about both variables and constants because almost all concepts that apply to variables also apply to constants in Swift. The text explicitly denotes times when there are differences between the two.*

Swift also allows you to use any Unicode character as a variable name—not just characters from the English alphabet. The following code is allowed in Swift:

```
let π = 3.14159
let r = 10.0
let area = π * r * r
```

Almost any Unicode character can be used in a variable name. There are some restrictions, however: Variable names cannot include mathematic symbols, arrows, private or invalid Unicode code points, or line- and box-drawing characters. Variable names cannot start with a number, either, although they may contain numbers after the first character. Even with these restrictions, however, variable names are certainly more flexible in Swift than in C and Objective-C.

Understanding Swift Data Types

Swift has its own version of all the fundamental data types you would expect from C and Objective-C, including various numerical, Boolean, and character types. It also includes its own support for `Array` and `Dictionary` container types, including a simple, straightforward syntax for declaring and working with those types. Swift also introduces a new data type, a tuple, which groups multiple values—possibly of different types—into a single compound type.

Using Numerical Types

Swift features three basic numerical data types: `Ints`, `Floats`, and `Doubles`. As you would expect, these match up with the same data types in C and Objective-C. `Ints` represent whole numbers with no fractional component, such as 1, 304, and 10,000. `Floats` and `Doubles` each represent a number with a fractional component, such as 0.1, 3.14159, and 70.0. As in C, they differ only in their precision: `Floats` are 32-bit types, whereas `Doubles` are 64-bit types. Because of their increased size, `Doubles` offer more precision than `Floats`.

> **NOTE** *Generally, it is better to prefer* `Doubles` *over* `Floats`, *unless you know for sure that you don't need the precision of a* `Double` *and you can't sacrifice the increased size necessary to store a* `Double`.

Numerical types in Swift are written identically to those in C and Objective-C. To increase readability, however, they may include underscores, which are typically used to separate a number into chunks. For example, the value 1,000,000 could be written like this:

```
let n = 1_000_000
```

Underscores can be used in `Ints`, as well as both `Floats` and `Doubles`.

Swift numerical types have all the arithmetic operators you would expect, including +, –, /, *, and %, as well as the increment (++) and decrement (–) operators from C. These operators are covered in more detail later in this chapter.

There is no functional distinction between "primitive types" and "objects," as exists in Objective-C. The numerical data types have methods associated with them. The Swift standard library offers a bevy of methods that work with numerical types.

You may have noticed the lack of more specific integral data types such as short and long. Unlike C and Objective-C, Swift only offers a single basic integral data type, the Int. The size, or bit width, of the Int matches the underlying platform: 32 bits on 32-bit processors, and 64 bits on 64-bit processors.

Swift also has data types for integrals of specific widths, as well as unsigned versions of each integral data type. These are named similarly to their C counterparts: `Int8`, `Int16`, `Int32`, and `Int64`. The `UInt` is the unsigned version of the `Int`, and like an `Int`, matches the size of the underlying platform. `UInt8`, `UInt16`, `UInt32`, and `UInt64` are also available if you need unsigned integers of a specific width.

Preferably, however, you won't need to worry about the specific size of integral data types. Swift's type inferencing system, described later in this section, is designed to work with the `Int` data type. Generally speaking, integers of a specific bit width are not necessary when programming in Swift, but they are available for the rare times when the need for them arises.

Boolean Types

Swift offers a single Boolean data type, `Bool`, which can hold one of two values: `true` or `false`.

Swift's `Bool` type differs a bit from similar types in C and Objective-C. C does not have a Boolean type at all, instead treating any nonzero value as true and any zero value as false. In C, ints, chars, and even pointers can be treated as true or false, depending on their value. Objective-C offers a Boolean type, `BOOL`, as well as the values `YES` and `NO`, but in Objective-C, a `BOOL` is really just an `unsigned char`, and `YES` and `NO` are just the values 1 and 0, respectively. And Objective-C follows the same "truthiness" rules as C, so any nonzero value in Objective-C is true in a Boolean context (such as an `if` statement), and zero is false—even when dealing with pointers.

Swift dispenses with this nonsense. You cannot assign any values other than true and false to a Swift `Bool`, and only a `Bool` type may be used in Boolean contexts, such as if statements. Comparison operators, such as == and !=, also evaluate to a `Bool`. This change adds a level of type safety to Swift programs, ensuring that you only use a Boolean value—and nothing but a Boolean value—in appropriate contexts.

Using Character Types

Two character-based data types are available in Swift: Strings and Characters. Characters represent a single Unicode character. Strings are a collection of zero or more Unicode characters. Both are denoted by double quotes:

```
let c: Character = "a"
let s: String = "apples"
```

Although conceptually similar to string and character types in C and Objective-C, Swift's String and Character types are substantially different in practice. Both the Character and String types are treated as objects and have methods associated with them, just like Swift's other types. More importantly, they are designed to interact with text in a Unicode-compliant way. Whereas C strings are essentially nothing more than collections of byte values, Swift strings should be thought of as an abstraction over encoding-independent Unicode code points.

This difference has some significant practical implications. One major concern is how Swift handles characters outside of the Basic Multilingual Plane, or BMP. These include emoji characters, which, with the advent of mobile messaging, are becoming more and more widely used. Cocoa's NSString class assumes that all Unicode characters can be represented with a 16-bit integer (specifically, a unichar, which is a type alias for an unsigned short integer). This is true of any character in the BMP, which can be represented in a 16-bit integer using UTF-16 (one of several encodings for Unicode text; the other popular alternative is UTF-8). But not all Unicode code points can be represented in 16 bits—emoji characters being one of them.

As a result, NSString objects that include Unicode code points outside of the Basic Multilingual Plane will not return an intuitive value for their length and will not intuitively enumerate over their characters. In fact, the length method will return the number of unichars required to encode a character. Consider the simple Objective-C program that follows:

```
NSString *s = @"\U0001F30D";
NSLog(@"s is %@", s);
NSLog(@"[s length] is %lu", [s length]);
NSLog(@"[s characterAtIndex:0] is %c", [s characterAtIndex:0]);
NSLog(@"[s characterAtIndex:1] is %c", [s characterAtIndex:1]);
```

This program contains a string with a single character: the emoji globe character, or 🌍. However, the second line of the program will print "2" for the string's length, because this is the number of unichars NSString uses to encode 🌍. The third and fourth lines will also print odd characters to the screen, because they are printing one byte out of the two bytes necessary to encode the 🌍 character.

Swift does not have this problem. An equivalent Swift program will correctly report that it has a length of 1. It will also correctly print the character at index 0 and crash if you try to print a character at index 1 (which does not exist). The equivalent Swift program is shown below:

```
let s = "🌍"
println("s is \(s)")
println("s.length is \(countElements(s))")
println("s[0] is \(s[advance(s.startIndex, 0)])")
println("s[1] is \(s[advance(s.startIndex, 1)])")
```

It is becoming increasingly important to work with Unicode text in programs. The fact that Swift correctly handles Unicode out of the box represents a huge win over NSString.

Strings can be concatenated using the + operator:

```
let s1 = "hello, "
let s2 = "world"
let s3 = s1 + s2
// s3 is equal to "hello, world"
```

You can also compare two strings to see if they are equal using the == operator:

```
let s1 = "a string"
let s2 = "a string"
let areEqual = s1 == s2
// areEqual is true
```

Naturally, you can see if two strings are unequal using the != operator:

```
let s1 = "a string"
let s2 = "a string"
let areNotEqual = s1 != s2
// areNotEqual is false
```

> **NOTE** *Operators like +, ==, and != are discussed in greater detail later in this chapter.*

Swift also dispenses with Cocoa's delineation between immutable and mutable strings, as seen in the NSString and NSMutableString types. Swift has one single string type that uses the power of Swift constants and variables to declare an instance as mutable or immutable:

```
let s1 = "an immutable string"
var s2 = "a mutable string"
s2 += " can have a string added to it"
```

An immutable string, on the other hand, cannot be appended to. The Swift compiler will emit an error if you try to append a string to an immutable string.

You can also create a new string from other data types using *string interpolation*. When creating a string literal, variables referenced in a \() construct will be turned into a string:

```
let n = 100
let s = "n is equal to \(n)"
// s is "n is equal to 100"
```

You can interpolate expressions in a string, too:

```
let n = 5
let s = "n is equal to \(n * 2)"
// s is "n is equal to 10"
```

Using Arrays

Arrays are an integral part of the Swift language. They are akin to the Foundation framework's NSArray and NSMutableArray classes, but Swift has syntactic support for the easy creation and manipulation of array data types. Swift's Array type also differs from Objective-C's NSArray. Most importantly, the values contained in a Swift Array must all be of the same type, as opposed to NSArray, which can contain instances of any class. As with Strings, Swift also uses the same Array type for both mutable and immutable instances, depending on whether the variable is declared using var or let.

Swift also provides a new syntax for initializing arrays. An array can be initialized by writing its elements between brackets, as shown here:

```
let shoppingList = ["bananas", "bread", "milk"]
```

Elements of an array can also be accessed using bracket notation:

```
let firstItem = shoppingList[0]
// firstItem is "bananas"
```

If an array is declared using the let keyword, it is immutable: Elements cannot be added or deleted from it. On the other hand, if an array is declared using the var keyword, you are free to add or delete elements from it, or change the element stored at a specific index. For example, in the code that follows, the second element is changed from "bread" to "cookies":

```
var shoppingList = ["bananas", "bread", "milk"]
shoppingList[1] = "cookies"
```

You can also change a range of elements:

```
var shoppingList = ["candy", "bananas", "bread", "milk", "cookies"]
shoppingList[1...3] = ["ice cream", "fudge", "pie"]
```

Afterwards, shoppingList will contain ["candy", "ice cream", "fudge", "pie", "cookies"]. You can also append elements to an array:

> **NOTE** *Range operators are discussed later in this chapter.*

```
var a = ["one", "two", "three"]
a += ["four"]
println(a)    // Will print ["one", "two", "three", "four"]
```

It is best to use immutable arrays, unless you absolutely need to alter an array's contents.

Using Dictionaries

Dictionaries are also a fundamental data type in Swift. They fill the same role as NSDictionary and NSMutableDictionary from the Foundation framework, albeit with a few implementation differences. As with arrays, Swift also has language syntax support for creating and manipulating dictionary instances.

Like Swift arrays, and unlike Cocoa's NSDictionary, dictionaries in Swift must use the same type for every key, and the same type for every value. Additionally, keys must be *hashable*. As with arrays, Swift also does not have separate types for immutable and mutable dictionaries. An immutable dictionary is declared using the let keyword, and a mutable dictionary is declared using var.

Dictionaries are initialized using a syntax similar to arrays. Syntactically, a dictionary looks like a list of key-value pairs enclosed in brackets; the key and value are separated with a colon, as shown here:

```
let colorCodes = ["red": "ff0000", "green": "00ff00", "blue": "0000ff"]
```

Individual keys of a dictionary can be accessed by putting the key in brackets after the variable name:

```
let colorCodes = ["red": "ff0000", "green": "00ff00", "blue": "0000ff"]
let redCode = colorCodes["red"]
```

If a dictionary is mutable, you can also change an element using the same bracket notation you use to access it:

```
var colorCodes = ["red": "ff0000", "green": "00ff00", "blue": "0000ff"]
colorCodes["blue"] = "000099"
```

Using Tuples

Swift has one new fundamental data type: the tuple. Tuples group multiple values into one single compound value. They are similar to arrays, but unlike arrays, the elements of a tuple may be of different types. For example, you can use a tuple to represent an HTTP status code:

```
let status = (404, "Not Found")
```

In the preceding example, status consists of two values, 404 and "Not Found". Both values are of different types: 404 is an Int, and "Not Found" is a String.

You can *decompose* a tuple into its constituent elements:

```
let status = (404, "Not Found")
let (code, message) = status
// code equals 404
// message equals "Not Found"
```

You can ignore one or more elements using an underscore (_) in the decomposition statement:

```
let status = (404, "Not Found")
let (code, _) = status
```

> **NOTE** *When decomposing tuples, you can use* var *instead of* let *if you plan to modify the decomposed elements.*

Tuples are most helpful when you want to return multiple values from a function or method. Functions or methods can only return a single value, but because a tuple *is* a single value (albeit one consisting of multiple values), you can use it to get around this restriction.

Working with Type Annotations

Swift is a *type safe* language, meaning that every variable has a type, and the compiler checks to ensure that you are assigning a value of the correct type to every variable and passing values or variables of the correct type to functions and methods. This ensures that your code is always working with an expected set of values and that it is not trying to perform an operation (such as calling a method) on a value that does not support that operation.

Type annotations are a method by which you, the programmer, communicate to the compiler the type of a variable. Annotations should be familiar to you if you have programmed in C or Objective-C. Consider the following code sample:

```
NSString *s = @"this is a string";
int x = 10;
```

In the preceding example, s and x are both variables. Each has a type annotation in front of the variable name: s is annotated with the type NSString, and x is annotated with the type int. These annotations are necessary to communicate to the compiler the types of values you expect s and x to hold. As a result, the compiler issues an error if you attempt to assign a value of some other type to the variable, as in the example that follows:

```
int x = 10;
x = @"this is a string";
```

Types help guarantee the correctness of code you write by ensuring that you are always working with a set of values that you expect. If a function expects an integer, you can't pass it a string by mistake.

Variables can be annotated in Swift, although the syntax differs from C and Objective-C. In Swift, you annotate a type by writing a colon and type name after the variable name. In the example that follows, ch is declared to be a Character:

```
let ch: Character = "!"
```

Essentially, the preceding declaration is the same as this declaration in C:

```
char ch = '!'
```

Type annotations can also be used in functions and methods to annotate the types of their arguments:

```
func multiply(x: Int, y: Int) -> Int {
    return x * y;
}
```

Here, both the parameters x and y have been declared to be of type Int.

> **NOTE** *Functions are covered in greater detail in the section "Working with Functions," found later in this chapter.*

Of course, annotating each and every variable with a type quickly becomes unwieldy, and places the burden on the programmer to ensure that all variables are annotated properly. Languages such as C and Objective-C also allow you to *cast* values from one type to another, eroding the foundation of the meager type safety afforded in those languages. All in all, explicitly annotating types is cumbersome and error-prone. Luckily, Swift offers a solution to this madness: its type inference engine.

Minimizing Annotation with Type Inference

Many programmers prefer dynamically typed languages such as Python and JavaScript because such languages do not require that programmers annotate and manage types for every variable. In most dynamically typed languages, a variable can be of *any* type, and so type annotations are either optional or not allowed at all. Objective-C took a hybrid approach: It required type annotations, but any variable pointing to an instance of an Objective-C class (which includes anything derived from NSObject, but not primitive types like ints, floats, and so on) could simply be declared with type id, and therefore point to *any* Objective-C instance type. Even when stricter annotations were used, the Objective-C compiler did not make any strict guarantees about the type of an Objective-C variable.

While dynamically typed languages are often considered more pleasant to work with than statically typed languages, the lack of strict type safety means that the correctness of programs cannot be guaranteed, and they are often more difficult to reason about, particularly when working with third-party code or code you wrote years ago.

Statically typed languages are not guaranteed to be any safer than dynamically typed languages, however. C has static types and requires type annotations, but it is trivial to circumvent C's limited type safety through the use of type casting, void pointers, and similar language-supported chicanery.

Swift takes the best of both worlds: Its compiler makes strict guarantees about the types of variables, but it uses *type inferencing* to avoid making programmers annotate each and every variable manually.

Type inferencing allows a language's compiler to deduce the types of variables based on how they are used in code. In practice, this means that you can forgo adding type annotations to most variables and instead let the compiler do the work of figuring out the type. Don't worry—even without annotations, your programs still have all the type safety afforded by Swift's type system.

Consider the following snippet of code:

```
let s = "string"
let isEmpty = s.isEmpty
```

Neither of these constants has been annotated with a type, but Swift is able to infer that s is a String and isEmpty is a Bool. If you try to pass in either of these constants to a function that takes Ints, you will get an error:

```
func max(a: Int, b: Int) -> Int {
    return a > b ? a : b
```

```
    }
    max(s, isEmpty)
```

The preceding code will generate the error message `'String' is not convertible to 'Int'`, demonstrating that Swift knows that `s` and `isEmpty` are not `Int` types.

While Swift's type inferencing system greatly reduces the number of annotations you have to make manually in your code, there are still times when you must declare types. When writing functions, you must declare the types of all parameters, as well as the return type of the function.

You may also have to annotate a type when the type of a variable is ambiguous. For example, both `Strings` and `Characters` are denoted by text surrounded by double quotes. The Swift compiler infers a single character in double quotes to be a `String`, not a `Character`. The code that follows will generate an error, because `c` is typed as a `String`:

```
    func cId(ch: Character) -> Character { return ch; }
    let c = "X"
    cId(c)
```

If you want `c` to be a `Character`, you have to explicitly declare it to be a character. The following snippet of code works:

```
    func cId(ch: Character) -> Character { return ch; }
    let c: Character = "X"
    cId(c)
```

However, such ambiguous cases are rare in Swift. Usually, the compiler has no trouble inferring the type you intend a variable to be, and you generally don't have to worry about explicit type annotations.

> **TYPE THEORY**
>
> Type inferencing is a huge topic in computer science and falls into the category of knowledge and research known as *type theory*. One important element of type theory is the Hindley-Milner type system, which forms the basis of many type inference engines. The type inference algorithm used in this system was intended as a way to describe types for the simply typed lambda calculus, a method of computation that is the foundation for many modern programming languages.
>
> A full discussion of type theory is far beyond the scope of this book, but interested readers are encouraged to peruse the plethora of material on the subject available online.

Clarifying Code with Type Aliasing

In some cases, it may be helpful from the standpoint of code clarity to refer to a type in more specific terms. Let's say you write a function to calculate speed:

```
    func speed(distance: Double, time: Double) -> Double {
        return distance / time
    }
```

Certainly this function does the job, but what is `distance`? Is it measured in feet? Meters? And what is `time`? Is it seconds, or minutes, or hours? The function isn't clear what it expects. It would be much nicer to write the function like this:

```
func speed(distance: Feet, time: Seconds) -> FeetPerSecond {
    return distance / time
}
```

Of course, `Feet`, `Seconds`, and `FeetPerSecond` are not data types in Swift. However, Swift has a facility for providing more expressive type names: *type aliases*. You may be familiar with `typedefs` from C and Objective-C. Type aliases act the same way: They allow you to specify aliases for existing types.

You can modify the preceding code so it will actually compile using type aliases:

```
typealias Feet = Double
typealias Seconds = Double
typealias FeetPerSecond = Double

func speed(distance: Feet, time: Seconds) -> FeetPerSecond {
    return distance / time
}
```

Type aliases allow you to write your function so it is more expressive and more readable. It is a powerful feature that you should feel comfortable using in your own code.

WORKING WITH OPERATORS

Swift includes a number of built-in operators for working with data types. For the most part, these are arithmetic operators, intended to work with the numerical data types (`Int`s, `Float`s, and `Double`s), but Swift also has an operator for string concatenation, as well as logical and comparison operators. Swift also introduces operators for representing and dealing with ranges of values. Almost all of them, with the exception of the range operators, are also a part of C and Objective-C, so you are undoubtedly familiar with most of them, and they behave nearly the same as their C and Objective-C counterparts.

Using Basic Operators

Swift supports four standard arithmetic operators:

➤ Addition (+)

➤ Subtraction (–)

➤ Multiplication (*)

➤ Division (/)

These operators behave exactly as you would expect, coming from C and Objective-C, with one minor difference: They do not allow overflow. That is, if a variable is the max value for its type (for example, the maximum value of an `Int`), and you try to add a value to it, an error will occur. If you want to overflow behavior you expect from C, you must use one of the overflow variants of these operators. Overflow operators are discussed in the next section.

As in C, applying the division operator (/) to `Int`s results in the maximum value that divides the second `Int` into the first:

```
let m = 11 / 5
// m is equal to 2
```

The addition operator (+) is also supported by strings. "Adding" two strings together concatenates them:

```
let s1 = "hello"
let s2 = ", world"
let s3 = s1 + s2
// s3 is now "hello, world"
```

Swift also has a remainder operator, `%`. The remainder operator returns the value left over after a division operation:

```
let rem = 11 % 5
// rem is equal to 1
```

The remainder operator is also supported for `Float`s and `Double`s, a departure from its behavior in C, which only allows the remainder operator to be used on `Int`s:

```
let rem = 5.0 / 2.3
// rem is equal to 0.4
```

> **NOTE** *In C and Objective-C, the* `%` *operator is commonly known as the modulus operator. Applying the modulus operation to negative numbers results in values that, while mathematically correct, are counter-intuitive to many programmers. Swift uses the more intuitive behavior when applying the operation to negative numbers, and so refers to* `%` *as the remainder operator instead. When applied to positive operands, the modulus and remainder operations yield essentially the same result.*

Finally, Swift also supports the increment (++) and decrement (–) operators, which increase or decrease a value by 1.

```
var i = 10
i++
// i is now equal to 11
```

These operators come in both prefix and postfix varieties. The prefix form yields the value of the variable *after* the operation is applied, whereas the postfix form yields the value of the variable *before* the operation was applied. The following code gives an example of this.

```
var i = 10
var j = i++
// j is now equal to 10, and i is equal to 11
var k = ++i
// i and k are both equal to 12
```

Using Compound Assignment Operators

You can combine an arithmetic operation with an assignment in one fell swoop using the compound assignment operators:

➤ Addition assignment (+=)

➤ Subtraction assignment (-=)

➤ Multiplication assignment (*=)

➤ Division assignment (/=)

➤ Remainder assignment (%=)

These operators perform their associated operation *and* set a variable to a new value in a single expression:

```
var x = 20
x += 10
// x is now equal to 30
```

Using Overflow Operators

Swift's arithmetic operators do not allow values to overflow. In other languages such as C, if a variable is at its maximum value and you add another value to it, the variable *wraps around* to its minimum value. In Swift, a runtime error occurs instead. However, there may be occasions in which you want the overflow behavior. Swift provides this with the overflow variants of its arithmetic operators:

➤ Overflow addition (&+)

➤ Overflow subtraction (&-)

➤ Overflow multiplication (&*)

➤ Overflow division (&/)

➤ Overflow remainder (&%)

You use these operators in exactly the same way as the basic arithmetic operators. The only difference is that they allow overflow (or underflow). For example:

```
var num1: Int8 = 100;
var num2: Int8 = num1 &+ 100;
println(num2);  // Prints -56
```

Using Range Operators

You can easily represent ranges in Swift using its range operators. Swift provides two ways to represent ranges: a closed range operator (...) and an open range operator (..<). Both take two integer operands and yield a range of values between them. The closed range operator includes both operands' values in the range, whereas the open range operator includes the first operand's value, but not the second operand's. They are often used as counters in loops:

```swift
for i in 1...5 {
    // i will contain the values 1, 2, 3, 4, 5
    println("\(i)")
}
for i in 1..<5) {
    // i will contain the values 1, 2, 3, 4
    println("\(i)")
}
```

Using Logical Operators

Swift has three logical operators: logical NOT (!), AND (&&), and OR (||). ! is a prefix operator and inverts a variable:

```swift
let b1 = true
let b2 = !b1
// b2 is false
```

&& and || both take two operands. && returns true if *both* operands are true, and || returns true if at least one operand is true.

```swift
let b1 = true
let b2 = false
let b3 = b1 || b2
// b3 is true
let b4 = b1 && b2
// b4 is false
```

Swift also has a ternary condition operator, inherited from C. This operator takes three parameters:

➤ A condition

➤ A value to return if the condition is true

➤ A value to return if the condition is false

Essentially, it is an inline if statement. It looks like this:

```swift
let flag = true
let res = if flag ? 1 : 0
// res is equal to 1
```

Unlike C and Objective-C, these operators *only* work on `Bool` values. You cannot use them on non-Boolean values, such as `Ints`.

Using Comparison Operators

There are six comparison operators in Swift:

- ➤ Equal to (`==`)
- ➤ Not equal to (`!=`)
- ➤ Greater than (`>`)
- ➤ Less than (`<`)
- ➤ Greater than or equal to (`>=`)
- ➤ Less than or equal to (`<=`)

Like the logical operators, the comparison operators *only* return `Bools`, although they operate on most data types, including the numerical types and even classes (if classes define a custom operator). Each comparison operator takes two operands, returning the result of the operation. They behave identically to their counterparts in C and Objective-C.

As an example, consider the following:

```
let a = 10
let b = 20
if (a > b) {
    println("a is greater than b")
} else if (a == b) {
    println("a is equal to b")
} else if (a < b) {
    println("a is less than b")
}
```

> **NOTE** *Conditional statements are covered in greater detail in the section "Using Conditional Statements."*

Using Custom Operators

You can also define your own custom operators in Swift. Custom operators are discussed more thoroughly in Chapter 8.

MAKING DECISIONS WITH CONTROL FLOW

A programming language would not be good for much if it did not have a way to make decisions based on certain conditions. Swift offers all the familiar control flow statements to allow your program to make decisions during its execution.

Using Conditional Statements

Swift has two basic conditional statements: if statements and switch statements. An if statement executes its body only if the condition is true:

```
let flag = true
if flag {
    println("This statement is executed")
}
```

If statements can also take an else block, which is executed if the condition is false:

```
let flag = false
if flag {
    println("This statement is not executed")
} else {
    println("This statement is executed")
}
```

If statements can be chained together. The first block for which the condition is true is executed:

```
let x = 10
if x < 5 {
    println("This statement is not executed")
} else if x < 10 {
    println("This statement is not executed, either")
} else if x < 20 {
    println("This statement is executed")
} else {
    println("This statement is not executed")
}
```

As with the basic if statement, chained if statements do not require an else block.

Swift also has switch statements. Switch statements operate on a value and compare it against numerous cases. The first case that evaluates to true is executed. Switch statements are essentially like chained if statements, in a more compact, easier-to-read form.

Switch statements' most basic form is much like C, with a slightly different syntax:

```
let n = 20
switch n {
case 0:
    println("This statement is not executed")
case 10:
    println("Neither is this statement")
case 20:
    println("But this one is!")
default:
    println("And this one isn't")
}
```

Aside from syntax, Swift's switch statements differ from C's in several key ways. For one thing, the value used in a Swift switch statement does not need to be an integer, or even a numerical type; strings, tuples, enumerations (discussed later in this chapter), optional types (discussed in Chapter 8), and even custom classes may be considered as well.

Each case may also take several matches, each one separated by a comma:

```
let ch: Character = "a"
switch ch {
case "a", "e", "i", "o", "u":
    println("\(ch) is a vowel")
case "y":
    println("\(ch) may be a vowel or a consonant")
default:
    println("\(ch) is a consonant")
}
```

Cases must have a body. However, instead of executable code, a case may have a `break` statement. The case is matched, but because there is no code to execute, execution jumps out of the `switch` statement:

```
let n = 10
switch n {
case 10:
    break
default:
    println("\(n) is not 10")
}
```

Ranges can also be matched in `switch` statements:

```
let n = 23
switch n {
case 0...10:
    println("\(n) is between 0 and 10")
case 11...100:
    println("\(n) is between 11 and 100")
case 101...1000:
    println("\(n) is between 101 and 1000")
default:
    println("\(n) is a big number")
}
```

Even tuples can be matched:

```
let color = (255, 0, 0)
switch color {
case (0, 0, 0):
    println("\(color) is black")
case (255, 255, 255):
    println("\(color) is white")
case (255, 0, 0):
    println("\(color) is red")
case (0, 255, 0):
    println("\(color) is green")
case (0, 0, 255):
    println("\(color) is blue")
```

```
default:
    println("\(color) is a mixture of primary colors")
}
```

In the case of tuples and many other composite data types, including enumerations and custom classes, it can be helpful to bind variables to specific elements of the data type. You can use Swift's *value bindings* to associate variables with variables and constants:

```
let color = (255, 0, 0)
switch color {
case (let red, 0, 0):
    println("\(color) contains \(red) red")
case (0, let green, 0):
    println("\(color) contains \(green) green")
case (0, 0, let blue):
    println("\(color) contains \(blue) blue")
default:
    println("\(color) is white")
}
```

The first case (`let red, 0, 0`) matches any tuple whose second and third elements are 0. The first element may match *any* value and is bound to the constant `red`.

You may also use variables in the binding, using the `var` keyword instead of `let`. If the binding is a variable, it may be modified in the case's body, just like any variable.

Case statements may also take a `where` clause to match on additional constraints outside of values:

```
let color = (255, 0, 0)
switch color {
case let (r, g, b) where r == g && g == b:
    println("\(color) has the same value for red, green, and blue")
default:
    println("\(color)'s RGB values vary")
}
```

In the first case, you can decompose a tuple to quickly bind the constants r, g, and b to the components of color.

Swift's switch statements do not implicitly fall through to the next statement in the switch block, as happens in C. Execution breaks out of a switch statement as soon as a case is matched and its body executed. You can explicitly fall through to another case with the `fallthrough` keyword:

```
let ch: Character = "y"
print("\(ch) is a ")
switch ch {
case "y":
    print("consonant, and also a ")
    fallthrough
case "a", "e", "i", "o", "u":
    println("vowel")
default:
    println("consonant")
}
```

Finally, the cases of a switch statement must be *exhaustive*; that is, the entire range of the condition's values must be accounted for. Otherwise, a compiler error will occur. A `default` case may be provided to cover the entire range of values, and the `break` statement may be used if no action should be taken on default values.

Using Loops

Swift offers two varieties of for loops: for-in loops, which enumerate over a set of values, and the more familiar for-condition loops, which loop over values until a certain condition is reached.

For-in loops may be unfamiliar to C programmers, and even Objective-C only got the feature with the release of Objective-C 2.0 in 2006. For-in loops, also referred to as "fast enumeration" in the Objective-C documentation, iterate over every element in a collection type, such as an array, dictionary, or even a `Range` object. At their most basic, for-in loops can utilize the range operators to loop over a set of monotonically increasing values:

```
for i in 1...5 {
    // iterates over the values 1, 2, 3, 4, 5
}
```

Instead of a range, you can also use a container type, such as an array or dictionary, to loop over a set of elements:

```
let fruits = ["lemon", "pear", "watermelon", "apple", "breadfruit"]
for fruit in fruits {
    // iterates over the values lemon, pear, watermelon, apple, breadfruit
}
```

You can also loop over a dictionary. Looping over a dictionary returns a 2-tuple containing each key and value. This 2-tuple can be decomposed into its constituent parts:

```
let nums = [0: "zero", 10: "ten", 100: "one hundred"]
for (num, word) in nums {
    // num will be 0, 10, 100
    // word will be zero, ten, one hundred
}
```

Swift's basic container types, such as arrays, dictionaries, and ranges, can all be iterated over in a for-in loop. Other objects that adopt the Sequence protocol can also be iterated over in a for-in loop. You will learn more about how to implement this protocol in your own classes in Chapter 8.

Swift also features for-condition loops, which are more familiar to those with C and Objective-C backgrounds. They are identical in spirit to C's for loop, although the syntax differs a bit:

```
for var i = 0; i < 5; ++i {
    // loops over 0, 1, 2, 3, 4
}
```

In for-conditional loops, variables are only valid within the scope of the loop; in the preceding example, `i` cannot be accessed outside of the loop. If you need to use `i` outside of the loop, you must declare it *before* the loop. The following code gives an example of this.

```
var i = 0;
for i = 0; i < 5; ++i {
    // loop body
}
```

If you do not wish to use the for loop's variable in a function, you can indicate this by using an underscore (_) as the variable name:

```
for _ in 1...10 {
    println("\n")
}
```

For-conditional loops are a bit superfluous because you can write the exact same construct using a for-in loop with a range, so you may not see them that often in practice. However, they are available if you decide you want to use them.

> **NOTE** *Some programming languages, such as Python, only have for-in loops. They dispense with for-condition loops entirely, instead relying on ranges to simulate for-condition loops. Some language designers consider for-in loops with ranges to be "safer" because they avoid issues with boundary conditions that are present in for-condition loops (commonly referred to as off-by-one errors). Swift still supports for-condition loops, but you may find it more convenient and less error-prone to use for-in loops in your code.*

For-in and for-conditional loops are considered to be *determinate* loops: They have a well-defined ending condition. Swift also offers two forms of *indeterminate* loops, or loops without a well-defined ending condition: while loops and their close cousins, do-while loops.

The bodies of while loops are simply executed until their condition becomes false:

```
var flag = true
var i = 1
while flag {
    println("i is \(i++)")
    if i > 10 {
        flag = false
    }
}
```

Do-while loops are similar, except that the body is always executed at least once, and the condition is checked at the *end* of the loop, rather than at the beginning:

```
var flag = false
var i = 1
do {
    println("i is \(i++)")
    flag = i <= 10
} while flag
```

Swift offers several varieties of loops, although all of them can be mimicked with the simple while loop. However, it may make your code clearer to use one of the other looping constructs. For example, when looping over a known range or set of items, a for-in loop communicates the intent much more clearly than a basic while loop.

Control Transfer Statements

Loops may contain statements that transfer control of code execution to different parts of code. These statements are identical to their behavior in C and Objective-C and may be used in all types of loops.

The `continue` statement causes execution to jump back to the top of the loop. The following code sample only prints odd numbers:

```
for i in 1...100 {
    if i % 2 == 0 {
        continue
    }
    println("\(i)")
}
```

The `break` statement causes a loop to immediately end. The following loop continues to execute until the user enters q:

```
while true {
    print("Enter 'q' to end: ")
    let input = getUserInput()
    if input == "q" {
        break
    }
}
```

Both `break` and `continue` statements break out of the innermost loop. However, you can label loops, which enables you to break out of an outer loop instead:

```
let data = [[3, 9, 44], [52, 78, 6], [22, 91, 35]]
let searchFor = 78
var foundVal = false
outer: for ints in data {
    inner: for val in ints {
        if val == searchFor {
            foundVal = true
            break outer
        }
    }
}
if foundVal {
    println("Found \(searchFor) in \(data)")
} else {
    println("Could not find \(searchFor) in \(data)")
}
```

GROUPING TYPES WITH ENUMERATIONS

Enumerations allow you to group related types together. In C and Objective-C, enumerations—designed with the `enum` keyword—are little more than constants grouped together. There is little compiler support to treat them as a "type" unto themselves. In Swift, on the other hand, enumerations are types unto themselves, giving them all the power of other types, such as structs and classes.

Like C and Objective-C, Swift enumerations are introduced with the `enum` keyword:

```
enum Direction {
    case North
    case South
    case East
    case West
}
```

Each enum case may also be written on the same line, separated by commas:

```
enum Direction {
    case North, South, East, West
}
```

You can easily use enums in switch statements, where each case can handle one of the enumerated types:

```
let dir = Direction.North
switch dir {
case .North:
    println("Heading to the North Pole")
case .South:
    println("Heading to the South Pole")
case .East:
    println("Heading to the Far East")
case .West:
    println("Heading to Europe")
}
```

> **NOTE** *Because the only cases associated with the* `Direction` *enum are North, South, East, and West, and the switch statement handles all of those cases, a default case is not necessary.*

Much like classes and structs, you can treat the individual cases in enumerated types as constructors and associate values with them. Associated values are similar to instance variables (or properties) in classes and structs (although even with this feature, enums are still not quite as powerful as classes). You can specify associated values when creating an enum case. For example, here is one way to describe JSON using enums:

```
enum JSValue {
    case JSNumber(Double)
    case JSString(String)
```

```
        case JSBool(Bool)
        case JSArray([JSValue])
        case JSDictionary([String: JSValue])
        case JSNull
    }
```

A `JSNumber` is not merely a data type: It also has a `Double` value associated it; a `JSString` has a `String` value associated; and so forth, for all types except for `JSNull` (which, by its nature, has no unique value associated with it).

You create an enum with an associated value similarly to how you would instantiate a class or struct:

```
    let val = JSValue.JSNumber(2.0)
```

You can decompose enumerated values in switch statements to get the associated value, just as you can with a tuple:

```
    let val = JSValue.JSNumber(2.0)
    switch val {
    case .JSNumber(let n):
        println("JSON number with value \(n)")
    default:
        println("\(val) is not a JSON number")
    }
```

Compared to C and Objective-C, enumerated types in Swift are very powerful. You can use them in many of the same ways you would use classes or structs. Enumerated types are covered in more detail in Chapter 3.

WORKING WITH FUNCTIONS

Swift functions are standalone blocks of code that you call to transform inputs into outputs, or simply to perform some action like writing to a file or printing output to the screen. Functionally they are the same as functions in C and Objective-C, although their syntax differs substantially. Functions can be top-level, or they can be nested within other functions (a feature not available in C or Objective-C). Functions can also be associated with classes, structs, and enums, in which case they are referred to as *methods*, although the syntax for declaring methods is more or less the same. (You learn more about classes and structs in Chapter 4.)

Declaring Functions

Every function has a name, which calls the function. Functions may also optionally take parameters. Functions are declared with the `func` keyword, followed by the name of the function. The name is followed by a set of parentheses; parameters may be declared within the set of parentheses. Finally, if a function returns a value, you specify the return value after a *return arrow* (->); you may omit this part of the function declaration if the function does not return a value. (Functions that do not return a value are called *void functions*.) The body of the function is specified in braces. Here is a simple definition for a function called `multiplyByTwo` that takes a single `Int` parameter, x, as input, and returns the parameter multiplied by 2:

```
func multiplyByTwo(x: Int) -> Int {
    return x * 2
}
```

Function calls look the same as in C and Objective-C:

```
let n = multiplyByTwo(2)
// n is equal to 4
```

If a function takes multiple parameters, the parameters are separated by commas:

```
func multiply(x: Int, y: Int) -> Int {
    return x * y
}
let n = multiply(2, 4)
// n is equal to 8
```

Functions with no return value can omit the return type:

```
func printInt(x: Int) {
    println("x is \(x)")
}
printInt(10)
// will print "x is 10" to the console
```

Functions can only return a single value. However, you can return multiple values by wrapping them in a tuple:

```
func makeColor(red: Int, green: Int, blue: Int) -> (Int, Int, Int) {
    return (red, green, blue)
}
let color = makeColor(255, 12, 63)
let (red, green, blue) = color
```

Specifying Parameter Names

Within a function, you use a variable by referencing the name specified in the parameter list. When calling the function, parameters are passed in the order they were declared in the function, and the caller does not need to specify the names of the parameters when calling the function.

Sometimes it may be useful to force the caller to specify parameter names. This can aid the readability of code that uses the function, for example. You specify the *external* parameter name before the *internal* parameter name:

```
func makeColor(red r: Int, green g: Int, blue b: Int) -> (Int, Int, Int) {
    return (r, g, b)
}
```

Within the `makeColor` function, the parameters are referred to as `r`, `g`, and `b`. However, *outside* of the function, they are specified as `red`, `green`, and `blue`. When calling a function with named parameters, you *must* specify the name:

```
let color = makeColor(red: 255, green: 14, blue: 78)
```

Often, you may want the internal parameter name and the external name to be the same. You can do this by prefixing the name with a hash symbol (#):

```
func makeColor(#red: Int, #green: Int, #blue: Int) -> (Int, Int, Int) {
    return (red, green, blue)
}
let color = makeColor(red: 255, green: 14, blue: 78)
```

Defining Default Parameters

You may also specify default values for function parameters. If you do not specify a value for such parameters when calling the function, the default value is used. You can still override the default value when calling the function, though:

```
func multiply(x: Int, by: Int = 2) -> Int {
    return x * by
}
let x = multiply(4)
// x is equal to 8
let y = multiply(4, by: 4)
// y is equal to 16
```

If you do not specify an external name for a default parameter, Swift uses the internal name as the external name as well. Regardless, you *must* use the external name when calling the function.

If you really do not want callers to use an external name when calling a default parameter, you can use an underscore (_) as its external name:

```
func multiply(x: Int, _ by: Int = 2) -> Int {
    return x * by
}
let x = multiply(4, 4)
// x is equal to 16
```

However, it makes your code more readable and is considered best practice to use an external name for default parameters.

Specifying Variadic Parameters

Functions may take a variable number of arguments. Variadic parameters are specified by placing three dots (. . .) after a parameter's type name:

```
func multiply(ns: Int...) -> Int {
    var product = 1
```

```
    for n in ns {
        product *= n
    }
    return product
}
```

Variadic parameters are passed as an array; in the multiply function in the preceding code, the type of the ns parameter is [Int], or an array of Ints. You call the function with a comma-separated list of variables or values for the parameter:

```
let n = multiply(4, 6, 10)
// n is equal to 240
```

A function can take no more than one variadic parameter, and it must be specified last in the list of parameters.

Specifying Constant, Variable, and In-Out Parameters

Just as you can use let or var to specify constants or variables, you can also use let or var in function parameter lists to specify if a parameter is a constant or variable. By default, all parameters are constants, so you cannot change their values in a function. The following is not allowed:

```
func multiply(x: Int, y: Int) -> Int {
    x *= y
    return x
}
```

However, if you declare the parameter using the var keyword, you can modify it within the body of the function:

```
func multiply(var x: Int, y: Int) -> Int {
    x *= y
    return x
}
```

Regardless of whether the parameter is a variable or a constant, changes to a parameter are seen only within the body of the function itself. The function does not change the value of variables outside of the function:

```
let x = 10
let res = multiply(x, 2)
// res is equal to 20, but x is still equal to 10
```

Sometimes it may be useful for a function to affect variables outside of the function. In such cases, you can specify the parameter as an inout parameter:

```
func multiply(inout x: Int, y: Int) {
    x *= y
}
```

When calling a function with an inout parameter, you prefix the inout parameter with an ampersand (&). This syntax is familiar if you've programmed in C or Objective-C: An inout parameter is similar to a pointer parameter in C and Objective-C. In those two languages, & is also used to get the address of a variable in memory, which returns a pointer to that variable. Swift has largely dispensed with the concept of pointers but uses a similar syntax for its familiarity.

Although the preceding multiply function does not return a value, it will still change the value of variables passed into it:

```
var x = 10
multiply(&x, 2)
// x is now equal to 20
```

You may only pass *variables* as inout parameters; passing a constant or value will result in a compiler error.

Function Types

Functions are types, just like Ints, Floats, Arrays, and everything else in Swift. However, there is not one unifying Function type. Rather, each unique function signature (that is, the combination of a function's parameter types and return type) represents a different, unique type. Take, for example, the following function:

```
func multiply(x: Int, y: Int) -> Int {
    return x * y
}
```

The type is "a function that takes two Int parameters and returns an Int" and is denoted with type signature (Int, Int) -> Int.

If a function has no parameters, its parameter types are specified as an empty set of parentheses, (). Although referred to as *void*, it is essentially just a tuple with 0 elements. Likewise, a function that returns no value has a return type of (). Therefore, the type signature for the following function is () -> ():

```
func printDash() {
    println("-")
}
```

As with other data types, you can declare a constant or variable that refers to a function:

```
func multiply(x: Int, y: Int) -> Int {
    return x * y
}
let m: (Int, Int) -> Int = multiply
let n = m(2, 4)
```

As the preceding code sample shows, you can call a variable or constant that refers to a function as though it were a function.

> **NOTE** *As with other variables, you do not need to specify the type of a variable that points to a function unless you do not initialize it immediately, as Swift can infer the variable's type, just as it can with other data types such as* Ints *and* Floats.

Because functions are objects, just like any other data type in Swift, you can specify a function as a parameter to another function and return a function from a function. For example, the function map that follows takes a function and an array of Ints, and multiplies each by 2:

```
func multiplyByTwo(x: Int) -> Int {
    return x * 2
}

func map(fn: (Int) -> Int, ns: [Int]) -> [Int] {
    var res: [Int] = []
    for n in ns {
        let n1 = fn(n)
        res.append(n1)
    }
    return res
}

let nums = map(multiplyByTwo, [1, 2, 3])
// nums is now [2, 4, 6]
```

You can also return a function from a function:

```
func subtract(x: Int, y: Int) -> Int {
    return x - y
}

func add(x: Int, y: Int) -> Int {
    return x + y
}

func addOrSubtract(flag: Bool) -> (Int, Int) -> Int {
    if flag {
        return add
    } else {
        return subtract
    }
}

let fn = addOrSubtract(false)
let res = fn(4, 2)
// res is equal to 2
```

Using Closures

Functions' ability to take other functions as parameters and return functions is especially powerful when coupled with Swift's *closures*. Like functions, closures are blocks of code that can be passed around as objects. They are so named because they *close over* the scope in which they are declared, meaning that they can refer to variables and constants that are currently in their scope. Unlike functions, however, closures do not have to be named or declared; they can simply be defined when they are used.

In fact, Swift functions are just special cases of closures, meaning they are treated the same way by the language (and its supporting infrastructure, such as the Swift compiler).

Other than named functions, closures are most commonly used in a *closure expression*, a bit of code that defines an anonymous closure. Closure expressions are written in braces. Like functions, they optionally take a list of parameters specified in parentheses and optionally have a return value specified after a return arrow (->). The body of a closure begins after the keyword in.

The addOrSubtract function defined before could be rewritten to use closures instead of named functions:

```
func addOrSubtract(flag: Bool) -> (Int, Int) -> Int {
    if flag {
        return { (x: Int, y: Int) -> Int in return x + y }
    } else {
        return { (x: Int, y: Int) -> Int in return x - y }
    }
}

let fn = addOrSubtract(false)
let res = fn(4, 2)
// res is equal to 2
```

In many cases, the types of a closure's parameters can be inferred from context and can thus be omitted from the declaration. Furthermore, if a closure has only a single statement, the return keyword may be omitted as well. This leads to greater brevity when using closures, which is important because they are commonly used in Swift programming. The map function from before could be written and used as follows:

```
func map(fn: (Int) -> Int, ns: [Int]) -> [Int] {
    var res: [Int] = []
    for n in ns {
        let n1 = fn(n)
        res.append(n1)
    }
    return res
}

let nums = map({ x in x * 2 }, [1, 2, 3,])
// nums is now [2, 4, 6]
```

For even greater ease of writing, closures can also use shorthand parameter names in their bodies. The parameter names are prefixed with a dollar sign ($). Parameter names are numbered starting at 0. The first is referred to as $0, the second as $1, and so on. The map function declared previously could be called like this:

```
let nums = map({ $0 * 2 }, [1, 2, 3])
```

Swift offers an additional syntax for closures passed last to a function: In such cases, the closure can be specified *outside* of the parentheses in the function call. Because of this elegant syntax, functions that take a single function as a parameter often specify that closure as the final parameter. You can rewrite map so the function parameter is last:

```
func map(ns: [Int], fn: (Int) -> Int) -< [Int] {
    var res: [Int] = []
    for n in ns {
        let n1 = fn(n)
        res.append(n1)
    }
    return res
}
```

The call to map can then be written like this:

```
let nums = map([1, 2, 3]) { $0 * 2 }
```

Closures are an incredibly powerful part of Swift. They are similar to blocks in Objective-C but much more flexible—and, more importantly, they have a much nicer, easier-to-remember syntax than Objective-C's blocks. Utilizing the full power and potential of closures is a topic unto itself and will be discussed in more detail in Chapter 8.

SUMMARY

This chapter provided a crash course in Apple's new Swift programming language. While this was not intended to be a complete introduction to Swift, hopefully you were able to re-acquaint yourself with the rudiments of the language. If you are still unfamiliar with Swift, you may want to check out a more thorough guide on the basics of the language before moving on to the advanced concepts presented in the rest of this book.

Writing a Swift Program

WROX.COM CODE DOWNLOADS FOR THIS CHAPTER

You can find the wrox.com downloads for this chapter at http://www.wrox.com/go/proswift on the Download Code tab. The code for this chapter is contained in the following files:

➤ SwiftIsFun.playground

➤ Swiftisms.zip

Swift is a new language, but luckily, little has changed when you develop and build applications in Xcode, even if you are writing your new application in Swift. This chapter gives a quick overview of the new Swift-related features in Xcode 6, the first version of Xcode to support Swift development. It builds on the skills and knowledge you have already acquired as an advanced iOS or OS X developer. You'll find that little has changed in the Xcode toolchain to support development of Swift applications.

SETTING UP XCODE

Xcode is Apple's integrated development environment (IDE) for OS X and iOS development. It supports the creation of programs in Objective-C, Swift, C, and C++, as well as a number of other less commonly used languages (such as Python). Xcode is based on Project Builder, an IDE you use to write programs for the NeXTSTEP operating system, the forerunner of Mac OS X, as well as Interface Builder, the environment for designing graphical interfaces on NeXTSTEP. As you can imagine, Xcode has changed substantially since its humble Project Builder days, and it now sports many modern features, as well as a suite of programs that support the creation and development of OS X and iOS programs, including debuggers and profiling tools.

HISTORY OF XCODE

Xcode traces its lineage back to Project Builder and Interface Builder on the NeXTSTEP operating system, the operating system that is the basis of both OS X and iOS. Most notably, Tim Berners-Lee used Interface Builder to design the graphical interface of the first World Wide Web browser. Project Builder and Interface Builder were rewritten for OS X, and rebranded as Xcode with the release of OS X 10.3 in 2003. In 2011, Interface Builder was combined into Xcode, and Apple ceased developing and distributing it as a separate application.

Downloading from Apple's Developer Portal

The first step in setting up Xcode is downloading it from Apple's developer portal. Before you can download Xcode, you must set up a developer account, if you haven't already. A developer account is free and gives you access to both Apple's developer tools, such as Xcode, and developer documentation for both iOS and OS X development. You must pay $99 per year if you want to test your iOS app on an actual device, rather than the device simulator that is packaged with Xcode. Testing on an actual device is highly recommended if you intend to distribute your app, and the $99 yearly fee is also required if you want to publish your app on Apple's App Store. A second, separate fee is required if you want to publish an OS X app on the Mac App Store, although you can write, test, and even distribute Mac applications (outside of the Mac App Store) without a fee.

A developer account is part of your Apple ID and is the account Apple uses for all of its services, including iCloud and the online store. If you haven't set up an Apple ID at all, you can sign up by going to `appleid.apple.com`. Follow the links on that page to set up your account. If you already have an Apple ID, you can log into Apple's developer portal at `developer.apple.com` using your existing ID.

Downloading Xcode

Once you have your Apple ID set up, you can download Xcode. The easiest way to get Xcode is from the Mac App Store. Search for "Xcode" on the Mac App Store and download it. You can also go to `developer.apple.com/xcode/downloads` to get a clickable link to Xcode on the Mac App

Store. Once you've started downloading Xcode, sit back and wait: It's over 2 gigabytes in size and may take a while to download. In the meantime, you can get a head start by reading the Swift documentation on Apple's developer portal, or the rest of this chapter.

When the download is completed, you can open Xcode from Launchpad or your computer's Application folder. You are greeted with the splash screen shown in Figure 2-1.

FIGURE 2-1

Note that there are two primary options:

➤ **Get started with a playground:** This is related to a brand-new feature integrated into Xcode with the release of Xcode 6.0: Playgrounds. As the name suggests, playgrounds are a way to test out application code without the need to create an application or even an Xcode project. They are akin to the read-eval-print loops (REPLS) of languages such as Python and Ruby, but they are much more powerful, and much more visual. Because playgrounds leverage the power of Swift and the Swift compiler, they are only available for the Swift language.

➤ **Create a new Xcode project:** This is self-explanatory: It allows you to dive right into development of your application.

Before you start writing a full-fledged application in Swift, let's take a look at Swift using a playground.

EXPERIMENTING WITH PLAYGROUNDS

Playgrounds, a new Xcode feature, allow you to experiment with code outside of an application or project. They are important because they:

➤ Allow you to examine different language and API features, as well as the results of executing select bits of code.

➤ Are fairly powerful in that not only do they show you the result of computation, but they can also show you how a variable changes over time (if, for example, you are changing its value in a loop).

➤ Can even visually show you the result of applying operations to graphical interface elements such as buttons and images.

➤ Utilize the full power of the Swift language and its compiler, so you can only experiment with Swift in playgrounds—no Objective-C allowed.

Xcode's playgrounds were heavily influenced by Light Table, a development tool designed to give programmers instant and visual feedback about their code. Playgrounds were also inspired by the work of Bret Victor, a programmer who designed the interface prototypes for the iPad and iPod Nano, as well as a number of other interface elements for Mac OS X and its bundled software, and who has continued to pioneer work in visual programming tools.

Xcode has historically emphasized the use of visual tools in its development suite. Interface Builder allows programmers to design interfaces by dragging user interface elements around on the screen, rather than by writing dozens of lines of code with no visual feedback. Apple's Instruments tool (covered more thoroughly in Chapter 10) gives programmers instant visual feedback about the state of a running program, allowing them to profile and debug code faster and easier than such tools traditionally allow. And now Swift allows programmers to experiment and interact with code in a visual way. Combined, these tools make OS X and iOS development accessible to a much larger pool of programmers.

Using Playgrounds in Xcode

Playgrounds are a new feature of Xcode. Playgrounds allow you to enter code into an editor and see the results of running that code immediately, rather than having to create a new Xcode project and compile the code. They have many of the features found in languages with an interactive interpreter, such as Python. This section shows a short demonstration of the usefulness and power of Xcode's playgrounds. You'll be able to experiment with code and see how it runs immediately.

You can also save a playground, just like any file, and even send it to your colleagues or friends. Recipients of a playground can open it up on their computer to see what you've done or to play around with your code on their own.

A Simple Example in Playground

To get started with a Swift playground, follow these steps:

1. **Launch Xcode.** You will be greeted with the splash screen.

2. **On the splash screen, click the Get started with a playground option to create a new playground (refer back to Figure 2-1).** You are prompted to select a platform for your playground: OS X or iOS (Figure 2-2). Swift itself isn't different across each platform, but the API features you have access to will be different; for example, on OS X you use AppKit for user interface elements, whereas on iOS you use UIKit. For now, let's play around with an iOS playground.

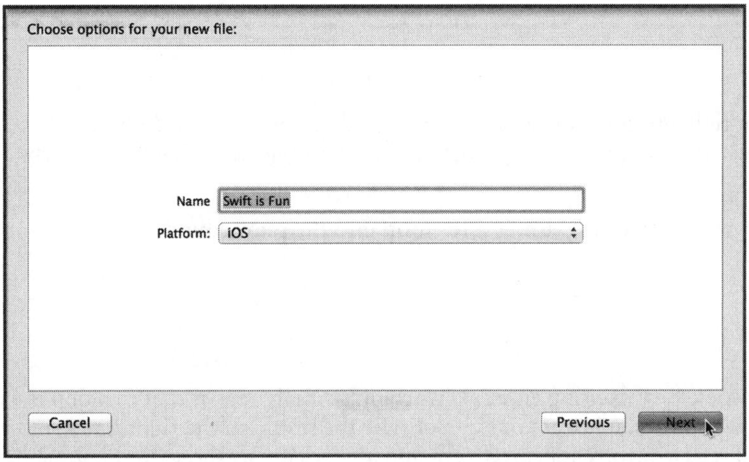

Choose options for your new file:

Name   Swift is Fun

Platform: iOS

Cancel   Previous   Next

FIGURE 2-2

3. **Select iOS from the drop-down menu, name the playground anything you want, and click Next.** You now see a new playground. It is not entirely empty, as Xcode has helpfully filled in a UIKit import for you and demonstrated the result of executing a single line of code, as shown in Figure 2-3. Otherwise, the canvas is fairly blank.

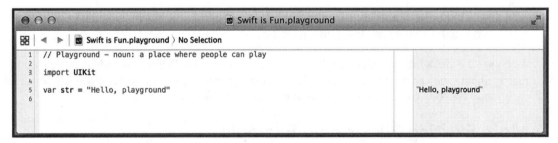

```
1   // Playground - noun: a place where people can play
2
3   import UIKit
4
5   var str = "Hello, playground"            "Hello, playground"
6
```

FIGURE 2-3

What is a blank canvas, after all, except an invitation to get started? You can type any bit of code into the playground.

4. **Enter a simple constant initialization:**

```
let num = 20
```

You will instantly see the result of the evaluation of that line of code, as shown in Figure 2-4.

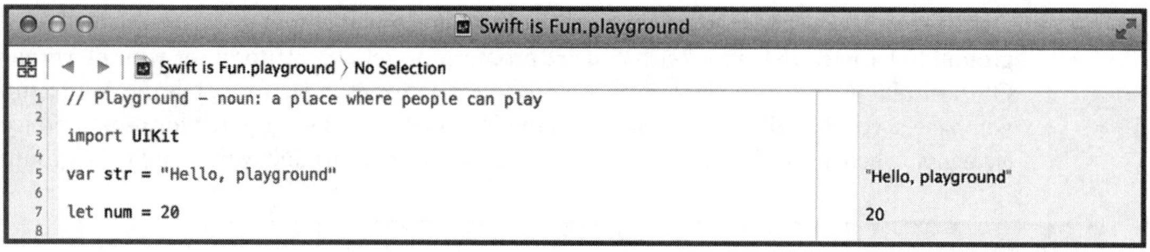

FIGURE 2-4

A simple constant initialization is boring, however. You'd be forgiven for doubting the power of playgrounds at this point—this playground hasn't done anything particularly exciting yet.

5. **Try something a bit more interesting. Enter a for loop into the playground:**

```
for i in 1...100 {
    let j = i * 10
}
```

Initially, this doesn't look very exciting either. Playgrounds simply report that the loop is executed 100 times. However, if you hover your cursor over the result on the right-hand side of the window, you will see two icons appear: an eye and a plus sign, as shown in Figure 2-5.

FIGURE 2-5

6. **Click the plus sign.** This brings up a third pane: a graph that shows how the value of j changed over time, as shown in Figure 2-6.

As Figure 2-6 demonstrates, j is steadily increasing, as expected. While this code is fairly easy to reason about, you can no doubt imagine that having a graph to show the value changing with each iteration of the loop could be very helpful in most day-to-day programming.

A More Exciting Playground Example

Let's try something even more exciting: working with UILabel objects. Enter the following code into a playground, line by line:

```
let label = UILabel(frame: CGRectMake(0, 0, 200, 80))
label.text = "Playgrounds are fun!"
label.backgroundColor = UIColor(red: 0.0, green: 0.75, blue: 0.95, alpha: 1.0)
label.layer.cornerRadius = 10
label.textAlignment = NSTextAlignment.Center
```

When working with UI elements, the plus sign icon turns into a circle with a dot in the middle. After entering each line, click the circle icon to see the result of applying various operations to a UILabel instance.

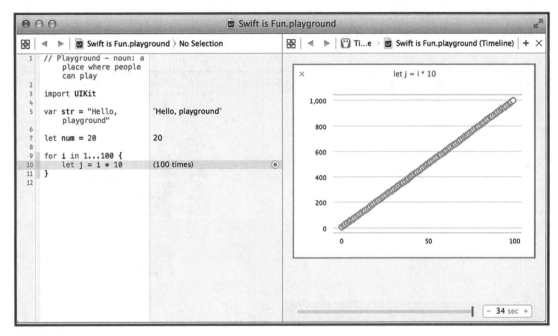

FIGURE 2-6

> **NOTE** *Note that the third line,* `label.layer.cornerRadius = 10,` *will not have a circle icon because that code operates on the label's layer, not the label itself.*

After entering the code and examining the results of the computation, you should see something like the output shown in Figure 2-7. Notice how the playground has shown how the label's appearance has been altered with each line of code, ultimately looking like the label shown in the last box of output.

Of course, such visualization is not limited solely to interface elements. You can do the same thing with any object. Figure 2-8 shows the result of modifying an instance of an `NSMutableAttributedString`.

Feel free to experiment with any object you like. `UIImages`, `NSRects`—everything is fair game in a playground!

WRITING SWIFT IN XCODE

Xcode's support for Swift goes far beyond playgrounds. Just like Objective-C, Xcode has full support for creating, compiling, and distributing an application written in Swift—or even in a combination of languages. For the most part, creating an Xcode project written partially or entirely in Swift is the same as creating an Xcode project written in Objective-C. Aside from a few button presses to create files, Xcode works more or less the same as you are used to. While Swift itself is new, Apple has taken great pains to ensure that the Xcode development toolchain is familiar to anyone who has written iOS or OS X applications already.

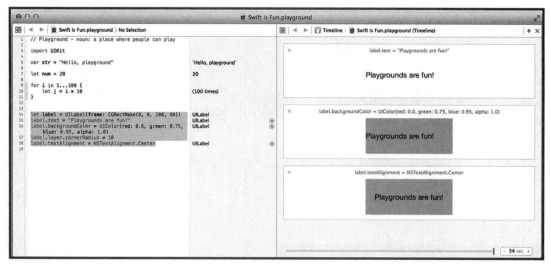

FIGURE 2-7

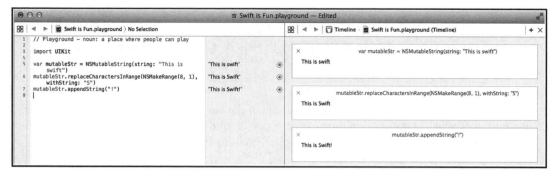

FIGURE 2-8

To demonstrate Xcode's support for Swift, this section walks you through the creation of a simple Swift project for iOS. It assumes that you already have some working knowledge of Xcode, and it highlights the use of Swift in a new project, rather than the finer details of Xcode. By the end of the section, you should have an idea of how to set up and create your own Swift applications in Xcode.

Creating a New Swift Project

Creating a project is simple. To do so, follow these steps:

1. **When Xcode launches, click the Create a new Xcode project option (Figure 2-9).** You are prompted to select a project template. The exact project template you choose depends on

whether you're creating an iOS or OS X application (or a library or other supporting code bundle for each). Each platform also has several different types of projects you can create; these dictate the template used to create your Xcode project.

Welcome to Xcode
Version 6.0 (6A279r)

Get started with a playground
Explore new ideas quickly and easily.

Create a new Xcode project
Start building a new iPhone, iPad or Mac application.

Check out an existing project
Start working on something from an SCM repository

☑ Show this window when Xcode launches

FIGURE 2-9

2. **For now, create a Single View Application for iOS.** You do this by selecting iOS and Application in the left-hand sidebar; then select Single View Application (see Figure 2-10) and click Next.

   You are presented with a sheet where you can configure metadata about your application.

3. **Name your project Swiftisms, and use whatever Organizational Identifier you want.** Just make sure that Swift is selected as the language, and click Next (see Figure 2-11). You are prompted to save your project.

4. **Save the project anywhere on your computer you like and click Create.**

ORGANIZATIONAL IDENTIFIERS

The operating system (either iOS or OS X) uses *bundle identifiers* to uniquely identify your application. Bundle identifiers are formed from an *organizational identifier* and your application's name. Generally, organizational identifiers are your *reverse domain name*. If your domain name is *example.com*, your organization

continues

continued

identifier would be *com.example*, and the bundle identifier for an app called "MyApp" would be *com.example.MyApp*.

Why your reverse domain name? The use of reverse domain names as identifying strings was popularized in the Java world to avoid name clashes in packages. The idea is that, if all developers prefix their package names with a domain name that they alone control, name clashes can be reduced—each developer (or organization) is responsible for avoiding name clashes in his or her code only. Reverse domain names were used to mimic the hierarchical nature of Java package names. The same technique is advised when creating bundle identifiers for iOS and OS X apps as well.

If you do not have a domain name, feel free to use any identifier that is unique to you. Many developers use an identifier in the form `lastname.firstname`, in lieu of a reverse domain name.

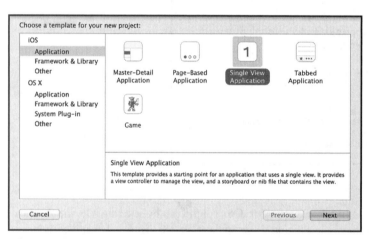

FIGURE 2-10

You now have a fully configured iOS project with some Swift file templates, including an app delegate, a view controller, and a test case, all written in Swift. Your file tree should look similar to the one shown in Figure 2-12. You can actually compile and run the project. It should work—although it doesn't actually do anything useful yet.

You can click any of the files to show them in the editor pane in the center of the main Xcode window (see Figure 2-13). Clicking `AppDelegate.swift`, for example, will show the source code for the app's delegate—implemented in Swift, of course. You can edit source code for your Swift files right in the editor pane, just like any text editor.

Creating the Swiftisms App

This section shows you how to create a simple iOS app using Swift. The app will consist of a single view with a text label and a button. Tapping the button will display one of several predefined strings in the text label.

Choose options for your new project:

Product Name:	Swiftisms
Organization Name:	Michael Dippery
Organization Identifier:	com.monkey-robot
Bundle Identifier:	com.monkey-robot.Swiftisms
Language:	Swift
Devices:	iPhone
	☐ Use Core Data

Cancel   Previous   Next

FIGURE 2-11

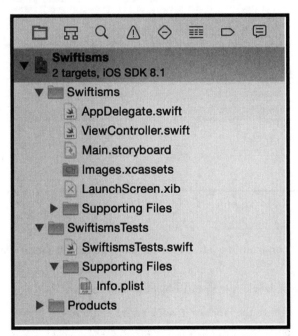

FIGURE 2-12

Creating the Interface

You start by laying out the interface:

1. Click `Main.storyboard` in the file list to show the main interface for the application. You will see a very plain-looking view in Xcode's center pane, as shown in Figure 2-14. The bottom of the rightmost editor pane is called the *object browser*.

```
     ⊞  < >  📄 Swiftisms ⟩ 📁 Swiftisms ⟩ 📄 AppDelegate.swift ⟩ No Selection
1    //
2    // AppDelegate.swift
3    // Swiftisms
4    //
5    // Created by Michael Dippery on 2/21/15.
6    // Copyright (c) 2015 Michael Dippery. All rights reserved.
7    //
8
9    import UIKit
10
11   @UIApplicationMain
12   class AppDelegate: UIResponder, UIApplicationDelegate {
13
14       var window: UIWindow?
15
16
17       func application(application: UIApplication, didFinishLaunchingWithOptions launchOptions: [NSObject: Any
18           // Override point for customization after application launch.
19           return true
20       }
21
22       func applicationWillResignActive(application: UIApplication) {
23           // Sent when the application is about to move from active to inactive state. This can occur for cert
24           // Use this method to pause ongoing tasks, disable timers, and throttle down OpenGL ES frame rates.
25       }
26
27       func applicationDidEnterBackground(application: UIApplication) {
28           // Use this method to release shared resources, save user data, invalidate timers, and store enough
29           // If your application supports background execution, this method is called instead of applicationWi
30       }
31
32       func applicationWillEnterForeground(application: UIApplication) {
33           // Called as part of the transition from the background to the inactive state; here you can undo man
34       }
35
36       func applicationDidBecomeActive(application: UIApplication) {
37           // Restart any tasks that were paused (or not yet started) while the application was inactive. If th
38       }
39
40       func applicationWillTerminate(application: UIApplication) {
41           // Called when the application is about to terminate. Save data if appropriate. See also application
42       }
43
44
45   }
46
47
```

FIGURE 2-13

2.   **In the object browser, click the third icon from the left.** This brings up the Object Library, as shown in Figure 2-15.

3.   **In the Object Library's search box, type** label. A `UILabel` object should appear.

4.   **Drag the object onto the storyboard.** Resize the label so it is the entire width of the view.

5.   **Search for "button" in the Object Library.** Drag the first item onto the storyboard.

6.   **Double-click the button's text and replace the default text with Show String.** When you're done, your storyboard's main view should look like the one shown in Figure 2-16.

Creating Connections between the View Controller and the Object

Now you need to create the connections between the app's view controller and the objects you just placed in the main view.

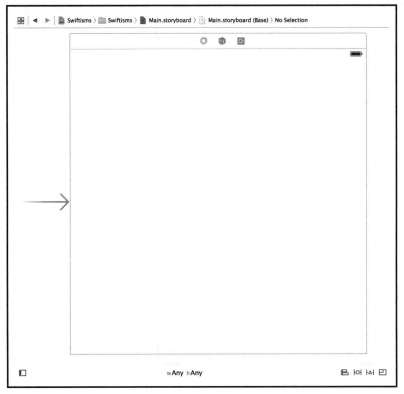

FIGURE 2-14

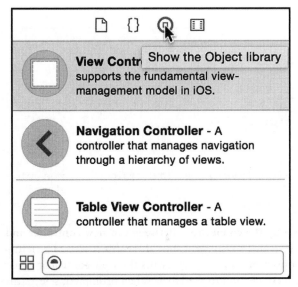

FIGURE 2-15

FIGURE 2-16

1. Select `ViewController.swift` in the file view and edit the file. When you're finished, it looks like Listing 2-1.

LISTING 2-1: ViewController.swift

```swift
import UIKit

class ViewController: UIViewController {
    @IBOutlet weak var label: UILabel!
    @IBOutlet weak var button: UIButton!

    override func viewDidLoad() {
        super.viewDidLoad()
        // Do any additional setup after loading the view, typically from a nib.
    }
}
```

2. Select `Main.storyboard` again and set up the connections between the view controller and the storyboard objects. Above the storyboard's view, you should see three icons. The leftmost one, a yellow circle with a white circumscribed square, represents the view controller object. Hold down the control key and drag a connection to the label. When prompted, select `label` in the popup to configure the connection for the view controller's `label` property. Do the same for the button.

3. Switch back to `ViewController.swift` and add a property called `strings` to store the strings. This will appear in the main view's label, as shown in Listing 2-2.

LISTING 2-2: ViewController.swift

```swift
import UIKit

class ViewController: UIViewController {
    @IBOutlet weak var label: UILabel!
    @IBOutlet weak var button: UIButton!

    let strings = [
        "Swift is fun!",
        "I like Swift",
        "This app was written with Swift",
    ]

    override func viewDidLoad() {
        super.viewDidLoad()
    }
}
```

4. Now you add a method to randomly select one of the strings to be displayed. This goal can be accomplished with just a few lines of Swift code:

```swift
func selectString() -> String {
    let idx = Int(arc4random_uniform(UInt32(strings.count)))
    return strings[idx]
}
```

5. Add this method to your `ViewController` class, as shown in Listing 2-3.

LISTING 2-3: ViewController.swift

```swift
import UIKit

class ViewController: UIViewController {
    @IBOutlet weak var label: UILabel!
    @IBOutlet weak var button: UIButton!

    let strings = [
        "Swift is fun!",
        "I like Swift",
        "This app was written with Swift",
    ]

    override func viewDidLoad() {
        super.viewDidLoad()
    }

    func selectString() -> String {
        let idx = Int(arc4random_uniform(UInt32(strings.count)))
```

continues

continued

```
            return strings[idx]
        }
    }
```

In `selectString`, you generate a random number in the range 0 to 3 inclusive using the function `arc4random_uniform`, and then use that as an index into the view controller's array of strings. You return the string at that index from the function.

Your app's view controller is nearing completion!

6.   **Now you need to hook up the main view's button.** Create an IBAction that takes in a UI element and sets the view's label to a random string, as shown in Listing 2-4.

LISTING 2-4: ViewController.swift

```swift
import UIKit

class ViewController: UIViewController {
    @IBOutlet weak var label: UILabel!
    @IBOutlet weak var button: UIButton!

    let strings = [
        "Swift is fun!",
        "I like Swift",
        "This app was written with Swift",
    ]

    override func viewDidLoad() {
        super.viewDidLoad()
    }

    func selectString() -> String {
        let idx = Int(arc4random_uniform(UInt32(strings.count)))
        return strings[idx]
    }

    @IBAction func buttonTapped(AnyObject) {
        let string = selectString()
        label.text = string
    }
}
```

The `buttonTapped()` method is marked as an `@IBAction` to let Xcode know that it can be the target of a UI element, such as a button. Because an IB action can take any object as a parameter, the method's argument is listed as `AnyObject`, which is roughly equivalent to an `id` in Objective-C. The parameter name was left out because you don't use the UI object in the method. A random string is retrieved using the `selectString()` method, and the label's text is set to the random string.

Connecting the Buttons and the Action

Now you need to hook up the button to the `buttonTapped()` action you just created. To do this, following these steps:

1. **Switch back to `Main.storyboard`.** While holding down the Control key, drag a connection to the view controller, selecting `buttonTapped()` as the action to invoke when the button is tapped. At this point, you can build and run your application in the simulator.

2. **Select your desired simulator.** You can find this on the simulator popup menu in the top left of the Xcode toolbar, as shown in Figure 2-17.

FIGURE 2-17

3. **Click Production ➤ Run, or press ⌘ +R.** You should see your app running in the iOS simulator, as shown in Figure 2-18.

4. **Click the Show String button—the label should display a random string each time you press the button.** When you're done, select Quit from the simulator's application menu.

Displaying Random Strings

There is one last loose end to tie up. When the application initially loads, the label simply reads "Label." It would be nice to have it prepopulated with a random string immediately when the application loads. You can accomplish that by adding the following line to the end of the view controller's `viewDidLoad()` method.

```
label.text = selectString()
```

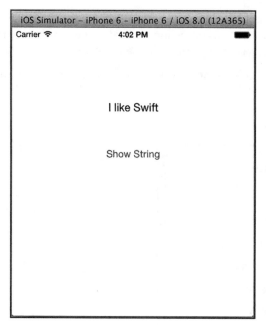

FIGURE 2-18

After you've added that line, the final version of `ViewController.swift` should look like the one in Listing 2-5.

LISTING 2-5: ViewController.swift

```
import UIKit

class ViewController: UIViewController {
    @IBOutlet weak var label: UILabel!
    @IBOutlet weak var button: UIButton!

    let strings = [
        "Swift is fun!",
        "I like Swift",
        "This app was written with Swift",
    ]

    override func viewDidLoad() {
        super.viewDidLoad()
        label.text = selectString()
    }

    func selectString() -> String {
        let idx = Int(arc4random_uniform(UInt32(strings.count)))
        return strings[idx]
    }
}
```

```
@IBAction func buttonTapped(AnyObject) {
    let string = selectString()
    label.text = string
}
}
```

Load up your app in the simulator to see it in action! Or, if you're a registered iOS developer, feel free to run it on an actual device and play around with it there. You've just finished your first Swift app!

What Next?

As you can see, developing a Swift app in Xcode is nearly identical to developing an Objective-C app—aside from using a completely different programming language, of course. The APIs are nearly identical (the only difference being the use of "Swiftisms" when calling APIs from Swift), and the look and feel of Xcode is the same. While learning a totally new language can be daunting, Apple at least took great pains to keep the overall development experience identical, enabling you to leverage the knowledge and experience gained while developing Objective-C applications in Xcode.

Of course, writing and running a program are not the only features Xcode offers. Xcode also has a fully integrated debugger that you can use to test and debug your Swift code—the same as your Objective-C code. Let's spend some time getting acquainted with Xcode's debugging tools.

DEBUGGING SWIFT APPLICATIONS

A debugger is a programming tool that lets you step through a program instruction by instruction. As the name suggests, you typically use one for debugging applications; you can load up a program and examine what the program is doing as it executes. You can also inspect the state of your program at any given time, yielding insight into how a program works, and highlighting areas that may be buggy. It is a powerful tool that greatly aids in finding problems and writing programs that function correctly.

Xcode ships with lldb, a debugger for the LLVM compiler suite that Xcode uses to build your programs for both iOS and OS X. Xcode has included a debugger since its inception; originally, it used gdb, the debugger developed alongside gcc (the compiler suite used by Xcode prior to LLVM), but with the transition to LLVM, Xcode began shipping with lldb instead. Conceptually, both tools are similar; if you are familiar with debugging with gdb, it is not too difficult to transition to lldb instead. The major difference is that lldb provides tighter integration with integrated development environments, including Xcode, and it provides better feedback to programmers when they use the tool. For the most part, however, lldb and gdb are the same.

LLVM

LLVM, the *Low-Level Virtual Machine*, is the set of tools that Xcode uses to compile your programs. You use it to compile both Objective-C and Swift code (as well as C and C++, if your program uses those languages) for iOS and OS X. LLVM began in 2000 at the University of Illinois at Urbana-Champaign, under

continues

continued

the direction of Chris Lattner, who now oversees the creation and maintenance of development tools at Apple. Despite the name, the project has evolved considerably and is no longer focused exclusively on virtual machines. It provides many of the tools used by Xcode developers, including compilers, debuggers, and profilers.

While Xcode's debugger is incredibly powerful, Apple has also gone to great lengths to ensure that it is so simple to use that programmers won't overlook this amazing tool.

Central to the use of the debugger is the concept of a *breakpoint*. A breakpoint indicates a line of code that, when hit during program execution, launches the debugger, enabling you to step through code and examine the state of your program.

Understanding Breakpoint Types

There are several different types of breakpoints:

➤ **Basic breakpoints:** This is set on a particular line of code; when that line of code is executed, you are dropped into the debugger.

➤ **Conditional breakpoints:** These load the debugger when a particular condition is met.

➤ **Symbolic breakpoints:** These load the debugger when a particular function is called.

This chapter will deal with only the basic, static types of breakpoints; Chapter 10 will cover the more advanced types of breakpoints in greater detail.

Setting Breakpoints

Before you execute your program with the debugger, you must decide which lines of code should invoke the debugger. After doing so, you follow these steps:

1. **Open up the `ViewController.swift` file in Xcode's code editor.** Along the left side of the code editor, you will see a gutter that shows line numbers for each line of code.

> **NOTE** *If you don't see line numbers for each line of code, you can enable them by selecting the "Text Editing" pane in Xcode's preferences and checking the box next to "Line numbers."*

2. **Click in the gutter to set a breakpoint on that line of code.** For this example, click the line with the text `let string = selectString()` in the code editor to set a breakpoint on that line of code, as shown in Figure 2-19.

When your program's execution hits that line, you are dropped into the debugger. Note that this line is part of the `buttonTapped()` function, so it will only be executed after tapping the main view's button.

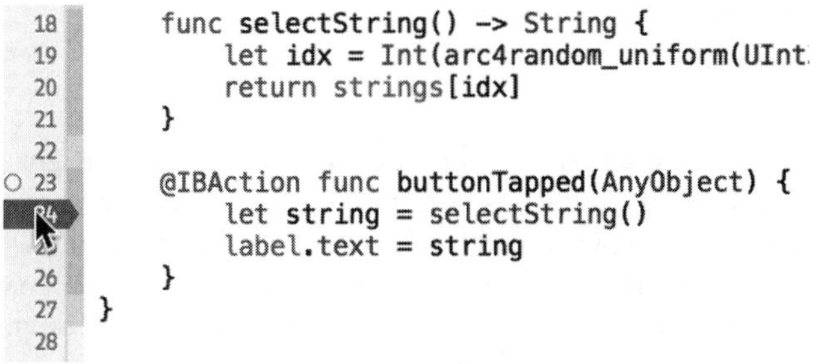

```
18      func selectString() -> String {
19          let idx = Int(arc4random_uniform(UInt.
20          return strings[idx]
21      }
22
23      @IBAction func buttonTapped(AnyObject) {
24          let string = selectString()
25          label.text = string
26      }
27  }
28
```

FIGURE 2-19

Using the Debugger

Build and run your program in the iOS simulator; then tap the Show String button.

Instead of changing the label to a new string, you are redirected back to Xcode and presented with the debugger view pane at the bottom of the code editor, as shown in Figure 2-20. The current line of code is highlighted in green in the code editor. This line of code has not been executed yet—the debugger is awaiting your command. You will also be unable to interact with your program in the iOS simulator because its execution has been halted by the debugger, which is now controlling the program.

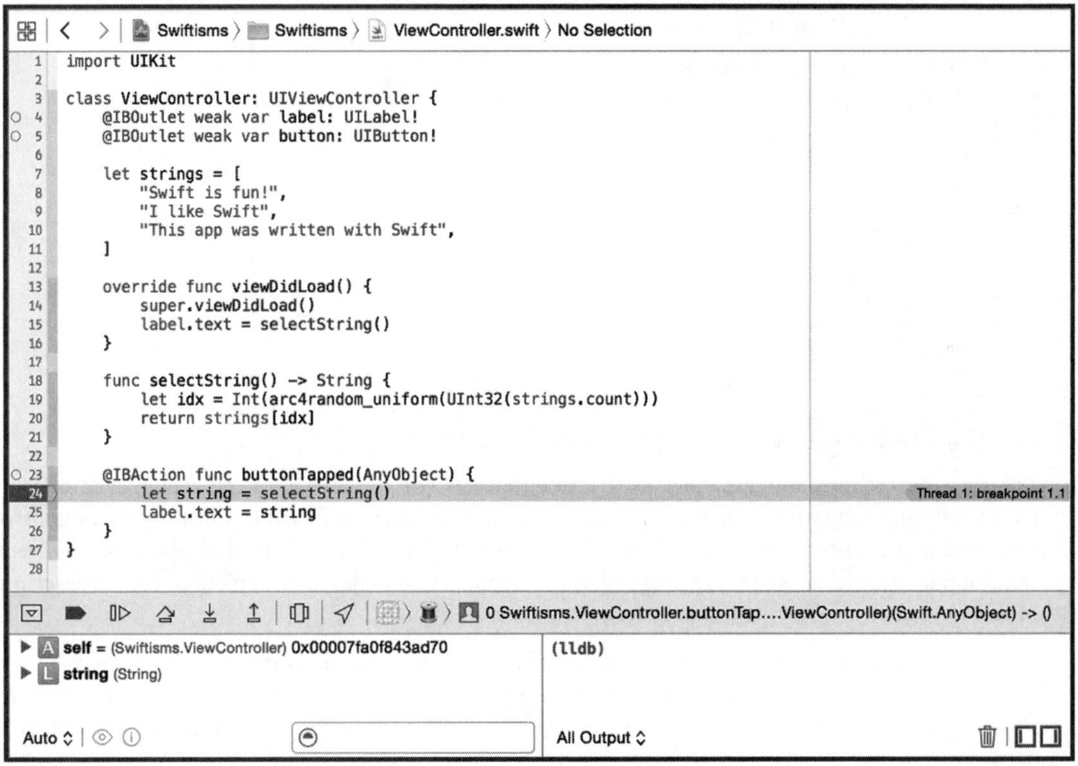

FIGURE 2-20

The debugger view consists of a toolbar and two separate panes.

Using the Hierarchical View

In the left pane, you see a hierarchical view of all the variables that are currently in scope. Right now, you should see two variables, "self" and "string". Each is also marked with its type and memory address. The variable "self" points to the view controller, the object that contains the breakpoint you set. "string" points to the variable `string` declared locally to the `buttonTapped()` function. Clicking on the disclosure arrow next to this variable will show a hierarchical list of view controller's instance variables. Each one of these, in turn, will have a sublist of all the variables that each of them contain. Play around with this view to get a feel for how the relevant variables are listed. The list should look similar to the one in Figure 2-21.

FIGURE 2-21

Using the Debugger View and the po Command

The right side of the debugger view is a console that lets you interact with the debugger. You can pass it various commands that are understood by the debugger and used to output data or control it. One common command is po, which is short for "print object." It is used to display a textual representation of a variable. Try typing **po self** at the debugger console now. You should see a description of the view controller printed in response, as shown in Figure 2-22.

You can examine any variable that is currently in scope using the po command. You can call methods or reference an object's properties using po, just as though you were writing code. Figure 2-23 shows how you can reference `self.strings` or even call `self.selectString()` in the debugger console.

> **NOTE** *Of course, you don't need to reference strings using* `self.strings` *in the debugger console because strings is already in scope. You could enter* po *strings directly to display the contents of the* `strings` *variable.*

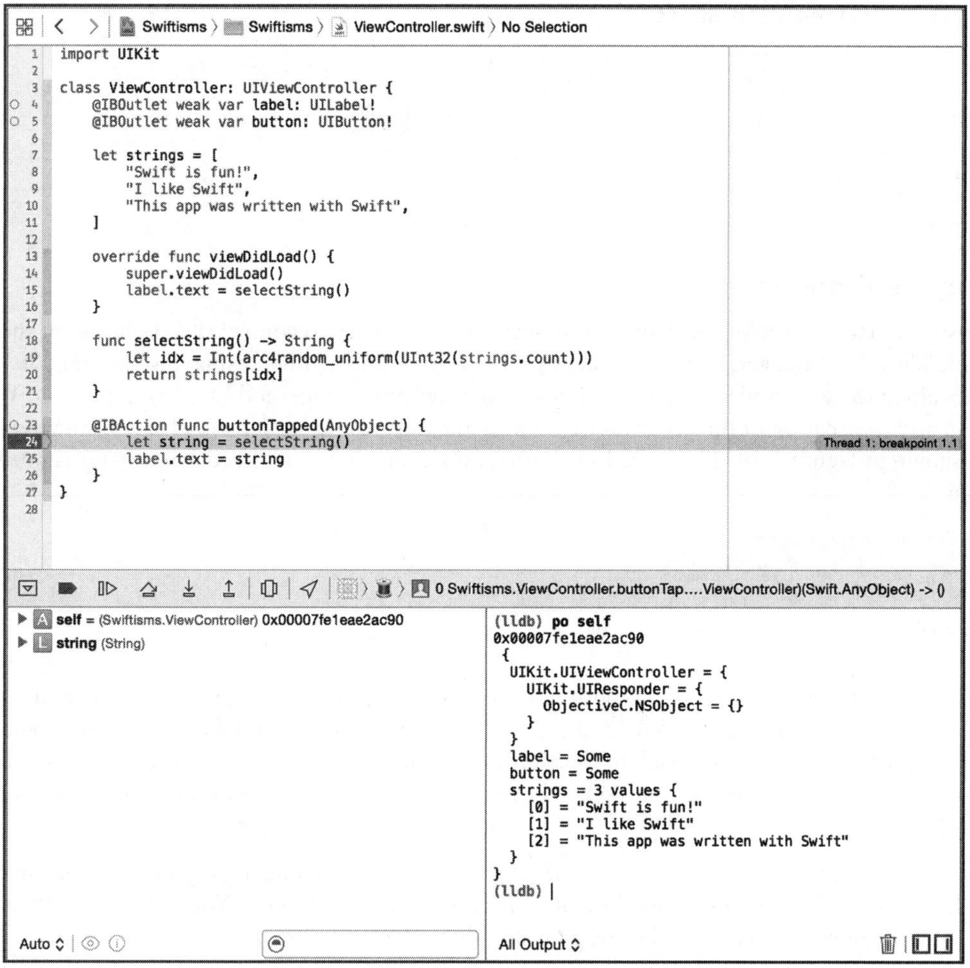
Swiftisms
Swiftisms
ViewController.swift
No Selection
import UIKit
class ViewController: UIViewController {
@IBOutlet weak var label: UILabel!
@IBOutlet weak var button: UIButton!
let strings = [
"Swift is fun!",
"I like Swift",
"This app was written with Swift",
]
override func viewDidLoad() {
super.viewDidLoad()
label.text = selectString()
}
func selectString() -> String {
let idx = Int(arc4random_uniform(UInt32(strings.count)))
return strings[idx]
}
@IBAction func buttonTapped(AnyObject) {
let string = selectString()
label.text = string
}
}
Thread 1: breakpoint 1.1
0 Swiftisms.ViewController.buttonTap....ViewController)(Swift.AnyObject) -> ()
self = (Swiftisms.ViewController) 0x00007fe1eae2ac90
string (String)
(lldb) po self
0x00007fe1eae2ac90
{
UIKit.UIViewController = {
UIKit.UIResponder = {
ObjectiveC.NSObject = {}
}
}
label = Some
button = Some
strings = 3 values {
[0] = "Swift is fun!"
[1] = "I like Swift"
[2] = "This app was written with Swift"
}
}
(lldb)
Auto
All Output

FIGURE 2-22

When displayed in the debugger console, objects generally print out their parent object (if they are subclassed) as well as the contents of their instance variables. Some special object types, such as arrays and dictionaries, will show their constituent elements instead. Strings will print out their contents, and numbers (integers and floating-point variables) will show their numerical values. Generally speaking, what is printed in the console with po is the most useful representation of an object.

```
(lldb) po self.strings
3 values
 {
   [0] = "Swift is fun!"
   [1] = "I like Swift"
   [2] = "This app was written with Swift"
}
(lldb) po selectString()
"This app was written with Swift"

(lldb) |
```

All Output ↕   🗑 | ☐☐

FIGURE 2-23

Executing the Program

The most powerful feature of the debugger, however, is the ability to control the execution of the program. With the debugger, you can execute your program line by line, displaying the state of variables along the way, and you can even jump into functions and methods as they are called. You can control the execution of the program by clicking the buttons on the left-hand side of the tool-bar, as shown in Figure 2-24. There are four buttons for controlling the execution of your running program.

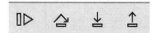

FIGURE 2-24

The first button, Continue program execution, simply continues to run the program. However, if you hit the breakpoint again, you will be dropped back into the debugger. Click Continue program execution and you are redirected back to the simulator. Click the Show String button and note that you are immediately dropped back into the debugger—line 24 was once again executed when you clicked Show String.

The second button, Step over, executes the current line of code—the one highlighted in green in the editor. Execution will stop on the next line of code. Click this button once. You will see that line 25 becomes highlighted in green. Clicking Step over again will execute line 25.

You can continue clicking Step over to your heart's content. Eventually, code execution will leave your own code, and jump into UIKit code. This represents the execution of your application's event loop, which is managed by the UIKit framework. When you jump into external code like UIKit, you will not have the elegant source code view as you have with your own code. Instead, you will be in decompiled code, and will only see the actual machine instructions that represent your program. However, you can still step through this code line by line if you want. You can even dump the contents of the simulator or device's registers by entering **register read** in the debugger console. For now, however, click the Continue program execution button to continue running your program.

Click Show String in your running app. Once again, you will be dropped back into the debugger, at line 24 of `ViewController.swift`. This time, click Step into, the third control button. Because you are calling a method, `selectString()`, in this line of code, the debugger will step forward one line *into* that method and pause execution. Line 19 in the code editor is now highlighted in green. You could continue using the same controls you used before: the Continue program execution button to leave the debugger and continue running your program, The Step over button to pause execution on line 20, or even the Step into button again to step into any functions called by line 19 of your code. However, now is a perfect time to introduce the final debugger control: Step out, the last of the four control buttons in the debugger toolbar. The Step out button jumps you *out* of the function or method you are currently examining, returning you back to the line of code that calls that function or method. Select the Step out, and note that you are back on line 24 of your program.

Play around with the debugger controls to get a feel for them. Xcode's debugger is an amazingly powerful tool, and using it is an important skill for any iOS or OS X developer to master. Chapter 10 covers the use of the debugger in much greater detail, including some of its advanced capabilities, but it's useful to have a working knowledge of it.

SUMMARY

In this chapter, you got acquainted with Xcode, the developer tool used to create iOS and OS X applications with both Objective-C and Swift. As you can see, little about the actual development process has changed with the transition from Objective-C to Swift. Ultimately, only the language itself is different. Your existing knowledge of iOS and OS X development is still as relevant as ever with regards to the tools offered by Apple.

The remaining chapters take a much more detailed look at the Swift programming language and how it can be used to write iOS and OS X applications with ease. You will continue to get a more in-depth look at Apple's developer tools and APIs as well, although they will continue to be as familiar when using Swift as they were when writing apps with Objective-C.

3
Classes, Structs, and Enums

WHAT'S IN THIS CHAPTER?

➤ Initializing and deinitializing classes and structs

➤ Adding properties to classes and structs

➤ Observing changes in property values

➤ Understanding methods

➤ Defining and using enumerated types

WROX.COM CODE DOWNLOADS FOR THIS CHAPTER

You can find the wrox.com downloads for this chapter at `http://www.wrox.com/go/proswift` on the Download Code tab. The code for this chapter is contained in the following files:

➤ `AlarmClock.swift`

➤ `BankAccount.swift`

➤ `Playgrounds.zip`

➤ `Square.swift`

This chapter covers the object-oriented programming features of the Swift language. Although Swift draws inspiration from a variety of programming languages and programming paradigms, it is, first and foremost, an object-oriented language. Writing programs in Swift requires a thorough understanding of object-oriented programming, and in particular, the object-oriented features available to Swift programmers. After reading this chapter, you should have the knowledge necessary to understand and write code that makes use of Swift's classes, structs, and enumerations.

Many of the examples given in this chapter are found in the `Playgrounds.zip` file available from the download section of this chapter. Feel free to load those playgrounds into Xcode and experiment on your own as you read the chapter.

WORKING WITH CLASSES AND STRUCTS

Like most object-oriented languages, including Objective-C, Swift supports two basic object-oriented data structures: classes and structs. Swift's classes are very similar to classes in Objective-C: They group pieces of data in *instance variables* and define an interface, or method, for working with that data.

Swift's structs, on the other hand, are substantially different from structs in Objective-C. In the latter, structs are the same as they are in C: discrete data structures that contain only variables and have no methods or other behavior associated with them. In Swift, however, structs function nearly identically to classes and are defined and used in much the same way. They support nearly the same features as Swift classes, including methods. The only major difference is in how they are copied in memory. The subtle differences between classes and structs are highlighted as this chapter progresses.

Swift also dispenses with the concept of header files used in Objective-C (as well as C and C++). There is no separation between the *declaration* and *definition* of classes, structs, and enums in Swift; both declaration and definition happen in the same file, in the same block of code. In Swift, as in Objective-C, it is considered good style to define only one class per file.

> **ONE CLASS PER FILE**
>
> In both Objective-C and Swift, you may define as many classes, structs, and enums as you want in a single file. However, programmers are encouraged to declare only one class per file, as this makes your code base much more organized and readable. Of course, like most rules, this can be broken from time to time if doing so would actually increase organization and readability. For example, many times, an abstract base class is declared in the same file as a subclass, particularly if that subclass is the only implementation of that abstract base class in the code base. Protocols are also often declared in the same file as a class that implements them. While you should strive to define only one class per file (and name the file after that class), feel free to do otherwise in certain instances if you think it makes more sense. This is not a hard and fast rule, and your own judgment wins out over any prevailing style.

Defining Classes and Structs

You define Swift classes using the `class` keyword, followed by the body of the class in a pair of curly braces. For example, the following code shows a class that describes a book.

```
class Book {
    var title = ""
    var author = ""
    var isbn = ""
}
```

> **NOTE** *A class's properties are declared identically to how you declare constants and variables in Swift. If this looks odd or unfamiliar right now, don't worry. Class and struct properties are described in much more detail later in the chapter.*

The preceding code block defines a simple `Book` class with three properties: `title`, `author`, and `isbn`. Properties can be thought of as the bits of data that make up individual instances of the class. They are much like *instance variables* in other object-oriented languages, such as Objective-C and Java. Basic properties, such as the ones mentioned previously, are declared just like constants and variables in Swift, although as you'll see later in the chapter, properties have a lot of other new features that make them more powerful than ordinary variables and constants. Together, instance variables and methods define the makeup and behavior of classes and structs in Swift.

Right now, the `Book` class has no behavior associated with it. Most often, a class exposes behavior and ways to work with its internal data structures in the form of *methods*. Methods are explored in greater detail later in this chapter.

Structs are defined in almost exactly the same way, except you use the `struct` keyword instead of `class`. Take a look at a simple struct to store the first and last name of a person:

```
struct Person {
    var firstName = ""
    var lastName = ""
}
```

Now that you have a `Person` struct defined, you can even modify the `Book` class so its author property references a `Person` struct:

```
class Book {
    var title = ""
    var author = ""
    var isbn = ""
}
```

Naming rules for classes and structs are the same as they are for constants and variables. They must start with an alphabetic character; after the initial character, they may contain letters or numbers, as well as some special symbols such as underscores. Unicode characters that fit this description are also allowed, just as they are in variable and constant names. Letters may be uppercase or lowercase, but typically class and struct names start with an initial capital letter and are written in CamelCase, rather than using separate characters such as underscores.

Classes and structs work together to define the data types and structure of a program. The preceding two examples are fairly simple data structures, but both classes and structs can be much more powerful than these simple examples. Let's take a look at the more advanced features of classes and structs in Swift.

Initializing Classes and Structs

Class and struct definitions aren't terribly useful in and of themselves. After all, you have *a* book, not just *book*. In order to make use of your class and struct definitions, you need to create instances of them. This process is referred to as *instantiation*. The syntax for creating new instances of a class or struct looks just like making a function call, with the name of the class or struct followed by a set of parentheses:

```
let book = Book()
```

The preceding line of code creates a new `Book` object, with the properties set to default values. (In the case of the `Book` class defined earlier, these properties are set to `nil` initially.)

But how are new instances of a class initialized? Methods called *initializers* create and initialize instances of classes and structs. Through initializers, you can also provide initial values for each of a class or struct's properties. By default, all structs have memberwise initializers. Memberwise initializers allow you to specify the values of the struct's properties when creating the struct by passing those values as named parameters during initialization. A new `Person` instance can be instantiated with your own property values using this memberwise initializer:

```
let author = Person(firstName: "Jane", lastName: "Doe")
```

This creates a new `Person` object with the `firstName` "Jane" and `lastName` "Doe."

Swift requires that all of a class or struct's properties are set to a value by the time the class or struct has finished being created. This differs from Objective-C, where instance variables received a default value of `nil` (or 0 for scalar types) if they were not explicitly initialized during construction of an object. You may initialize a Swift object's properties by providing either of the following

➤ An initial value in the declaration of a property

➤ An initializer that sets a property to a value

Creating an Initial Value

When declaring a property, you can set it to a value, just like a variable or constant declaration. For example, you can modify the `Book` and `Person` classes to have default values:

```
struct Person {
    var firstName = "Jane"
    var lastName = "Doe"
}

class Book {
    var title = "The Great American Novel"
    var author = Person()
    var isbn = "978-3-16-148410-0"
}
```

Both the `Person` struct and `Book` class are created with these initial values. In the case of the `Person` struct, you can still override these values in the memberwise initializer. You can also change the value of these properties after creation if you want.

By default, all structs have a memberwise initializer. Classes, on the other hand, have a default initializer only if all of its properties are set to an initial value—otherwise, you must provide one yourself. You may also override the initializer for structs if you do not want to use the default initializer that is created automatically by the Swift compiler.

Defining Your Own Initializer

Of course, providing default values makes your classes and structs fairly inflexible. You probably don't want *all* of your `Book` objects to have a title of "The Great American Novel," and changing that title after creation is both cumbersome and error-prone. There is a better way: Swift allows you to provide your own initializer. Just like functions, initializers can take arguments that allow you to modify the values of a class or struct's properties when they are created.

Defining your own initializer is easy: You provide an `init()` method in the definition of your class or struct. (You learn more about methods later in this chapter.) You define an `init()` method just like a function, but it appears in the body of the class or struct. Experienced Objective-C developers no doubt recognize this method name: A method called `init()` is also used to initialize instances of Objective-C classes as well. Unlike the similarly named methods in Objective-C, however, an `init()` method in Swift does not return a value—you use it exclusively for setting up a new instance of a class or struct.

OBJECTIVE-C'S INIT METHOD

Initializers are often referred to as *constructors* in other object-oriented languages such as Java. Objective-C also has object constructors in the form of `init` methods. However, in Objective-C, there is nothing special about these methods. Conventionally, programmers set up the initial state of an object in `init` methods, but in reality they are just like any other method. Because they are like any other Objective-C method, programmers have to explicitly return the newly initialized object from the `init` method. Typically, these methods simply return their receiver (often the last line is `return self;`), but it is possible to return a completely different object (this is often the case in so-called "class clusters," such as `NSString`).

Swift's initializers act more like constructors in Java. You use them exclusively to set up a new instance of a class or struct, and you do not return an object or any other value from a Swift initializer.

You can modify the `Book` class from before to set its properties to values passed in by the caller:

```
class Book {
    var title: String
    var author: Person
    var isbn: String
```

```
    init(title: String, author: Person, isbn: String) {
        self.title = title
        self.author = author
        self.isbn = isbn
    }
}
```

You specify these parameters when creating an instance of the `Book`:

```
let book = Book(title: "The Great American Novel",
                author: Person(firstName: "Jane", lastName: "Doe"),
                isbn: "978-3-16-148410-0")
```

Note that you specify the names of the parameters when instantiating the class. Recall from Chapter 2 that function parameters can be named. When calling initializers, you *must* specify the names of the parameters to the `init()` method. This is because classes and structs can actually have multiple `init()` methods, each of which may take parameters that mean different things, and perform different operations on these parameters. Because the `init()` methods are called implicitly, Swift requires that you specify the parameter names so the compiler knows which `init()` method to invoke.

Writing an Initializer

Consider, for example, a `Distance` class, which stores distances in meters. It may be handy to write initializers that take distances in meters, centimeters, and inches, and convert them to distances in meters. A simple struct for storing this data looks like this:

```
struct Distance {
    var meters = 0.0

    init(meters: Double) {
        self.meters = meters
    }

    init(centimeters: Double) {
        self.meters = centimeters / 100.0
    }

    init(inches: Double) {
        self.meters = inches / 39.3701
    }
}
```

All three `init()` methods take a single parameter, a `Double`, so you must specify the parameter name so Swift knows which `init()` method you should use to create the object:

```
let d1 = Distance(meters: 1.0)
let d2 = Distance(centimeters: 100.0)
let d3 = Distance(inches: 39.3701)
```

As with functions, you can specify both an external and internal parameter name. (Recall that if you do not specify an external name, it is the same as the internal name.) Often, this can enhance the readability of a function or method (including an initializer). With this in mind, you could rewrite your `Distance` class:

```
struct Distance {
    var meters = 0.0

    init(inMeters meters: Double) {
        self.meters = meters
    }

    init(inCentimeters centimeters: Double) {
        self.meters = centimeters / 100.0
    }

    init(inInches inches: Double) {
        self.meters = inches / 39.3701
    }
}
```

As with functions, the first part of the parameter name is the external name, the name callers use when calling the method; the second part is the name within the method body to refer to the parameter. You can instantiate instances of `Distance` like this:

```
let d1 = Distance(inMeters: 1.0)
let d2 = Distance(inCentimeters: 100.0)
let d3 = Distance(inInches: 39.3701)
```

You must instantiate a Swift object with named parameters, even if the class or struct has only one initializer. However, you can suppress this behavior by specifying an underscore ("_") as the external name. You can rewrite the `Distance` struct so that the first initializer has no external name:

```
struct Distance {
    var meters = 0.0

    init(_ meters: Double) {
        self.meters = meters
    }

    init(inCentimeters centimeters: Double) {
        self.meters = centimeters / 100.0
    }

    init(inInches inches: Double) {
        self.meters = inches / 39.3701
    }
}
```

With this change, you no longer have to use a named parameter when creating a distance in meters:

```
let d1 = Distance(1.0)
```

You may only suppress named parameters when doing so does not create an ambiguous `init()` method. Otherwise, the Swift compiler will emit an error. In the `Distance` struct example, the second two `init()` methods must have named parameters. However, if you modified the version that takes inches to take an `Int` instead of a `Double`, it, too, could have an unnamed parameter. It is best practice, however, to use parameter names with class and struct initializers, and only suppress named parameters when it is not confusing to do so.

Working with Multiple Initializers

If your class or struct has multiple initializers, you may call a different initializer from within another one. In fact, it is best practice to have one "designated initializer" that "convenience initializers" ultimately call after performing their own calculations. The `Distance` class could be modified to defer initialization to the first initializer:

```
struct Distance {
    var meters = 0.0

    init(_ meters: Double) {
        self.meters = meters
    }

    init(inCentimeters centimeters: Double) {
        self.init(centimeters / 100.0)
    }

    init(inInches inches: Double) {
        self.init(inches / 39.3701)
    }
}
```

Designated initializers are in no way required by the language, but they can make your code much clearer and more maintainable. (Swift does, however, have special support for designated and convenience initializers, particularly for the benefit of class inheritance, which will be described in the section "Understanding the Difference between Classes and Structs" later in this chapter.)

There is one caveat to the rule that initializers do not return a value: An initializer can return `nil` to indicate that creation of a class or struct failed. Such initializers are denoted with a question mark and return an optional type. Consider the `Distance` struct you created earlier. Distances cannot be less than 0, so you can modify the struct to fail if a negative distance value is used to instantiate the class:

```
struct Distance {
    var meters = 0.0

    init?(_ meters: Double) {
        if meters < 0.0 {
            return nil
        }
        self.meters = meters
    }

    init?(inCentimeters centimeters: Double) {
        self.init(centimeters / 100.0)
    }
```

```
        init?(inInches inches: Double) {
            self.init(inches / 39.3701)
        }
    }
```

With the preceding changes, instantiating distance will actually return an optional type, requiring you to unwrap the optional type:

```
    if let d = Distance(inCentimeters: -100.0) {
        println("Distance is \(d.meters) meters")
    } else {
        println("Could not create distance")
    }
```

You can instead define an `init!()` method (with an exclamation point instead of a question mark) that will return an implicitly unwrapped type instead.

UNWRAPPED TYPES

Swift introduces the concept of an optional type. Optional types are analogous to `nil` types in Objective-C: They represent a value that may or may not exist. Unlike `nil`, however, Swift's optional types are designed to complement its type system. In Swift, you are forced to deal explicitly with variables that are optional (that is, they may have a value, or they may be `nil`). This prevents many bugs that arise from the improper use of nonexistent values in Objective-C.

Related to the concept of optional types are wrapped and unwrapped values. A *wrapped* value is a value that is actually an optional type. An *unwrapped* value represents a value that was an optional type, but the actual value (if it exists) has been *unwrapped* from the optional.

Because any value coming from Objective-C may be `nil`, many Objective-C APIs actually return optional types. These optional types can be unwieldy to work with, so Swift allows you to assume they are not optional—that is, a value actually exists. When used as parameters to functions or methods, or as values returned from a function or method, these values are said to be *implicitly unwrapped*.

Optional types are covered in greater detail in Chapter 8.

One other caveat about failable initializers: A class must initialize all of its properties (either by defining default values or by setting them in the initializer) *before* failing. Structs (and enums, covered later in this chapter) do not fall under this requirement.

Deinitializing Classes

Just as classes can be initialized, so, too, can they be *deinitialized*. Classes are deinitialized when they are *deallocated*, or removed, from memory. Unlike Objective-C, Swift does not require you, the programmer, to manually manage memory. The compiler and runtime take care of memory management concerns for you. Behind the scenes, however, memory is still being allocated and deallocated, in accordance with the runtime's *automatic reference counting* system, so you do not need to concern yourself with freeing memory when your Swift objects are deallocated.

However, there may be times when you need to free up resources when an object is removed from memory. If you are working with files or communicating over a network, your object may have open file handles or network sockets that need to be closed when the object is no longer being used. Or you may have other non-memory resources that need to be freed.

To facilitate this, classes can implement a `deinit` method that is called when the object is removed from memory. The `deinit` method takes no arguments and returns no value. You cannot invoke this method yourself; it is invoked only by the Swift runtime. Here is a simple implementation of a `deinit` method, which prints a message when an object is removed from memory:

```
class Something {
    deinit {
        println("Removing object from memory")
    }
}
```

You may only implement `deinit` methods on classes. Structs and enums do not support the use of `deinit` methods.

WORKING WITH PROPERTIES

Properties are much like instance variables in other object-oriented languages. The major difference is that properties can have additional behavior associated with them. They can "wrap" instance variables, providing a controlled way to access the internal data of a class or struct. In essence, they are a combination of both instance variables and methods and have features in common with both. In fact, Swift dispenses with the concept of a discrete instance variable entirely, relying solely on properties to store an object's internal data.

Properties were first introduced to OS X and iOS programmers with the release of Objective-C 2.0 in 2006. Even so, they were essentially just syntax sugar for the more traditional method-based mechanism for accessing and mutating instance variables in Objective-C. Swift, on the other hand, has first-class support for properties, making them every bit as powerful and flexible as their Objective-C counterparts in a way more native to the language itself.

Using Simple Properties

In their simplest form, properties can simply be declared the same way you would declare variables, within the body of the class or struct you are defining. This code declares a simple `Color` struct that holds three red, green, and blue values that are initialized to 0.0:

```
struct Color {
    var red = 0.0
    var green = 0.0
    var blue = 0.0
}
```

You can also declare them without initial values. If you do not specify an initial value, however, you must supply a type, because without initial values, Swift cannot infer the type of a property:

```
struct Color {
    var red: Double
    var green: Double
    var blue: Double
}
```

Properties can be accessed or set using the familiar dot syntax:

```
var color = Color()
color.red = 1.0
color.blue = color.red
color.green = color.blue
```

As with variables, if a property is declared using the `var` keyword, then it is mutable; it can be changed after instantiation, as shown the preceding code. You can also declare variables using the `let` keyword, in which case they are immutable—they cannot be changed after creation:

```
struct Color {
    let red: Double
    let blue: Double
    let green: Double
}
```

If properties are declared as constants, however, you must set them when instantiating the object by passing initial values into the initializer:

```
let color = Color(red: 1.0, green: 0.0, blue: 0.5)
```

Constant values cannot be changed after instantiation, even within the class itself. However, if you do not initialize constants to a default value, you are allowed to set their value in initializer methods—but nowhere else:

```
struct Color {
    let red: Double
    let blue: Double
    let green: Double

    init(fromRed red: Int, green: Int, blue: Int) {
        self.red = Double(red) / 255.0
        self.green = Double(green) / 255.0
        self.blue = Double(blue) / 255.0
    }
}
```

One final caveat: If a struct's properties are mutable (they are declared with the `var` keyword), but you assign the object to a constant (using the `let` keyword), you cannot change the properties after creation—even though they were declared as variables. This restriction does not apply to classes, however.

Using Lazy Properties

Lazy properties are properties whose values are not computed or created until the property is first used. Properties with complex data structures or properties that may never be accessed and used are often declared as lazy to reduce the amount of time it takes to instantiate the object. Values that rely on outside data that may not be known until after instantiation are also excellent candidates for lazy properties. In Swift, it's trivial to denote a property as lazy: They are simply marked with the `lazy` keyword:

```
class DataObject {
    lazy var connection = DatabaseConnection()
}
```

New `DataObject` instances have a `connection` property, but the value is not set up until it is first used. If code never calls the `connection` property, it isn't created at all.

Lazy properties must always be declared as variables, not constants, because they may not be initialized until after the class or struct's `init()` method runs.

Using Computed Properties

You may want to define properties that are based on the state of the object when the property is accessed or set. Swift provides support for this operation in the form of computed properties. Computed properties are essentially a set of methods, one that computes the property and one that handles modifying the property. These methods are referred to as `get` and `set`, respectively, and you create a computed property by specifying these methods with a special syntax. Consider the case of a simple `Square` struct:

```
struct Square {
    var lengthOfSide: Int
}
```

You realize that you often want to get the perimeter of the square. Exposing this as a property would make your code simpler. Because it is a square, you can also compute the length of a single side given the perimeter of the entire shape. Putting this together, you can use computed properties to get the perimeter of a square, as well as set the length of a side:

```
struct Square {
    var lengthOfSide: Int
    var perimeter: Int {
        get {
            return self.lengthOfSide * 4
        }
        set(newPerimeter) {
            self.lengthOfSide = newPerimeter / 4
        }
    }
}
```

You can now modify an instance of a `Square` via the `perimeter` property (as well as the `lengthOf-Side` property), as shown in the code that follows.

```
var square = Square(lengthOfSide: 10)
let p1 = square.perimeter      // p1 == 40
square.perimeter = 100
let s1 = square.lengthOfSide      // s1 == 25
square.lengthOfSide = 4
let p2 = square.perimeter      // p2 == 16
```

Swift also offers a shorthand for declaring the setter for a computed property. You can specify the setter with no arguments. The setter has access to an implicit argument called `newValue` that represents the new value for the property. `Square` could be modified to utilize that shorthand notation:

```
struct Square {
    var lengthOfSide: Int
    var perimeter: Int {
        get {
            return self.lengthOfSide * 4
        }
        set {
            self.lengthOfSide = newValue / 4
        }
    }
}
```

You can also omit the setter for a computed property, in which case the property will be read-only. If you omit the setter, you can simply write the getter's body in a set of braces without the `get` keyword. You can modify `Square` to make it a read-only struct:

```
struct Square {
    var lengthOfSide: Int
    var perimeter: Int {
        return self.lengthOfSide * 4
    }
}
```

Note that even if a computed property is read-only, it is still declared as a variable, using the `var` keyword. This is because the property is not created until *after* the object's initializer runs.

Observing Property Changes

In addition to computed properties, Swift also has property observers. You can attach an observer to a property to execute an action either immediately before or after the property's value is changed. Although they fill a similar role as computed properties, property observers may make your code more clear, and in many cases they are more flexible than computed properties.

Property observers are created by attaching two methods, `willSet` and `didSet`, to a property, similarly to how `get` and `set` are attached to computed properties. `willSet` takes one argument that represents the new value that a property will be set to. `didSet` takes one argument that represents the old value that a property had before it was changed. As with computed properties, Swift offers a shorthand for working with these arguments: If no argument is specified, the new value can be referred to as `newValue` in the body of `willSet`, and the old value can be referred to as `oldValue` in the body of `didSet`.

Among other uses, you can use property observers to alert other objects to changes in an object's data. This is similar to the function of key-value observing (KVO) in the Cocoa and Cocoa Touch frameworks. For example, you can modify the Square struct you created earlier to alert observers to changes in the length of a side, as shown in Listing 3-1. The program described in Listing 3-1 prints "New value: 50" to the console when executed.

LISTING 3-1: Square.swift

```
struct ObservableSquare {
    var lengthOfSide: Int {
        willSet {
            println("New value: \(newValue)")
        }
    }

    init(lengthOfSide: Int) {
        self.lengthOfSide = lengthOfSide
    }
}

var square2 = ObservableSquare(lengthOfSide: 10)
square2.lengthOfSide = 50
```

KVO AND SWIFT

Unlike Objective-C classes, Swift classes do not have native support for KVO, but you can easily accomplish the same goal in a typesafe way using property observers. However, classes that inherit from NSObject *do* have support for KVO. If you need your class to support KVO but you do not want to use property observers, you can still inherit from NSObject in order to use KVO. Unfortunately, even when inheriting from NSObject, KVO is not automatic; properties you wish to observe with KVO must be marked with the dynamic keyword in order for KVO to be available in a Swift class.

UNDERSTANDING METHODS

Methods describe the behavior of a class or struct and allow outside code to interact with it in a safe, controlled way. Many consider this interface to be the cornerstone of object-oriented programming.

Simply put, methods are just functions that are tied to a specific class. Just as properties are declared almost identically to free variables and constants, methods, too, are declared like functions with the body of a class. The only thing really special about methods is that they receive an implicit argument, self, which refers to the object on which the method was called.

You can see methods in action in this simple definition of a BankAccount in Listing 3-2.

LISTING 3-2: BankAccount.swift

```swift
class BankAccount {
    let name: String
    var balance: Int

    init(name: String, initialBalanceInCents balance: Int) {
        self.name = name
        self.balance = balance
    }

    func toDollars() -> Double {
        return Double(self.balance) / 100.0
    }

    func deposit(amount: Int) -> Int {
        self.balance += amount
        return self.balance
    }

    func withdraw(amount: Int) -> Int {
        self.balance -= amount
        return self.balance
    }
}
```

There are three methods defined on `BankAccount`:

➤ `toDollars()`: Converts the balance (stored internally in cents) to a `Double`.

➤ `deposit()`: Takes in an amount and adds that to `balance`, returning the new balance.

➤ `withdraw()`: Takes an amount and subtracts that from `balance`, returning the new balance.

> **NOTE** *Just like functions, methods are not required to return a value. You can have a method that simply omits a return type and returns no value.*

You can call a method on an object using the familiar dot syntax:

```swift
var account = BankAccount(name: "John Doe", initialBalanceInCents: 100)
let balance = account.toDouble()
var newBalance = account.deposit(100)
newBalance = account.withdraw(150)
```

Note that the first parameter in a method is not a named parameter, so you do not need to specify a name when calling the method. However, method arguments after the first *do* have external names, which must be specified when calling the method. Listing 3-3 shows a simple `AlarmClock` with a method that takes multiple parameters.

LISTING 3-3: AlarmClock.swift

```swift
class AlarmClock {
    var alarmHour: Int = 0
    var alarmMinute: Int = 0

    func setAlarmForHour(hour: Int, minute: Int) {
        self.alarmHour = hour
        self.alarmMinute = minute
    }
}
```

To set the alarm, you call the `setAlarmForHour()` method, passing `hour` as an unnamed parameter and `minute` as a named parameter:

```swift
var alarm = AlarmClock()
alarm.setAlarmForHour(12, minute: 0)
```

At first glance, calling methods this way seems a bit odd. However, if you recall from Objective-C that method parameters were actually a part of the method name itself, you'll see that Swift's creators designed method calling in this fashion for compatibility with Objective-C. (The equivalent Objective-C method would be `setAlarmForHour:minute:`.)

As with functions, it is possible to specify your own external name for named parameters. You can even force callers to use a name for the first parameter by specifying an external name, and you can suppress the naming of subsequent parameters by using an underscore ("_") as the external name. But most idiomatic Swift code will use the default way of naming method parameters, as that most closely aligns with Objective-C.

UNDERSTANDING THE DIFFERENCE BETWEEN CLASSES AND STRUCTS

As you can see, in terms of features, there are very few differences between structs and classes in Swift. Both may have properties and methods, and at first glance, they largely seem to be interchangeable. Objective-C, on the other hand, also had both classes and structs, but they were substantially different—Objective-C's structs were just a vestige of its C inheritance, and only classes had object-oriented programming features. Why, then, include both in Swift?

There are a few key differences between structs and classes in Swift:

➤ Classes can inherit from other classes, taking on the behavior of a superclass. Structs cannot inherit from other classes.

➤ You can check the type of a class at runtime. You cannot check the type of a struct at runtime.

➤ Classes can have deinitializers to free up non-memory resources when instances of it are deallocated. Structs do not have deinitializers.

Perhaps the biggest difference between the two, however, is the way memory is handled. In Swift, classes are reference types, meaning that multiple variables or constants can point to the same object in memory. This is akin to how objects are handled in Objective-C and how pointers are handled in C. Structs, on the other hand, are value types. Multiple variables or constants do not point to the same instance of a struct in memory; rather, if a variable is set to the value of another variable, the struct is actually copied in memory, and the two variables point to distinctly different copies of the object. Mutating methods called on one of the variables will not alter the state of the other variable. To see this in action, take a look at Listing 3-4.

LISTING 3-4: References.playground

```
class Foo {
    var x = 0
}

struct Bar {
    var x = 0
}

var foo1 = Foo()
var foo2 = foo1
foo1.x     // 0
foo2.x     // 0
foo1.x = 10
foo1.x     // 10
foo2.x     // 10

var bar1 = Bar()
var bar2 = bar1
bar1.x     // 0
bar2.x     // 0
bar1.x = 10
bar1.x     // 10
bar2.x     // 0
```

You can load the code in Listing 3-4 into a playground to see the effects in action. Foo is defined as a class, whereas Bar is a struct. In the first set of code, a Foo object is instantiated and assigned to foo1. foo1 is then assigned to foo2. Because they are classes, the Foo instance only exists *once* in memory. foo1 and foo2 both point to the same instance of that class. This becomes evident when the property x is changed to 10 on foo1. After that change, the property x is equal to 10 on *both* foo1 and foo2—because they're pointing to the same object in memory.

This is not the case for Bar, which is a struct. In the second bit of code in Listing 3-4, an instance of Bar is created and assigned to bar1. bar1 is then assigned to bar2—but because it is a struct, the instance is actually copied in memory, and bar2 has its own copy. This becomes evident after changing the x property on bar1. After changing x, bar1.x is equal to 10, but bar2.x is still equal to 0. They are distinctly different objects.

This feature of Swift has ramifications not only for mutable objects (such as `Foo` and `Bar`, in this example), but for general program performance as well. Classes are not copied in memory, and they are passed around to functions and methods, and assigned to other variables, without incurring an additional memory cost (or the time to copy the object). Structs are *always* copied—when assigning them to other variables, or passing them to functions or methods—which comes with a slight cost in terms of memory usage and performance. Of course, structs are also easier to work with and reason about, and simpler, too, because they dispense with some object-oriented features such as class inheritance.

When designing your own program or library, you must decide whether your data types should be structs or classes. In most cases, you should use classes: They are more powerful than structs. Structs are best suited to basic data types, such as a simple grouping of values (perhaps to represent a point in 3D space, for example) with little behavior of their own, and no need to inherit behavior from other types. However, the choice of which to use is ultimately up to you, and is dictated by how you—and anyone using your code—plans to use your data structures.

WORKING WITH ENUMERATIONS

Swift offers one more composite data type: the enumeration, or enum for short. An enumeration groups together related types of objects, allowing you to work with categorical data in a typesafe way.

Thanks to its C heritage, Objective-C also had enumerations, but Swift's enumerations are much more powerful. A far cry from the simple constants of Objective-C, Swift enumerations have many of the same features as classes and structs. They even adopt some of the features found in unions in C. While they are not intended as a replacement for either classes or structs, they are a rich system unto themselves that can greatly improve the clarity—not to mention the type safety—of your Swift programs.

An enumerated type is created with the `enum` keyword. In its simplest form, it is nothing but a set of types that define the values for the enum. Consider a simple Color enum:

```
enum Color {
    case Red
    case Orange
    case Yellow
    case Green
    case Blue
    case Indigo
    case Violet
}
```

This enum defines eight cases, each representing one color of the rainbow. The cases are a single type, `Color`, and that type can contain any one of those eight values—but no other values. You reference a particular value using the type name followed by a dot and finally the value:

```
var color = Color.Red
```

If Swift is able to infer the type—such as when you change the value of an existing variable—you can leave out the type name and simply prepend the value with a dot:

```
var color = Color.Red
color = .Violet
```

Enumerated types are especially useful in switch statements. In a switch statement, you can write a case to handle each of an enum's values. The code that follows prints "color is violet" to the console:

```
var color = Color.Red
color = .Violet

switch color {
case .Red:
    println("color is red")
case .Violet:
    println("color is violet")
default:
    println("color is neither red nor violet")
}
```

The power of enums lies in their type safety. If you do not handle all of an enum's values and emit a default case, the Swift compiler emits an error and refuses to compile your code. This ensures that your code is correct and will run properly under all conditions.

SUMMARY

This chapter covered the ins and outs of Swift's object-oriented programming support. You learned how to create classes and structs, and the differences between the two. You learned how enums can be used to encapsulate a set of values in your program. Swift's rich type system gives you all the features you need to elegantly express the structure of your program and make certain guarantees about the type safety of the code you write. The following chapters will build on this foundation to show you how Swift, in combination with Cocoa and Cocoa Touch, makes writing OS X and iOS programs easy and even fun.

Concurrency in Swift

WROX.COM CODE DOWNLOADS FOR THIS CHAPTER

You can find the wrox.com downloads for this chapter at `http://www.wrox.com/go/ proswift` on the Download Code tab. The code for this chapter is contained in the following files:

➤   `async.swift`

➤   `threads.swift`

➤   `timers.swift`

➤   `gcd.swift`

Concurrency is the process by which a computer or individual program can perform multiple tasks simultaneously, including executing tasks or processes in the background. Modern computers have many programs running at the same time. Even "single task" operating systems such as iOS have many unseen programs running in the background, in addition to any user-facing programs that may be open. Each individual programs can run multiple actions at the same time. It is difficult and constraining to design and write iOS and OS X programs without an understanding of the concurrency primitives used by both operating systems.

This chapter introduces you to the foundations for concurrency programming used by OS X and iOS: classes such as NSTimer and NSThread, as well as libraries like Grand Central Dispatch. It also discusses the importance of concurrency, particularly in the use of asynchronous methods, in modern applications. By the end of the chapter, you will be well-versed in multitasking.

WHAT IS CONCURRENCY?

Consider the case of a computer with a single processor. Because it has only a single processor core, such a computer can only execute a single thread of computation at a time. Of course, modern computers are generally running dozens of tasks simultaneously, and even a single program may be performing multiple actions at the same time. If your theoretical computer has only a single processor, how can it run many programs? This single-processor computer can achieve this desired level of parallelism by having the processor switch between the multiple running programs rapidly.

Modern processors can execute multiple programs by allowing each to run for a short period of time—often as short as several milliseconds or even microseconds—and then switching to another process. While this may seem inefficient, a modern processor can execute several billion instructions per second, so a program running for even a millisecond—one one-thousandth of a second—can execute over a million instructions in that time frame. Rapidly switching processes gives the user the illusion that the computer is running many programs and performing many tasks simultaneously, even though the processor is only doing a single thing at any given time.

Of course, modern computers generally have more than one processor. iMacs, for example, have *four* processor cores, and even the iPhone 6 has two processor cores. The Mac Pro can have up to *six* processor cores. Multiple processor cores mean that the computer can, in fact, execute multiple tasks at the same time—one for each processor core. Even with multicore computing, it's useful to run more computing tasks than the number of processor cores. The conceptual model highlighted in the discussion of a single-processor computer can be helpful for understanding how even the most modern computer systems handle concurrency.

It is also important to note that concurrency can exist on two levels. As already mentioned, it is useful for a computer to be able to run multiple programs at the same time. This is more accurately described as *multiprocessing*. It's also useful for multiple threads of execution to exist with a single program. This is what programmers generally mean when they say *concurrency*. A program may have multiple threads of execution so that it may remain responsive when performing time-consuming computations, reading a large amount of data from a file, or communicating with remote services over a network, among other useful tasks.

Before delving deeply into the specific ways OS X and iOS handle both multiprocessing and concurrency, you might find it useful to clearly understand the different concepts used in each.

Understanding Processes

A *process* is a single instance of a computer program. Processes are often thought of as user-facing programs; Mail, Safari, and Calendar are all processes. Operating systems generally run numerous processes in the background, as well, which are useful for various system functionalities. Whereas a computer program is a static set of instructions that describe a computation, a process is a specific running instance of a program. An individual program can also be loaded into memory and executed multiple times; each instance of that program is another, separate process.

> **NOTE** *In general, multiple instances of a single program can be loaded into memory and run. However, on OS X, generally only one instance of a graphical program can be run at a time; attempting to launch a second instance of a graphical program brings the currently running process to the foreground.*

Processes are isolated into their own memory space and cannot interfere with the memory space of other processes running on the system. Processes also have their own set of open *descriptors*, or handles to files and other system resources such as network connections, allowing multiple processes to open up the same file or connection. The operating system manages the allocation of these resources to prevent interference from other processes, which can result in *deadlock*, a condition in which multiple code paths attempt to use the same file or other resource. Process isolation is also central to the operating system's security model.

Isolation between processes helps the system mitigate problems within a process, increasing both the stability and security of the system as a whole. Because one program cannot affect the state of another, a buggy program may crash but does not bring other processes down with it. Because of this isolation, however, individual processes cannot communicate directly with one another, so the operating system must provide a method of *interprocess communication* so that one process can share data with another.

INTERPROCESS COMMUNICATION ON OS X AND iOS

OS X is a collection of various operating system technologies drawn from the Mach kernel, the BSD operating system, and the Foundation framework used by the NeXTSTEP operating system. As a result, it provides a number of methods for interprocess communication (IPC):

➤ The Mach port primitive from the Mach kernel

➤ Pipes, named pipes, sockets, and shared memory from BSD

➤ Higher-level concepts provided by the Foundation framework, including distributed objects, distributed notifications, and the pasteboard.

OS X also provides a comprehensive framework, called Grand Central Dispatch, as an interface for interprocess communication. (Grand Central Dispatch is discussed in more detail later in this chapter.) Starting with Lion, many of these technologies are abstracted into a single interface known as XPC, which allows easy communication between running processes.

continues

continued

In the interest of security, iOS is much more restricted in the interprocess communication mechanisms available to developers. On iOS, only Grand Central Dispatch and the pasteboard are available.

Strictly speaking, this chapter is about concurrency, not multiprocessing, and interprocess communication is not vital to implement concurrent programs. Because of the limited communication features available on iOS, iOS developers especially do not make extensive use of IPC in their programs. The interprocess communication facilities of iOS and OS X are not covered in great detail here, but you may find it helpful to be aware of them.

Understanding Threads

A single program may have multiple paths of execution. These paths are known as *threads*. Threads are much like processes: Abstractly, they represent different computation sequences, and they are scheduled independently by the operating system. However, individual threads within a process are not isolated to the same degree as processes. They share the same memory space as their parent process and thus have access to the data structures of other threads. They also share other resources common to the process, such as open files and network handles. They can also communicate directly with each other (for example, a thread can call a method on an object created by another thread), so there is no need for the more complex interprocess communication facilities provided to processes.

Threads are most commonly used to allow an individual program to perform several tasks at once. Using threads, a program can open a large file, query a remote web service, and handle input from the user, all at the same time.

Of course, this simplified model of concurrent computation means that the isolation provided to processes by the operating system is nonexistent when dealing with threads. Individual threads are completely able to interfere with the memory of other threads, such as by deallocating another thread's objects or by changing the data referenced by another thread. Therefore, programs with multiple threads must take great care to protect critical areas of memory from other threads.

Threads are also scheduled in much the same way that the operating system schedules processes. A program cannot guarantee when or in what order threads are run. This can result in *race conditions* if two or more threads are accessing the same data structures, and the result of computation is dependent on which one accesses the data structure first (or last). Programmers must take care to ensure that computation is not dependent on two threads executing in a predictable order, or, if such an order is required, programmers must use data structures such as *semaphores* to guarantee that threads only operate on data in a specific order. Of course, if handled incorrectly, the use of semaphores can result in dead lock.

> **NOTE** *Luckily, many of the difficulties inherent in concurrent programming with threads are handled elegantly by the Grand Central Dispatch library available on both OS X and iOS, making multithreaded programming much easier for programmers. But even with the help of this library, there are many pitfalls to be aware of when writing concurrent programs.*

Because threads are not isolated in the same way as processes, a bug in one thread can easily affect other threads, or even cause an entire program to crash.

Why Concurrency?

Given the possible pitfalls inherent in multithreaded programming, you would not be remiss if you asked the question, why bother with concurrent programming at all? There are numerous reasons why you might want, or even need, to write a concurrent program. A multithreaded program can perform time-consuming computations without blocking the main thread of the program, allowing the program's user interface to remain responsive even while the program is performing complex calculations. Time-consuming computations may include math-heavy calculations that take a long time to run. It may also include simpler, but slow, tasks, such as reading a file from the disk or making a call to a remote web service. A program may even use concurrency to several small operations at once. For example, a web browser may create several threads so it can make multiple web requests at the same time, cutting down on the time it takes to download resources for a web page.

There is no doubt that concurrent programming is complex and error-prone. Luckily, Apple provides various libraries and frameworks to ease concurrent programming, but writing a concurrent program is still much more complex than single-threaded programming. However, concurrent programming can greatly increase the performance of your application, and there are times when writing a multithreaded program is simply unavoidable.

Designing Concurrent Programs

You must take care when writing a multithreaded program: It must still run correctly, protect critical data structures, and still run predictably, or not rely on predictability at all. You will probably find it beneficial to design a program to take advantage of concurrency—by offloading time-consuming tasks to separate threads and by ensuring that your classes and functions are designed with concurrency in mind.

When dealing with concurrent programming, many programmers take care to ensure that their methods and functions are *asynchronous*. Asynchronous programming is closely related to concurrent programming, and asynchronous code is often a fundamental part of any concurrent program. Unlike "normal" methods and functions, asynchronous methods do not directly return a value to the caller through a `return` statement. Rather, they accept a *callback* as an argument, perform their computation (perhaps on another thread, or even by calling an external program), and return the value by passing it to the callback function provided by the caller. Presumably, this callback function will in turn do something useful with the value provided by the asynchronous method. These callbacks are often closures or anonymous functions. Because closures are so easy to create and use, Swift offers great support for this style of asynchronous programming.

CONCURRENCY IN iOS AND OS X

As both the OS X and iOS platforms have evolved, concurrent programming has become more and more central to writing software for these systems. The increasing reliance on remote web services has only increased the importance of multithreaded programming, as has the increase of the number of processor cores available to programmers writing software for both operating systems. In modern iOS and OS X development, it is nearly impossible to avoid writing concurrent code.

But why is concurrent programming so important on OS X and iOS? Obviously it would be more straightforward—not to mention less error-prone—to write a single-threaded program. To understand the importance of concurrency in Mac and iOS programs, it is vital to understand how graphical programs work at a fundamental level in these environments.

Understanding Event Loops

Central to understanding the model of the development of graphical programs on OS X and iOS is the event loop. The event loop forms the basis of how programs receive input from the user (or from sources like the network), process those inputs, and perform computations.

Conceptually, programs in both environments run in a main event loop. The main event loop receives input from the user. On OS X, this can be mouse clicks and drags, menu selections, and keyboard presses, to name a few types of events. On iOS, these events may be swipes, button presses, or keyboard entry, among others. These events are received and dispatched to parts of your code that are set up to respond to them. These event handlers, in turn, may jump to other parts of your code that perform necessary computations. Once your code has handled a particular event, other events are dispatched; then the loop starts over again. This process repeats until the user exits your program.

On OS X and iOS, the main event loop runs on the *main thread*. Any code set up to handle events also runs on this main thread. This includes methods and functions that the event handlers may call to perform additional computations. This model is fairly simple, and it is easy to write code that executes only on the main thread. In fact, many simple programs never have to worry about spawning additional threads, and thus do not have to worry about the issues inherent to concurrent programming at all.

The problem, of course, is that long-running computations that are dispatched synchronously (the "classic" way to call methods and functions) block the main thread until they finish executing. This means that your program's user interface becomes unresponsive until this time-consuming operation is completed. On OS X, this is signified by the infamous spinning beach ball; even worse, on iOS, there is often no indication that an operation is taking a while to complete. An unresponsive interface is obviously frustrating to the user, so it is desirable to avoid this condition entirely.

Understanding Run Loops

Each thread is associated with a *run loop*. Run loops are encapsulated by objects provided by OS X and iOS, and generally you do not need to create run loops yourself—you simply need to provide the code used by the run loop, and the appropriate data structures are created for you. The main thread's run loop, appropriately referred to as the *main run loop*, is even created automatically by the machinery that sets up your program's environment, so you do not need to worry about its creation or structure at all.

Run loops can be thought of as an implementation of the general concept of the event loop described before. They receive events from the user and dispatch those events to the appropriate handler. While the main run loop generally handles user interface events (such as mouse clicks or swipes), the run loops for other threads can handle input from other sources, such as timers (discussed later in this chapter).

> **NOTE** *While every thread has a run loop, you don't always have to set up the run loop yourself. In fact, you only need to specify the code used to create the actual loop if your thread needs to process incoming events. If you are simply using another thread to perform a background task, you don't need to configure the actual loop at all.*

Understanding Asynchronous Methods

Asynchronous methods (or functions) are methods that do not directly return a value (through the use of the `return` keyword); rather, they accept a *callback* as a parameter, and the method—after performing its own computations—invokes that callback, perhaps passing it some value it has calculated. In this way, values can be returned to the caller without the caller having to block on the function. Asynchronous methods make use of Swift's closures, providing an easy syntax for defining and calling the callback parameter.

Listing 4-1 shows a simple implementation of asynchronous functions in Swift.

LISTING 4-1: Async.swift

```
func asyncFunction(callback: () -> ()) {
    println("Called asyncFunction()")
    callback()
}

func asyncFunctionWithReturnValue(callback: (Int) -> ()) {
    println("Called asyncFunctionWithReturnValue()")
    callback(100)
}

asyncFunction({
    println("Called asyncFunction's callback")
```

continues

continued

```
    })

    var val = 0
    println("Before callback: val is \(val)")
    asyncFunctionWithReturnValue({ x in
        val = x
    })
    println("After callback: val is \(val)")
```

The code in Listing 4-1 defines two functions. The first, `asyncFunction()`, takes a single parameter, a callback. The callback is a function (or a closure—a function is really just a special case of a closure in Swift) that takes no parameters and returns no value. `asyncFunction()` simply calls the callback.

The second function, `asyncFunctionWithReturnValue()`, demonstrates how an asynchronous function may return a value to the caller. It, too, accepts a callback function as a parameter; however, this callback takes one parameter, an `Int`. This integer is passed to the callback function when it is invoked by `asyncFunctionWithReturnValue()`.

In the main body of the program, the calls to these asynchronous functions are made. The first simply passes in a closure that, when invoked, prints "Called asyncFunction's callback" to the console.

The call to `asyncFunctionWithReturnValue()`, on the other hand, is a bit more complicated. First, you initialize the variable `val` to 0. You then pass in a callback that takes a single parameter, x. In the callback, `val` is set to the value x passed to your callback function.

Running the program in Listing 4-1 should result in the following being written to the console:

```
Called asyncFunction()
Called asyncFunction's callback
Before callback: val is 0
Called asyncFunctionWithReturnValue()
After callback: val is 100
```

It is important to note that asynchronous methods and functions do not in and of themselves implement any sort of concurrency. The callbacks are still invoked on the same thread as the caller. However, asynchronous functions and closures are integral to the use of Grand Central Dispatch, discussed later in this chapter. Using Grand Central Dispatch, you *can* implement concurrency in your program.

RUNNING SWIFT COMMAND-LINE PROGRAMS

The program in Listing 4-1 is intended to be run as a command-line program. You can import it into an Xcode command-line tool project and run it from there, but it is simple to run from the command line itself. You can run a Swift file as a command-line program by executing `xcrun swift /path/to/file.swift` from your favorite terminal application.

Understanding NSTimer

The Foundation framework in both OS X and iOS provides a high-level, abstract way to make a program's operations concurrent: the NSTimer class. An NSTimer instance allows you to schedule a method call at some point in the future, on a given run loop, which may be the main run loop or an alternative run loop.

It is worth noting that NSTimer is not in and of itself a concurrency mechanism. NSTimers are simply ways to trigger a method call at some point in the future. However, because NSTimer instances can be scheduled for a given run loop (or run loop mode), you can use them in conjunction with run loops to provide concurrency in an application. Regardless of whether NSTimers are used as part of concurrent programming or not, it's useful to be aware of them and know how to use them.

Creating and scheduling an NSTimer is fairly simple. Listing 4-2 shows a complete program that schedules and runs a timer.

LISTING 4-2: Timers.swift

```swift
import Foundation

@objc class SayTime {
    var count = 0

    func sayOne(timer: NSTimer!) {
        count++
        NSLog("One second!")
        if count == 15 {
            NSLog("Fifteen seconds")
            timer.invalidate()
            exit(0)
        }
    }

    func sayFive(timer: NSTimer!) {
        NSLog("Five seconds!")
    }

    func sayTen(timer: NSTimer!) {
        NSLog("Ten seconds!")
    }
}

let hello = SayTime()
let timer1 = NSTimer(timeInterval: 1.0,
                     target: hello,
                     selector: "sayOne:",
                     userInfo: nil,
                     repeats: true)
let timer2 = NSTimer(timeInterval: 10.0,
                     target: hello,
                     selector: "sayTen:",
```

continues

continued

```
                        userInfo: nil,
                        repeats: false)
    let timer3 = NSTimer(timeInterval: 5.0,
                        target: hello,
                        selector: "sayFive:",
                        userInfo: nil,
                        repeats: false)
    NSRunLoop.currentRunLoop().addTimer(timer1, forMode: NSDefaultRunLoopMode)
    NSRunLoop.currentRunLoop().addTimer(timer2, forMode: NSDefaultRunLoopMode)
    NSRunLoop.currentRunLoop().addTimer(timer3, forMode: NSDefaultRunLoopMode)
    NSRunLoop.currentRunLoop().run()
```

Listing 4-2 creates a simple class, `HelloWorld`, that implements three methods, each of which prints a message to the console at certain intervals. Because you are working with classes from the Foundation kit, namely `NSTimer` and `NSRunLoop`, Foundation is imported (using the `import` keyword) on the first line of the program. Because methods of the `HelloWorld` class are invoked from `NSTimer`, a class implemented in Objective-C, `HelloWorld` must be a class that is compatible with Objective-C, so it is marked with the `@objc` attribute. (Chapter 9 covers interoperating with Objective-C from Swift in more detail.)

In the body of the program itself (shown below the class definition), you first create an instance of `HelloWorld`, and then three instances of `NSTimer`. The first instance, `timer1`, invokes the `sayOne()` method every second (until the method explicitly exits, using the `exit()` function, of course). `timer2` invokes `sayTen()` after ten seconds, and `timer3` invokes `sayFive()` after five seconds. You then add the timers to the current run loop and kick off the run loop.

> **NOTE** *Typically, you don't have to call* `run()` *on the current run loop. However, this is necessary when scheduling* `NSTimer` *instances in a command-line program, like the one in Listing 4-1. In graphical programs, you generally do not have to worry about this.*

When you run the program in Listing 4-2, you should see "Hello, world!" printed to the console every second for fifteen seconds. Every five seconds, a different message is printed. As you can see, despite the fact that the timers were created and added to the run loop in different orders, the messages indicating five, ten, and fifteen seconds should be printed in the proper order, and interlaced appropriately with the other messages that are printed.

Although this example is very simple, timers are fairly versatile. They can be scheduled to run on *any* run loop (not just the current one, as the program in Listing 4-2 does). You can configure them to repeat or only run once, and you can pass additional context to the target method using the `userInfo` parameter. However, it must be stressed that timers—while very useful—do not in and of themselves grant your program concurrency. They are actually dispatched as part of the event loop, just like other input sources, and their target methods are called synchronously, so the execution of the event loop will be blocked until the target method returns. However, in conjunction with run loops, timers are often used in concurrent programming, and general knowledge of them is useful no matter the structure of your program.

> **NOTE** *Timers are not guaranteed to run at precisely the interval you specify in their constructor. OS X and iOS attempt to run the timer at the given interval, but because timers are synchronous and operate similarly to other input sources in the event loop, it is possible they will not fire exactly when you specify. For example, when running the program in Listing 4-2, you may see that the "Hello, world!" message is sometimes printed slightly more or slightly less than one second apart.*

Understanding NSThread

The Foundation framework also provides a class, NSThread, to encapsulate the details of creating and running new threads in a program. The NSThread class makes it easy to create a new thread in an object-oriented fashion. It manages the setup and disposal of threads for you. It does *not* manage the protection and isolation of critical data structures, so the pitfalls surrounding multi-threaded programming discussed earlier in this chapter are still up to you, the programmer, to deal with. Even so, the class does greatly simplify the creation and management of new threads in your program.

Listing 4-3 shows a simple, but complete, example of how the NSThread class can achieve parallelism.

LISTING 4-3: Threads.swift

```
import Foundation


@objc class SayFunction {
    func sayOne() {
        NSLog("First method invoked after 0 seconds")
    }

    func sayTwo() {
        NSThread.sleepForTimeInterval(10.0)
        NSLog("Second method invoked after 10 seconds")
    }

    func sayThree() {
        NSThread.sleepForTimeInterval(5.0)
        NSLog("Third method invoked after 5 seconds")
    }
}

let hello = SayFunction()
let thread1 = NSThread(target: hello, selector: "sayOne", object: nil)
let thread2 = NSThread(target: hello, selector: "sayTwo", object: nil)
let thread3 = NSThread(target: hello, selector: "sayThree", object: nil)
thread1.start()
```

continues

continued

```
thread2.start()
thread3.start()
while (true) {}
```

Listing 4-3 again creates a simple class with three methods. Unlike the NSTimer example in Listing 4-2, however, each method is invoked only once. This is because threads, unlike timers, do not automatically repeat—they simply execute a method. (If you want a method to repeat forever, you must implement that repetition in the method you call from the thread, generally as a loop.)

As in Listing 4-2, you create an instance of the HelloWorld class called hello. You then create three threads configured to execute the three methods defined in the HelloWorld class. Finally, you start the threads. The final line of the program is also a loop that repeats forever. If you don't create such a loop in the main body of the program, the program will exit immediately, and in doing so, terminate the thread you created because it is a child of your main program.

When you run the program in Listing 4-3, you should see the following lines printed to the console:

```
First method invoked after 0 seconds
Third method invoked after 5 seconds
Second method invoked after 10 seconds
```

The key difference between the program in Listing 4-3 and the one in Listing 4-2 is that the code is actually running in a separate thread.

Understanding Grand Central Dispatch

While NSThread is an elegant way to implement concurrency in your program, it certainly has its drawbacks. It is not particularly versatile, requiring the definition of a class, and a method that acts as the loop for a class. This makes it cumbersome to use from C code and isn't particularly elegant to use from Swift, either. It also requires the programmer to implement many of the lower-level details of multithreading, including locks around critical memory structures and areas of code. Finally, it's not particularly efficient and requires the programmer to be mindful of performance issues when writing multithreaded code.

To address these concerns, Apple introduced Grand Central Dispatch in Mac OS X 10.6 and iOS 4. Grand Central Dispatch provides an interface for doing fine-grained, versatile multithreading. It essentially allows programmers to specify "work," or tasks, to be performed as functions or blocks, and it takes care of properly scheduling those blocks on multiprocessor architectures. Behind the scenes, it provides an implementation of *thread pools*, which greatly improve the performance of multithreaded code in many situations. Nowadays, it is the primary means to implement concurrent programs on both OS X and iOS.

THREAD POOLS

Many programs dynamically spawn dozens or even hundreds of threads. For example, a web server may spawn a new thread to handle each incoming request and then dispose of that thread once the request has completed. Creating a new thread comes with a certain amount of overhead: It requires the creation (and eventually the disposal) of data structures in the kernel itself, and it requires a certain amount of setup. While the kernel is very efficient at setting up new threads, programs that require a lot of threads can still hit a performance bottleneck.

Thread pools are designed to mitigate this problem. When a program starts up, it may create a number of threads and store them in a thread pool. When it needs a new thread, it will grab one from the pool, use it to perform its work, and then put it back. With thread pools, the overhead of spawning new threads can be minimized.

NSThread itself does not provide any pooling of threads, so prior to Grand Central Dispatch, programmers had to handle thread pooling themselves. With the introduction of Grand Central Dispatch, however, thread pooling is handled behind the scenes, making the use of even hundreds of threads very efficient and optimized for the specific hardware on which a program is running.

Unlike NSThread, Grand Central Dispatch is provided as a C interface, making it easy to call Grand Central Dispatch functions from Objective-C, C, Swift, or even other languages like C++. In fact, Grand Central Dispatch functions are mapped almost seamlessly into Swift, and calling into Grand Central Dispatch from Swift looks almost the same as it does in Objective-C and C—and it is much simpler than setting up an NSThread object from Swift.

Listing 4-4 shows a simple implementation of our "Hello, world!" programming, using Grand Central Dispatch instead of NSThread.

LISTING 4-4: Gcd.swift

```swift
import Foundation

func one() {
    NSThread.sleepForTimeInterval(1.0)
    NSLog("This is function one()")
}

func two() {
    NSThread.sleepForTimeInterval(10.0)
    NSLog("This is function two()")
}

func three() {
    NSThread.sleepForTimeInterval(5.0)
    NSLog("This is function three()")
}

NSLog("Starting")

dispatch_async(dispatch_get_global_queue(DISPATCH_QUEUE_PRIORITY_DEFAULT, 0), {
    three()
```

continues

continued

```
    })

    dispatch_async(dispatch_get_global_queue(DISPATCH_QUEUE_PRIORITY_DEFAULT, 0), {
        two()
    })

    dispatch_async(dispatch_get_global_queue(DISPATCH_QUEUE_PRIORITY_DEFAULT, 0), {
        one()
    })

    while (true) {}
```

In the version shown in Listing 4-4, concurrency is achieved in a simple, elegant way. Gone is the need to create a class; rather, you use a Swift closure to directly implement the functionality desired (a loop that prints "Hello, world!" every second). As in the NSThread version from Listing 4-3, you implement an infinite loop in the main program body so that the program doesn't exit immediately. When running this program, you should see the following console output after the program has run for fifteen seconds:

```
Starting
This is function one()
This is function three()
This is function two()
```

Although several techniques exist for implementing a multithreaded program on OS X and iOS, modern programs almost exclusively use Grand Central Dispatch. Thanks to its performance optimizations, as well as its near-universal interface, Apple advocates Grand Central Dispatch as the preferred mechanism for writing concurrent programs, and there is rarely a reason to fall back to older techniques like NSThread.

SUMMARY

Concurrent programming is vital to writing and understanding programs for OS X and iOS. In this chapter, you learned about the concepts behind multithreaded programs, including the important aspects of the design of concurrent programs and the problems inherent to the use of threads on Apple's platforms. As this chapter demonstrated, Swift is an excellent fit for both asynchronous and concurrent programming on OS X and iOS. Thanks to its automatic memory management features, multithreaded programming is even easier with Swift, although there are still some pitfalls that are important for programmers to be aware of. In the next chapter, you will put much of this knowledge to use in the design of programs that communicate with remote web services.

5

Interfacing with Web Services

WHAT'S IN THIS CHAPTER?

- ➤ Reviewing common web service architectures
- ➤ Communicating with remote web services
- ➤ Processing responses from web services
- ➤ Displaying data from web services

WROX.COM CODE DOWNLOADS FOR THIS CHAPTER

You can find the wrox.com downloads for this chapter at `http://www.wrox.com/go/proswift` on the Download Code tab. The code for this chapter is contained in the following file:

- ➤ `Album.zip`

Web services expose data and operations over HTTP. They can range from simple websites serving static web pages, to major e-commerce platforms, and even portals into commercial data stores on the Web. Almost all modern-day software makes use of the Web in some way. Web services are especially critical for mobile apps because mobile devices are limited in both computing and storage capacity and often rely on web services for data processing and storage. Knowledge of network programming is essential for iOS developers and even people writing software for OS X.

UNDERSTANDING WEB SERVICES

A web service is a website or server that exposes data or operations over the Web, that is, via HTTP. This can simply be a service that exposes a few points of data, such as a website that publishes news articles, or a more complex system, such as an e-commerce platform that allows customers to search for items, buy goods, and track orders. The key is that these operations are exposed over HTTP, and thus work with any device capable of making a standard web (or

HTTP) request. Often, web services expose URLs in a consistent, easily discoverable manner and return data in a consistent format that is easy for computer software to parse and process.

While ad-hoc, informally defined web services can certainly be found, they often follow a standard set of protocols or architecture practices that define how URLs are exposed to clients, the format in which data is sent back to the client, and how the service handles data received from the client. One of the earliest such protocols was SOAP, or *Simple Object Access Protocol*. SOAP was an RPC, or *remote procedure call*, mechanism that worked over HTTP. Generally, only one *endpoint*, or URL, was exposed to clients. Messages that were passed between the server and the client (in either direction) were encoded into XML *envelopes*. As with most XML documents, the schema for doing so was well-defined. SOAP was very popular for use in web services in the early 2000s, and many libraries were written to automatically create clients from a well-defined schema (known as a WSDL, or *web services description language*, specification).

Despite its name, SOAP was a very complex protocol. Even though it was designed to be easy to use, it had many pitfalls. An alternative at the time was XML-RPC, which was very similar to SOAP, but much simpler (and, as a result, it had a somewhat limited functionality when compared to SOAP).

Nowadays, most web services are designed using the principles of the REST, or *Representational State Transfer*, architecture. REST is an architecture proposed by Roy Fielding, one of the principal authors of the HTTP specification. It is much simpler (and more freeform) than either SOAP or XML-RPC and makes extensive use of the features of HTTP itself to expose data and operations to web clients. It particular, REST dictates that data be exposed as sets of *resources*, identified by URLs. For example, a magazine may expose articles at URLs like /articles/article-title. /articles exposes a *collection* of articles, and /articles/article-title exposes a specific article, identified by its title, in that collection. An e-commerce platform may have /orders, the collection of all orders known to the system, and /orders/245, a specific order identified by an ID number.

Various operations can act on these resources. The most common operations are getting the representation of a resource, creating a new resource, deleting an existing resource, and modifying an existing resource. These operations each map to an HTTP *verb*, or a type of request defined in the HTTP specification: GET, POST, DELETE, and PUT, respectively. For example, given a magazine web service, getting the text of an article would involve making an HTTP GET request to /articles/article-title. To create a new article, a client would make a POST request to /articles with the text of the new article in the POST request's body; the server would generally respond with the URL of the newly created article. A client could delete an article by making a DELETE request to /articles/article-title. Finally, a client could modify an existing article by making a PUT request to /articles/article-title with the modified article text. A web service may only allow a specific subset of these operations and may only allow authorized clients to make certain types of requests. For example, an anonymous user shouldn't be able to make DELETE or PUT requests to any article she wants!

Unlike SOAP and XML-RPC, REST services generally expose data in a simple, human-readable way. Because REST works within the scope of HTTP, pretty much every website can be thought of as a REST service (although conformance with the original specification differs wildly)—even a website serving static HTML content. However, REST web services that are specifically geared toward working with clients such as iPhone apps generally use XML or JSON as their data representation. Originally, most services used XML, but today, most use JSON, as it is simpler and more human-readable than XML. JSON, or *JavaScript Object Notation*, was originally conceived as a way to serialize JavaScript objects into a format suitable for transmission over a network, but because of its simplicity and ubiquity, most web services serialize their responses into JSON, making it easy for downstream software clients to parse and process.

While there were never extensive SOAP or XML-RPC client libraries available in Objective-C, there are many libraries for parsing and processing JSON responses available to iOS and OS X programmers. In fact, the Foundation framework includes its own class for handling JSON data: NSJSONSerialization. This class is, of course, available to Swift programs as well. Furthermore, at the time of this writing, there are many programmers hard at work on Swift-centric JSON libraries as well. It is a data format with wide support in the iOS and OS X worlds.

IMPLEMENTING A WEB SERVICES CLIENT

In order to demonstrate how to create an iOS app that communicates with a remote service, you'll use Firebase.com. Firebase.com provides a way for you to store arbitrary pieces of data on a remote web server and save and retrieve data from that server using a simple REST API. Specifically, you'll create an iOS app that lets you record your favorite music albums. That data is saved on Firebase.com and is retrievable from any device on which you use the Albums app.

Signing Up for a Firebase Account

To use Firebase, you must first sign up for an account. Firebase offers a free tier that allows you to interact with the service. The free tier is limited but more than sufficient for this demonstration app. To sign up for firebase.com follow these steps:

1. **Visit Firebase.com in your web browser.** Click the "Sign Up" button on the top right of Firebase's home page. Enter your email address and preferred password and click "Create My Account." That's it! You've created a free account. After signing up, you'll be redirected to your Firebase dashboard. A placeholder application should have been created for you.

2. **Set up your account.** You can click on the placeholder application name to change it to something more appropriate ("Albums," for example), or you can leave it as-is. Below the name is your application's URL, which should be something like "boiling-inferno-4018.firebaseio.com." (Firebase applications initially have a randomly-generated URL. Paid account holders can modify that URL or even use their own custom domain, but for the purposes of this exercise, the randomly-generated URL will be fine.)

3. **Go to the application's dashboard.** Click the title of the application. You are taken to the application's dashboard, which, by default, shows you all the data currently stored in the Firebase application. Right now, you have no data, so the dashboard will be empty. You're about to create an app to add some data!

> **NOTE** *After entering the dashboard, Firebase may prompt you to take a tour or watch a tutorial. Feel free to take the tour in order to get a better feel for how Firebase works.*

Laying Out the User Interface

Before writing the code that will communicate with the Firebase web service, you should first lay out the app's user interface. The Albums app is fairly simple, consisting of a main table view that shows all of the data you have saved in your Firebase app. Once you have designed the user interface, you can begin work on the code itself.

> **NOTE** *Whenever you are starting a new app, you have a choice between focusing either on the user interface or code first. Both approaches have merits, and individual developers take different approaches to their apps. It is often easiest to start with the interface first, so you can easily get feedback about how the app is working once you start writing the code.*

Because the Albums app is fairly simple, there's not much to the user interface. Completing the design of the interface should be fairly simple:

1. **Launch Xcode.** Click the Create a new Xcode project button. In the template selection window, select the Single View Application option from the iOS Application templates, and click Next, as shown in Figure 5-1.

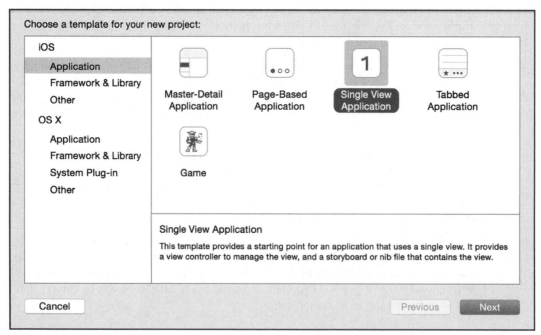

FIGURE 5-1

2. **In the project setup window, give your application the name** Albums. Make sure you select the Swift option in the Language drop-down menu, and select Device ➤ iPhone. Click Next to create your project. Save your project somewhere on your hard drive when prompted.

3. **Click once on Main.storyboard in the file tree.** This brings up the user interface in Xcode's main editor window.

4. **Replace the default view with a table view.** Because the Albums app will display data in a table, the main view should be a table instead of a generic view. Expand the View Controller Scene in the main editor window and select the `View` object, as shown in Figure 5-2. Delete it. In its place, drag a `Table View` object from the Object Library in the lower right corner of the Xcode editor window, and place it in the existing view controller instance.

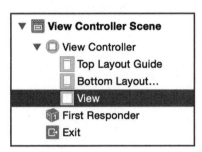

FIGURE 5-2

5. **Drag a Table View Cell from the object library onto the table view you just placed.** Select the new Table View Cell. In the Attributes inspector, change its Identifier to **AlbumCell**, as shown in Figure 5-3.

Table View Cell

Style	Custom
Identifier	AlbumCell
Selection	Default
Accessory	None
Editing Acc.	None
Indentation	0 10
	Level Width
	☑ Indent While Editing
	☐ Shows Re-order Controls
Separator	Default Insets

FIGURE 5-3

6. **Add a Navigation Controller to the storyboard.** Select the View Controller instance in the editor's object navigation pane. Then, click Editor ➤ Embed In ➤ Navigation Controller. This adds a Navigation Controller as the storyboard's entry point.

7. **Set the main view's title.** Double-click the center of the header in the main view (the table view you added in Step 4) and change the title to **Albums**.

8. **Add a + button to the main view.** Drag a Bar Button Item from the editor's object library. Place it on the right hand side of the table view's navigation bar. In the Attribute inspector, change its Identifier to Add, as shown in Figure 5-4. You will use this button to add new records to your app.

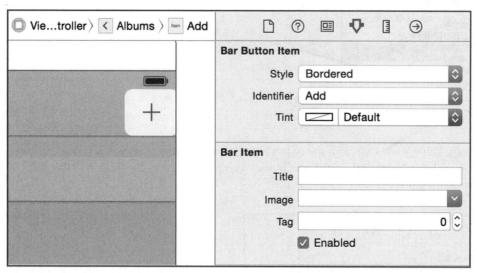

FIGURE 5-4

9. **Add another Navigation Controller to the scene.** Drag a Navigation Controller from the object library and place it to the right of the table view. This actually adds two items: another Navigation Controller and another Table View Controller.

10. **Link the first table view to the Navigation Controller you just created.** Hold down the Control key and drag a connection from the + button to the new Navigation Controller instance. Select Present Modally from the popup menu. Pressing the + button now invokes the Navigation Controller's view (the second table view that is linked to it).

11. **Change the second table view to use static cells.** You'll use the table view to lay out the form for adding new albums, so it doesn't have to have dynamic content or a data source. In the table view's Attributes inspector, change the Content to Static Cells. You should also change the Style to Grouped and configure the table view to have two sections as shown in Figure 5-5.

12. **Label the first table section Album Title.** Select the first table row. In its Attributes inspector, change the number of rows to 1 and change the header to Album Title, as shown in

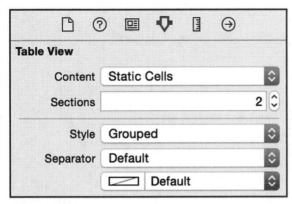

FIGURE 5-5

Figure 5-6. Select the second table section and change its rows to 1 and its header to Band.

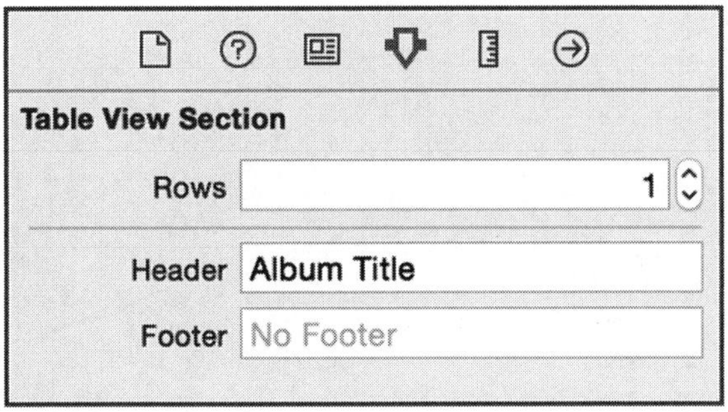

Table View Section

Rows | 1

Header | Album Title

Footer | No Footer

FIGURE 5-6

13. **Add a text field so users can enter the title of the album.** From the object library, drag a text field object to the storyboard and drop it over the content view for the Album Title section. Resize the text input so it is the same size as the existing content view. In the Attributes inspector, remove the text input's border. Deselect the Adjust to Fit option. Finally, change the font to System 17.0. The text field's attributes should be like those shown in Figure 5-7.

14. **Add a text field so users can enter the album's band.** Do the same thing you did when you added a text field to the Album Title section in Step 13, but for the Band section instead. When you're done, the new album view should look like the one shown in Figure 5-8.

Hooking Up the Add Album View Controller

You need to create a view controller for the album creation view you just generated. This view controller will manage the display of the album creation modal window as well as manage the movement of data between the album creation modal and the main view controller.

FIGURE 5-7

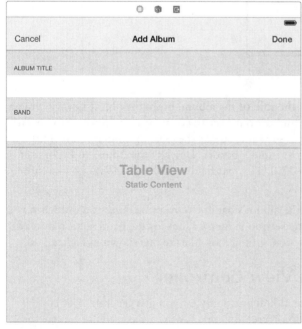

FIGURE 5-8

Adding the Album Creation View Controller

The album creation view controller is pretty simple to create.

1. **Add a new view controller.** In the file navigator pane, right-click the Albums group and select New File. Double-click the Swift File template. Save the file as `AddAlbumViewController`.

2. **Copy the code in Listing 5-1 into the new file you just created.**

LISTING 5-1: AddAlbumViewController.swift

```swift
import UIKit

class AddAlbumViewController: UITableViewController {
    @IBOutlet weak var albumTitleField: UITextField!
    @IBOutlet weak var bandField: UITextField!
}
```

The `AddAlbumViewController` class adds two interface outlets: `albumTitleField` and `bandField`. As their name suggests, these two outlets will be hooked up to the text fields you added to the album creation view in the previous section.

You must modify the main view controller so that it is a table view controller, instead of just a generic view controller. You also need to add methods for handling the segue between the album creation view and the main table view.

3. **Change the superclass.** Open the `ViewController.swift` file into Xcode's code editor, and change the superclass of `UIViewController` to `UITableViewController`.

4. **Add methods to handle the album creation view segue.** The two methods you should add are `cancel` and `add`. These methods will be attached to buttons that you will soon add to the album creation view to handle the dismissal of the view. When you're done, `ViewController.swift` should contain the code shown in Listing 5-2.

LISTING 5-2: ViewController.swift

```swift
import UIKit

class ViewController: UITableViewController {
    // MARK: Add album

    @IBAction func cancel(segue: UIStoryboardSegue) {
    }

    @IBAction func add(segue: UIStoryboardSegue) {
        dismissViewControllerAnimated(true, completion: nil)
    }
}
```

Hooking Up the Segue

Now you are ready to finish the album creation view and hook up the segue.

1. **Select Main.storyboard in the file navigator to edit the storyboard.**

2. **Select the view controller instance for the album creation view.**

3. **Change the controllers's title.** Double-click the view controller's title in the navigation bar (it should say Root View Controller by default) and change it to Add Album.

4. **Add a button to cancel the album creation view.** Drag a Bar Button Item instance from the object library and drag it to the left side of the navigation bar in the album creation view. Double-click the title and change it to Cancel.

5. **Add a button to submit the new album.** Drag a Bar Button Item instance from the object library and drag it to the right side of the navigation bar. Double-click the title and change it to Add.

6. **Hook up the buttons.** Control-drag a connection from the Cancel button to the Exit icon along the top of the view controller instance. Select `cancel:` as the target of the action. Control-drag another connection from the Add button to the Exit icon, and select `Add` as the target, as shown in Figure 5-9.

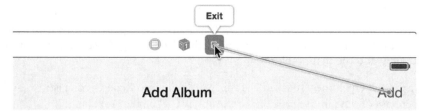

FIGURE 5-9

7. **Give the segues unique identifiers.** Select the first segue from the object hierarchy, as shown in Figure 5-10. Bring up the Attributes inspector. This segue should be pointing to the `cancel:` action. Change the identifier to `CancelAlbum`. Select the second segue and change its identifier to `SaveAlbum`.

The Album app's interface should now work properly (although it won't do anything useful, such as saving album data, yet). If you want, you can build and run the app to see the interface in action.

Creating the Album Model

Now that the user interface has been laid out, you can create the data model that will store information about the albums you have entered. The actual `Album` model itself is fairly simple.

1. **Create a new Swift file.** Right-click the Albums group in the file navigator and select New File. Double-click the Swift File template. Save the file as `Album.swift`.

2. **Copy the code from Listing 5-3 into the Album.swift file.**

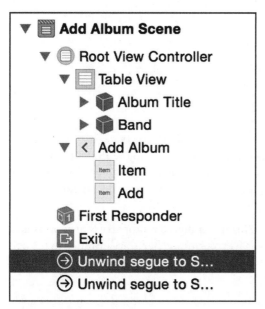

FIGURE 5-10

LISTING 5-3: Album.swift

```swift
class Album: Printable, Comparable {
    let band: String
    let title: String
    var id: String? = nil

    var description: String {
        return "\(band): \(title)"
    }

    init(band: String, title: String) {
        self.band = band
        self.title = title
    }

    func toJSON() -> [String: String] {
        return ["band": band, "title": title]
    }
}

func <(left: Album, right: Album) -> Bool {
    if left.band == right.band {
        return left.title < right.title
    }
    return left.band < right.band
}
```

continues

continued

```
func ==(left: Album, right: Album) -> Bool {
    if left.band == right.band {
        return left.title == right.title
    }
    return false
}
```

The code is pretty simple. It has three instance variables: an album title, the name of the band that recorded the album, and an ID. The ID is used when communicating with the Firebase web service. Firebase assigns an automatically-generated ID number to any record you create, which allows for easy tracking of records. In particular, it is useful when you implement code for deleting records.

The Album class also has a description property. This is a computed property that returns a string containing the band and album name. You can use it when printing an Album instance to the console, such as when using NSLog() or println(). Strictly speaking, it's not necessary but can make debugging a bit easier.

The Album class also has a toJSON() method that can return a JSON object that represents an Album instance. You will use this when communicating with the remote Firebase service. Firebase offers a REST API, and data is passed to and from Firebase using JSON. This method makes it easier to convert an Album instance into a JSON string.

A couple parts of this code may raise a few eyebrows. After the definition of the Album class, there are two functions named < and ==. These implement the comparison and equality operators for Album instances. Implementing these comparison operators makes it easier to sort arrays of Album instances by band name and album title. This is a feature known as *operator overloading*, covered in more detail in Chapter 8.

The Album class also implements two protocols: Printable and Comparable. These protocols allow Swift to make use of the description property, as well as the overloaded operators. Protocols are covered in more detail in Chapter 7.

Communicating with Firebase

The most crucial part of the Albums app is the code that will actually communicate with the remote Firebase web service. Using this connector code, you can query the service for albums that the user creates and saves, as well as delete album records that the user is no longer interested in.

Because Firebase uses JSON to transfer and store data, JSON parsing is an important part of the Firebase connector code. The rest of the code communicates with the remote Firebase web service over HTTP. Cocoa and Cocoa Touch both have ample support for making HTTP requests, as well as handling JSON data returned from these requests.

Creating the Firebase Connector

To start, you must create a new Swift file. Name it **Firebase.swift** and save it. The contents of Firebase.swift should contain the code shown in Listing 5-4.

LISTING 5-4: Firebase.swift

```swift
import Foundation


typealias FirebaseSaveCompletion = (String?, NSError?) -> Void
typealias FirebaseFetchCompletion = ([Album]?, NSError?) -> Void
typealias FirebaseDeleteCompletion = (NSError?) -> Void


class Firebase {
    let hostname: String
    var albumsURL: NSURL {
        return NSURL(scheme: "https", host: hostname, path: "/albums.json")!
    }

    init(hostname: String) {
        self.hostname = hostname
    }

    func fetchAlbums(completionHandler: FirebaseFetchCompletion) {
        var request = NSURLRequest(URL: albumsURL)
        NSURLConnection.sendAsynchronousRequest(
            request, queue: NSOperationQueue.currentQueue()) {
                (response, data, error) in
            if let error = error {
                completionHandler(nil, error)
                return
            }

            var err: NSError?
            let json: AnyObject? = NSJSONSerialization.JSONObjectWithData(
                data,
                options: NSJSONReadingOptions(0),
                error: &err)
            if let err = err {
                completionHandler(nil, error)
                return
            }

            if let json: AnyObject = json {
                if let json = json as? [String: AnyObject] {
                    var albums: [Album] = []
                    for (key, item) in json {
                        if let item = item as? [String: String] {
                            var album = Album(band: item["band"]!,
                                            title: item["title"]!)
                            album.id = key
                            albums.append(album)
                        }
                    }
                    completionHandler(albums, nil)
```

continues

continued

```
                    return
                }
                completionHandler(nil,
                    NSError(domain: "albums", code: 100, userInfo: nil))
                return
            } else {
                completionHandler(nil,
                    NSError(domain: "albums", code: 101, userInfo: nil))
                return
            }
        }
    }
}

func saveAlbum(album: Album, completionHandler: FirebaseSaveCompletion) {
    var err: NSError?
    let data = NSJSONSerialization.dataWithJSONObject(
        album.toJSON(),
        options: NSJSONWritingOptions(0),
        error: &err)
    if let err = err {
        completionHandler(nil, err)
        return
    }

    var request = NSMutableURLRequest(URL: albumsURL)
    request.HTTPMethod = "POST"
    request.HTTPBody = data

    NSURLConnection.sendAsynchronousRequest(
        request, queue: NSOperationQueue.currentQueue()) {
            (response, data, error) in
        if let error = error {
            completionHandler(nil, error)
            return
        }

        err = nil
        let obj: AnyObject? = NSJSONSerialization.JSONObjectWithData(
            data,
            options: NSJSONReadingOptions(0),
            error: &err)
        if let err = err {
            completionHandler(nil, err)
            return
        }
        if let obj: AnyObject = obj {
            if let albumDict = obj as? [String: String] {
                let albumID = albumDict["name"]!
                completionHandler(albumID, nil)
            }
        } else {
            completionHandler(
                nil, NSError(domain: "albums", code: 102, userInfo: nil))
```

```
                }
            }
        }

        func deleteAlbum(album: Album, completionHandler: FirebaseDeleteCompletion) {
            if album.id == nil {
                completionHandler(NSError(domain: "albums", code: 103, userInfo: nil))
                return
            }

            let deleteURL = NSURL(scheme: "https",
                                    host: hostname,
                                    path: "/albums/\(album.id!).json")!
            var request = NSMutableURLRequest(URL: deleteURL)
            request.HTTPMethod = "DELETE"

            NSURLConnection.sendAsynchronousRequest(
                request, queue: NSOperationQueue.currentQueue()) {
                    (response, data, error) in
                if let error = error {
                    completionHandler(error)
                } else {
                    completionHandler(nil)
                }
            }
        }
    }
}
```

Take a look at the code you added to `Firebase.swift`. There are several key parts to this code. The top of the file contains several *type aliases*. Type aliases are much like typedefs in C and Objective-C: They associate a name with a type so that you can use the name when declaring types, instead of the more verbose type signature. In this case, the type aliases all denote a closure. A closure is much like a block in Objective-C. It represents an executable bit of code that can take parameters, just like a function, and return values. In the case of the Firebase connector code, they are *void* closures, meaning they don't return a value. They do, however, take parameters.

Making Asynchronous Web Requests

Why do we use closures here? In Cocoa and Cocoa Touch, web requests are asynchronous. That means that the actual web request happens in the background. You see later in the code that web requests are made using the method `sendAsynchronousRequest()` in the `NSURLConnection` class. This method does not actually return the result of the request. Instead, it happens in the background. In order to work with the result of the request, you must supply a callback—a closure—that is executed after the request has been made and data has been returned.

> **NOTE** *Closures and callback functions were covered in more detail in Chapter 4. Refer back to that chapter if you need a refresher.*

The `Firebase` class exposes three methods for working with the remote Firebase service. `fetchAlbums()` returns all of the albums you have saved in Firebase. It starts off by making a web request to the Firebase service using `NSURLConnection.sendAsychronousRequest()`. The `sendAsynchronousRequest()` takes a callback function. In the case of the `fetchAlbums()` method, this callback is a closure that takes three parameters: an `NSURLResponse` representing the response to the web request, an `NSData` object containing the data returned from the response, and an `NSError` instance containing information on any errors that occurred while making the response. All three of these parameters are optional types.

The callback closure first checks to see if an error occurred by unwrapping the `error` optional and passing it to the completion handler (another closure supplied by the caller of the `fetchAlbums()` method). It uses a pattern that you'll see elsewhere in the `Firebase` class:

```
if let error = error {
    completionHandler(nil, error)
    return
}
```

In the code above, `error` is unwrapped into another constant, using the `let` keyword. The same name, `error`, is used for the unwrapped variable; you could use another name, but in the interests of not having to come up with tons of unique names for essentially the same variable, the name is reused. If `error` is successfully unwrapped—that is, it is actually an `NSError` object, and not `nil`— then the completion handler is passed the unwrapped error, and the closure exists early.

Processing JSON Data

If an error did *not* occur, you can proceed to process the returned data. Firebase returns its data in the JSON format, so you first must unpack that data using the `NSJSONSerialization` `.JSONObjectWithData()` method provided as part of the Foundation framework. `JSONObject-WithData()` takes a pointer to an `NSError` instance and sets it if an error occurs while parsing the data, so next you check to see if that error object (named `err`) is `nil`; if it is, the completion handler is once again passed the error object and the closure returns.

> **NOTE** *The Firebase REST API is documented at* `https://www.firebase.com/docs/rest/api/`.

If not, then you can proceed to pull data out of the parsed JSON. Processing a JSON data structure in Swift is a bit odd, however. Swift cares a lot more about types than JSON. A top-level JSON object can be either an array or a dictionary. This freeform structure is not exactly compatible with Swift's strict typing, and so processing a JSON data structure is a bit cumbersome in Swift. `JSONObjectWithData()`, in particular, returns an object of type `AnyObject?` (that is, an optional `AnyObject`), although it is either an `NSArray` or an `NSDictionary`, and the Firebase API notes that a dictionary will be returned from this type of request. The first thing to do, then, is to unwrap the returned `AnyObject?` into an actual `AnyObject`, which is done with this line of code:

```
if let json: AnyObject = json {
```

If that line of code succeeds, you can continue parsing the returned JSON data structure. The next step is to try to coerce the `AnyObject` into a dictionary that maps `String` keys to `AnyObject` values:

```
if let json = json as? [String: AnyObject] {
```

If that succeeds, you know you can start processing the data and making `Album` objects out of the JSON you received back from Firebase. The code then enters a for loop, iterating over the key-value pairs of the dictionary. The first line of the for loop attempts to cast the value as a dictionary mapping `String` keys to `String` values (which, again, the Firebase API says is the structure of the data it returns):

```
if let item = item as? [String: String] {
```

If this works, then you have the data you need, and you can create an `Album` instance out of that data, which is done with the following code:

```
var album = Album(band: item["band"]!,
    title: item["title"]!)
```

Because `item` has been coerced to a dictionary, you can grab the values of that dictionary by indexing into the `item` variable. Of course, Swift, being as typesafe as it is, returns an optional value when you index into a dictionary. But you can be reasonably sure that the Firebase API returned data in the documented structure that you expected, so you can forcibly unwrap the value by suffixing the indexing operation with an exclamation point.

After an `Album` is created, it is added to the albums array. When all the data is processed, that array of `Albums` passes back to the caller via the `completionHandler` closure.

> **NOTE** *In the next section, you complete the* `ViewController` *class, which will demonstrate how the completion handlers are defined and used in conjunction with the* `Firebase` *class.*

Creating New Albums

Fundamentally, the `saveAlbum()` method works in the same way. `saveAlbum()` takes an `Album` instance (as well as a completion handler, albeit of a different type than `fetchAlbums()`). `saveAlbum()` first calls the `Album` instance's `toJSON()` method, which returns a dictionary representing the album. `NSJSONSerialization.dataWithJSONObject()` is then called to convert that album into JSON data, in the form of an `NSData` instance. `dataWithJSONObject()` is, of course, the opposite of `JSONObjectWithData()`; the former turns a JSON object (a `Dictionary` or `Array`) into an `NSData` instance, whereas the latter turns an `NSData` instance into a JSON object.

After some basic error handling, `saveAlbum()` creates a new request object. Unlike the GET request in `fetchAlbums()`, `saveAlbum()` is going to make a POST request to the Firebase web service. In REST APIs, this is generally how data is sent to a remote service: a POST request with the new JSON data being the body of the request. This request is then sent using `NSURLConnection.send-AsynchronousRequest()`, just as the request was made in `fetchAlbums()`. As in `fetchAlbums()`, the request is then parsed using `JSONObjectWithData()`. When making a POST request, however, the response is much simpler: The Firebase API specifies that the response is a dictionary containing a single key, "name", mapped to an ID. The Firebase service uses the ID to identify records added to its database. If the request was successful (that is, you could create a record in Firebase), the completion handler passes the new album ID. Otherwise, errors are handled similarly as to how they are handled in the `fetchAlbums()` method.

Deleting Albums

The final method, `deleteAlbum()`, allows you to delete a record from the Firebase database. This one is slightly different than the others: Rather than making a GET or POST requests to the `/albums.json` endpoint, you make a DELETE request to the `/albums/:id.json` endpoint, where `:id` is the ID of the record you want to delete. The DELETE request has no body. It doesn't return any relevant data in its response body, either, so you simply have to check whether `sendAsynchronousRequest()` returned an error or not and pass that data along to the completion handler.

Wiring Up the View and Data Models

The last major task is implementing the code in the main view controller (the `ViewController` class) that will take actions from the user interface and perform the relevant operations on the data layer. The data layer is essentially the data stored in Firebase, so this code invokes the actual requests that you just created in the `Firebase` class (in the `Firebase.swift` file).

Copy the contents of Listing 5-5 into `ViewController.swift`.

LISTING 5-5: ViewController.swift

```swift
import UIKit

class ViewController: UITableViewController {

    let firebase = Firebase(hostname: "your-hostname.firebaseio.com")
    var albums: [Album] = []

    override func viewDidLoad() {
        super.viewDidLoad()
        self.reloadData()
    }

    private func reloadData() {
        firebase.fetchAlbums { (albums, error) in
            if let error = error {
                self.showAlert(error)
            } else {
                if let albums = albums {
                self.albums = albums
                self.albums.sort { $0 < $1 }
                self.tableView.reloadData()
            }
        }
    }
}

    private func showAlert(error: NSError) {
        let alert = UIAlertView(
            title: "Oops!",
            message: "Could not fetch albums data.",
```

```swift
            delegate: nil,
            cancelButtonTitle: "OK")
        alert.show()
}

// MARK: Table view data source

override func tableView(tableView: UITableView,
                        numberOfRowsInSection section: Int) -> Int {
        return albums.count
}

override func tableView(tableView: UITableView,
                        cellForRowAtIndexPath indexPath: NSIndexPath)
        -> UITableViewCell {
        var cell = tableView.dequeueReusableCellWithIdentifier(
            "AlbumCell") as UITableViewCell?
        if cell == nil {
            cell = UITableViewCell(
                style: UITableViewCellStyle.Default,
                reuseIdentifier: "AlbumCell")
        }
        cell!.textLabel?.text = albums[indexPath.row].description
        return cell!
}

override func tableView(tableView: UITableView,
                        canEditRowAtIndexPath indexPath: NSIndexPath)
        -> Bool {
        return true;
}

override func tableView(
        tableView: UITableView,
        commitEditingStyle editingStyle: UITableViewCellEditingStyle,
        forRowAtIndexPath indexPath: NSIndexPath) {
        if editingStyle == UITableViewCellEditingStyle.Delete {
            let album = albums[indexPath.row]
            firebase.deleteAlbum(album, completionHandler: { (error) in
                if let error = error {
                    self.showAlert(error)
                } else {
                    self.albums.removeAtIndex(indexPath.row)
                    self.tableView.deleteRowsAtIndexPaths([indexPath],
                        withRowAnimation: UITableViewRowAnimation.Automatic)
                }
            })
        }
}

// MARK: Add album

@IBAction func cancel(segue: UIStoryboardSegue) {
```

continues

continued

```
    }

    @IBAction func add(segue: UIStoryboardSegue) {
        let detailController = segue.sourceViewController as AddAlbumViewController
        firebase.saveAlbum(detailController.album) { (albumID, error) in
            if let error = error {
                self.showAlert(error)
            } else {
                self.reloadData()
            }
        }

        dismissViewControllerAnimated(true, completion: nil)
    }
}
```

> **WARNING** *It is essential that you make one change. You should change the line that declares the firebase property so it has your own Firebase URL:*
>
> ```
> let firebase = Firebase(hostname: "your-hostname.firebaseio
> .com")
> ```
>
> *You can find your Firebase application's URL by logging in to the Firebase dashboard. The application's URL is listed along with the rest of the application's data in the dashboard.*

The `ViewController` now has two new methods, `reloadData()` and `showAlert()`.

`reloadData()` simply requests the list of albums stored in Firebase. It updates its own internal list of albums with the data from Firebase and requests that the table view be reloaded. This ensures that the table view is always in sync with the Firebase data. It fetches this data via the `fetchAlbums()` method you created in the `Firebase` class. Recall that `fetchAlbums()` is an asynchronous method that takes a completion handler. The completion handler is invoked once `fetchAlbums()` has made a web request and has data to return. `fetchAlbums()` takes care of parsing that data, so its completion handler is given an array of `Album` instances (or an error, if an error occurred). `reloadData()` updates its albums property with this array and signals that the table view should be redrawn. It also sorts the array of albums so they appear in alphabetical order (which is why you needed to define an ordering for `Album` instances by overloading the `<` and `==` operators).

`showAlert()` is a helper method that takes an error object and presents an error dialog to the user.

`ViewController` also includes several methods for updating its table view in response to user input. These methods are fairly standard when working with table views.

`tableView(tableView:numberOfRowsInSection:)` lets the table view know how many rows should be drawn. There is one row per album, so the size of the `albums` property is returned here.

`tableView(tableView:cellForRowIndexAtPath:)` retrieves the proper table view cell for a given row. It sets the cell's text to be the band name and title of the album and returns it.

> **NOTE** `UITableView` *instances improve performance by caching table cells in memory. A cached cell can be returned using the table view instance's* `dequeueReusableCellWithIdentifier()` *method. If that method returns* `nil`, *a new table cell instance should be created; otherwise, an existing table view cell can be reused by changing its text.*

Finally, you want to allow the user to delete albums they're not interested in anymore. The user should be able to delete an album by swiping left on the album, which will reveal a delete button the user can press to remove an album.

According to the `UITableViewController` API, to allow rows to be deleted, you must supply two methods: `tableView(tableView:canEditRowAtIndexPath:)` and `tableView(tableView:commitEditingStyle:forRowAtIndexPath:)`.

`tableView(tableView:canEditRowAtIndexPath:)` simply returns true, meaning that editing the row is, in fact, allowed.

`tableView(tableView:commitEditingStyle:forRowAtIndexPath:)` is a bit more complicated, as it actually does the work of deleting a row. If the `editingStyle` is `UITableViewEditingStyle` `.Delete`—that is, the user pressed the delete button—then the album is deleted using the `delete-Album()` method and is removed from the view controller's albums array. `deleteAlbum()` is, of course, an asynchronous method, so the work of handling the delete is done in the completion handler passed to `deleteAlbum()`.

Finally, you have to update the `add()` method to handle the creation of a new album. Remember, this method is invoked after the user presses the Add button on the album creation view. In this method, the album is retrieved from the segue's `AddAlbumViewController` instance and saved using the `saveAlbum()` method in the `Firebase` class.

Wiring Up the Segue

A few more changes have to be made to allow the album creation view to work and to manage the segue between the album creation view and the main view controller. First of all, the `AddAlbumViewController` class should override the `prepareForSegue()` method. In this method, it should create a new Album instance to track the data entered by the user, saving it in its own album property. Modify the `AddAlbumViewController` class so it looks like the one shown in Listing 5-6.

LISTING 5-6: AddAlbumViewController.swift

```swift
import UIKit

class AddAlbumViewController: UITableViewController {
    @IBOutlet weak var albumTitleField: UITextField!
```

continues

continued

```
@IBOutlet weak var bandField: UITextField!
var album: Album!

override func prepareForSegue(segue: UIStoryboardSegue, sender: AnyObject?) {
    if segue.identifier == "SaveAlbum" {
        album = Album(band: bandField.text, title: albumTitleField.text)
    }
}
}
```

You should also change the album creation view's controller so it is an instance of the AddAlbumViewController class. Open Main.storyboard in the storyboard editor. Select the album creation view (Add Album Scene), then select the scene's view controller (Add Album) from the object hierarchy, as shown in Figure 5-11. In the Identity inspector, change the class to AddAlbumViewController.

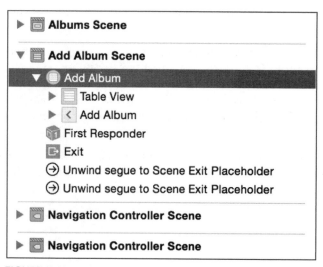

FIGURE 5-11

Finally, you'll have to wire the UI outlets in the AddAlbumViewController to the proper text fields in the album creation view. Control-drag a connection from the view controller to album title text field, selecting albumTitleField as the outlet, as shown in Figure 5-12. Control-drag another connection from the view controller to the band name text field, selecting bandField as the outlet.

Run the Application

You should now have a fully-functional iPhone application to keep tracking of music albums. Build and run the application and experiment with it a bit. You should see that you are able to add albums, which then appear in the main table view. You can also delete albums from the main table view. Your application should look similar to Figure 5-13.

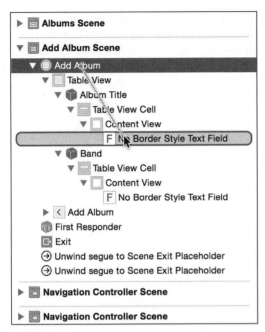

FIGURE 5-12

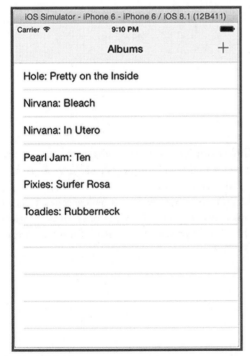

FIGURE 5-13

It is important to note that both your creation and deletion operations will be mirrored in your Firebase application's database. If you log in to your Firebase dashboard and click on your application, you can view all the data being stored in your application's database, similar to what you see in Figure 5-14. As you create and delete albums, you should see them appear and disappear from the Firebase application view as well.

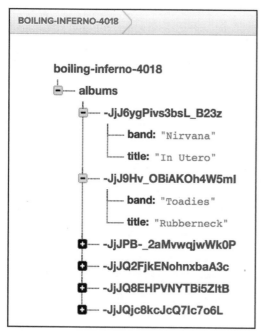

FIGURE 5-14

SUMMARY

Communicating with web services is an essential skill for both iOS and OS X programmers. In this chapter, you learned how to write a Swift program that can make web requests to a service. You also learned how you can process the data returned by that web service into a form suitable for consumption by a user of your app. More importantly, you saw how Swift can be leveraged to communicate with remote services over HTTP, a ubiquitous protocol that forms the basis of network communication in nearly all modern-day software. This should provide you with a foundation for writing your own Swift apps that communicate over HTTP.

Storing Data with Core Data

WHAT'S IN THIS CHAPTER?

- ➤ Understanding the purpose of Core Data
- ➤ Creating a graphical Swift program for OS X
- ➤ Inserting new records into Core Data
- ➤ Fetching existing records from Core Data
- ➤ Displaying Core Data records in a table view

WROX.COM CODE DOWNLOADS FOR THIS CHAPTER

You can find the wrox.com downloads for this chapter at `http://www.wrox.com/go/proswift` on the Download Code tab. The code for this chapter is contained in the following file:

- ➤ `Birthdays.zip`

Since its introduction in OS X 10.4, Core Data has rapidly become an integral part of many OS X and iOS programs. It is rare for both Objective-C and Swift developers to encounter programs that do not use Core Data in some way. Core Data is frequently used as both a caching layer (particularly in iOS apps), as well as a way for programs to store its most important data. While Core Data is implemented in Objective-C and designed from an Objective-C mindset, working with Core Data from Swift is just as easy as working with it from Objective-C. This chapter is a primer on how you can use Swift in conjunction with Core Data to easily write data-driven programs.

This chapter assumes some familiarity with Core Data, even if you've only worked with Core Data in Objective-C. It is an introduction to Core Data from a Swift perspective and does not cover all the finer details of working with Core Data. Core Data is a robust framework with many useful features, and entire books have been written on the topic. However, by the end of this chapter, you should have a more thorough understanding of how to use Core Data in your own Swift programs.

WHAT IS CORE DATA?

Core Data is an object persistence framework released with OS X 10.4 in 2005. It became an important part of iOS with the release of the iPhone in 2007, as well. Core Data provides a uniform way for OS X and iOS programs to save, or *persist*, an object graph. Programs on both OS X and iOS can be thought of as a collection of objects that communicate with one another. This structure is known as an *object graph*. It consists of instances of classes (objects) and connections between these objects.

Programs generally need to save data to a permanent data store, such as a hard drive. This data may be in the form of files (such as text files or JPEGs) or in the form of temporary cache files needed during program execution. (The latter need is especially common on iOS devices because they are often working with poor or no Internet connections.) It is also quite common for a program to have a need to store some or all of its internal state so that users can continue working where they left off when they quit the program.

Core Data provides an easy way to persist the state of a program to disk, store data used by the program, and cache data required by the program. For these purposes, it is unwieldy for a programmer to design their own file format, along with the code required to load and save those files that are used exclusively by the program. Core Data makes such persistence work much easier and more maintainable for programmers.

Moreover, Core Data also provides an easy, elegant way to organize and work with data that is loaded into memory and used during the runtime of a program. A program can easily query its object graph for specific pieces of data, as well as sort it in an efficient way. Core Data also manages the work of loading and purging data from memory as-needed, allowing programs to work with large datasets in an efficient way.

The power of Core Data allows for several key technologies in the Cocoa framework, including Cocoa Bindings, a feature that allows programmers to hook up user interface elements, such as table views, to data sources. With Cocoa Bindings, programmers can wire up many interface elements to data sources without having to write a single line of code themselves.

Behind the scenes, Core Data often uses the SQLite database as a backing store. It may seem, then, that Core Data is simply an abstraction over database querying—a glorified object relational mapper, or ORM. However, Core Data should not be thought of as an ORM. The fact that it often stores data in SQLite is nothing more than an implementation detail.

> **NOTE** *Programs that use Core Data most commonly configure Core Data to use SQLite as its backing store. However, Core Data can also use its own XML- or binary-based stores as well. You can also write your own backing store.*

THE CORE DATA STACK

Core Data can be thought of as two key components: an object graph manager and a persistence coordinator. The object graph manager takes care of maintaining objects and the connections between them, as well as managing the memory used by those objects. The persistence coordinator does the work of saving and loading the object graph (or parts of the object graph) to and from disk. Together, these two components work in conjunction to make Core Data work.

The object graph manager consists mainly of two key classes: NSManagedObject and NSManagedObjectContext. NSManagedObject represents a type of data stored in the object graph. These are generally your own custom data types that store and manage the data used by your program. For example, if you were writing a program to store book collections, Book, Author, and Library may be managed object subclasses you would create. These are often referred to as *entities* in the Core Data literature. These managed objects live in a "space" known as a managed object *context*, which is, of course, represented by the NSManagedObjectContext class.

On the other side of the fence, the persistence coordination layer also consists of two key classes: NSPersistentStore and NSPersistentStoreCoordinator. NSPersistentStore represents the actual backing store used by Core Data; generally, this is a SQLite database, but may be other types of stores as well. An NSPersistentStoreCoordinator acts as an intermediary between a persistent store and a managed object model. In essence, it works similarly to a controller in Cocoa's MVC structure.

Of course, these aren't the *only* classes in the Core Data. Many base classes have several subclasses, and a programmer may even subclass NSManagedObject to provide additional functionality for the entities they create as part of their program's Core Data model. Together, however, these basic classes form the engine on which Core Data runs.

USING CORE DATA WITH SWIFT

Like other frameworks on OS X and iOS, Core Data is available to programs written in Swift, as well. Much of Core Data depends on the dynamic nature of Objective-C; despite this issue, however, Swift works nearly seamlessly with Swift code. In fact, Xcode 6 contains a number of templates that make the creation of Core Data–backed programs written in Swift a breeze.

SWIFT AND CORE DATA

Core Data is often associated with a number of technologies that make writing iOS and OS X programs that use Core Data simple. One of these is Cocoa Bindings, a technology that allows programmers to wire user interface elements, such as table views, up to Core Data object graphs. This makes it easy to display and interact with data in iOS and OS X programs. Using Cocoa Bindings, a programmer can quickly create rich interfaces that create, edit, and delete data, as well as sort, format, and display that data in standard Cocoa views.

Cocoa Bindings often form the central controllers used in programs that make use of Core Data. Bindings are so pervasive and well-supported in the Cocoa framework that programmers making use of these data bindings often don't have to write a single line of code to manipulate and display data. Because of this simplicity, it is considered best practice to use Cocoa Bindings wherever possible, rather than write your own data controllers by hand.

continues

continued

Unfortunately, because Cocoa Bindings cuts down drastically on the amount of code written by programmers, its use does not make for a good example to demonstrate the interaction between Swift and Core Data. As such, the example used in this chapter does not make use of Cocoa Bindings, even though it easily could—and *should*. Remember that it is generally best to use Cocoa Bindings, even though this chapter's example will demonstrate how to write your data controllers by hand.

Setting Up the Birthdays Application

To demonstrate the use of Swift with Core Data, we'll create "Birthdays," a simple program for storing and displaying friends' and family members' birthdays.

1. **Launch Xcode and click Create a new Xcode project.** In the project selection window, select Application under the OS X header, and then select Cocoa Application and click Next, as shown in Figure 6-1. Enter **Birthdays** for the product name. Make sure Swift is selected as the language, select the Use Core Data box, and ensure the Use Storyboards checkbox is not selected. Click Next when you are done. Save your project.

> **NOTE** *Although you are creating an OS X application in this example, Core Data is largely the same across both the OS X and iOS platforms, and the same concepts will apply to the use of Core Data on each platform.*

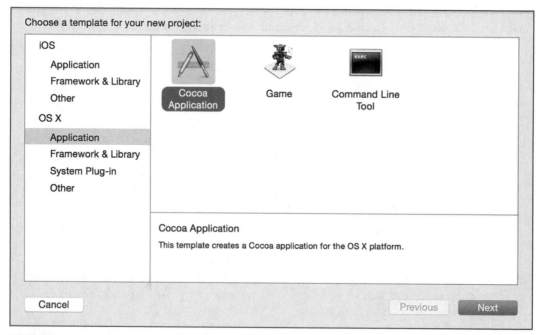

FIGURE 6-1

Xcode will open in the project view. You will see a number of files already created for your project in the file viewer on the left-hand side of the project viewer.

2.   **Click once to select the file `Birthdays.xcdatamodeld`.** This is the Core Data object configuration. It will display in the Xcode editor pane. The data model file now lists all the entities associated with your application.

> **NOTE** *An entity is much like a class: It has properties called attributes and can even have methods associated with it, just like a class. Unlike a generic class, however, it is managed by Core Data, which means you can query the Core Data object graph for instances of an entity, as well as save them to and load them from the persistent store.*

3.   **Your Birthdays application will have one entity: a Birthday.** To add this entity, click the Add Entity button at the bottom of the editor pane. A new item will appear under the Entities header, as shown in Figure 6-2. Change its name to **Birthday** and press Return.

4.   **Add two attributes to the `Birthday` entity: `name` and `birthday`.** Make sure `Birthday` is selected, and click the + button under the Attributes section to add a new attribute. Change its name to `name`, and set its type to `String`. When you are done, add another entity. Call it `birthday`, and set its type to `Date`. Your data model configuration should look like that shown in Figure 6-3.

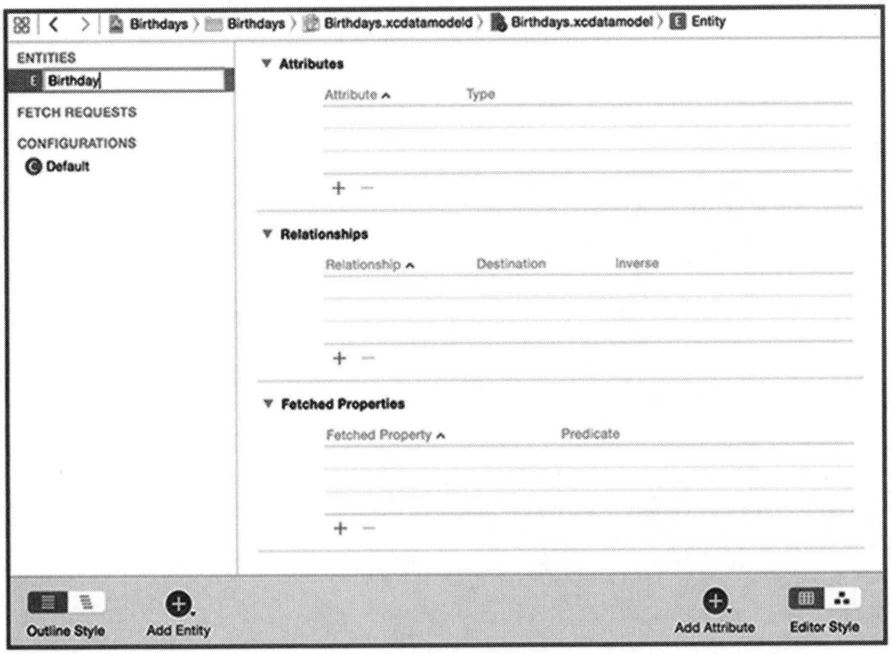

FIGURE 6-2

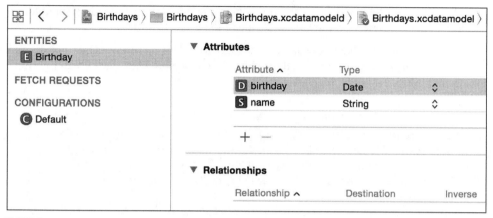

FIGURE 6-3

5. **Set up the user interface.** Select `MainMenu.xib` in the Project navigator to show the application's main XIB file in the Xcode editor. The user interface for Birthdays will be fairly simple: a basic table view in the primary window, coupled with a dialog sheet that can be used to add birthdays. You should notice that the Xcode template has already set up much of the user interface for you. It already contains an application delegate instance, a main window, and a main menu.

6. **Select the main window.** You do this by clicking the second icon from the bottom in the left-hand toolbar.

7. **Add a table view to the main window.** From the editor's object library, drag and drop a table view instance onto the main window, as shown in Figure 6-4. Use the editor's guides to resize it to fill the main window.

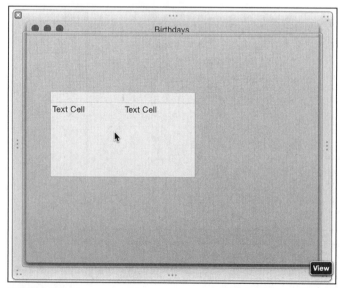

FIGURE 6-4

8. **If you want, you can also add constraints, so that the table view maintains its proportions as you resize the window.** Click the Pin button at the bottom of the editor view; then click the four lines shown at the top of the Pin popup, as shown in Figure 6-5. This will allow the table view to resize as the window is resized.

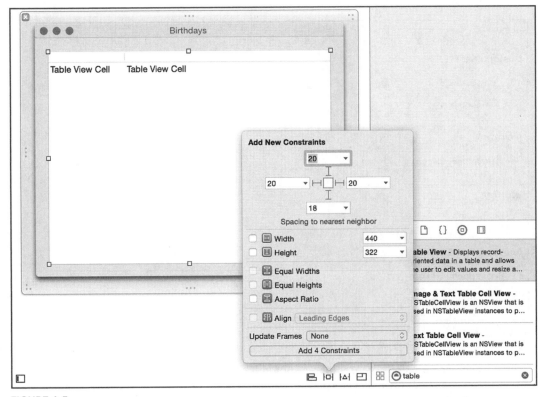

FIGURE 6-5

By default, the column headers are blank. Your application will look much nicer if you name the column headers.

9. **Double-click the leftmost header and label it Name.** Change the rightmost header's label to Birthday.

> **NOTE** *For the purposes of this demonstration application, it is not strictly necessary to add constraints. The worst that can happen is that the table view will not grow or shrink with the window as you resize it in the running application. If you do not add constraints, you will get a warning when building your application, but this warning can be safely ignored. Production-ready applications should take care to add constraints; however, the ins and outs of constraints in Cocoa UI programming is outside the scope of this chapter.*

10. **You should also change the table columns' identifiers to be human-readable.** This is because by default, Cocoa assigns them a machine-generated name that is unwieldy to work with. Double-click the leftmost column. In the Identity inspector, change the identifier to name, as shown in Figure 6-6. Change the rightmost column's identifier to `birthday` using the Identity inspector, as well.

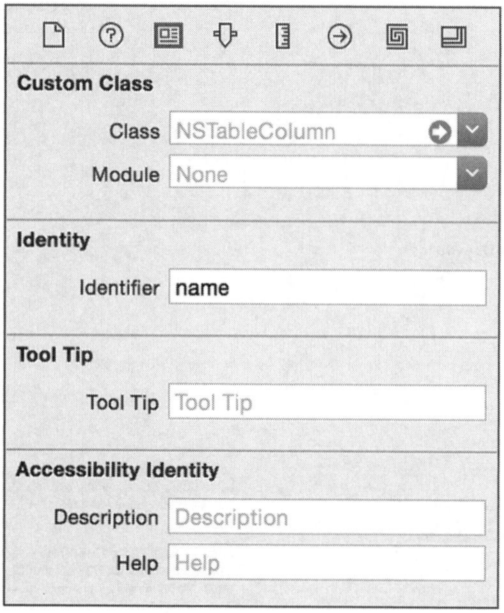

FIGURE 6-6

When you are done, your window should look like the one shown in Figure 6-7. The table view will be used to display all the names and birthdays you've stored using the application.

11. **Change the table view to be cell-based.** A cell-based table view will draw the values for its cells from its data source. Select the table view. In the Attributes inspector, change the Content Mode to Cell Based.

12. **Format the birthday column.** You may want to format the birthday column so a simple date is shown (instead of the full date and time). Drag a Date Formatter object from the object library onto the birthday column. In the Attributes inspector, select Short Style for the Date Style, and No Time Style for the Time Style.

13. **You will need a way to add new names and birthdays, of course.** To accomplish this, you'll create an NSPanel to use as a dialog sheet to add new birthdays to the application. Begin by dragging an NSPanel instance from the object library onto MainMenu.xib's canvas, as shown in Figure 6-8.

    By default, this panel will be shown when the application launches.

14. **You're just using the panel as a dialog sheet, so select it and clear the Visible At Launch checkbox in its Attributes inspector, as shown in Figure 6-9.**

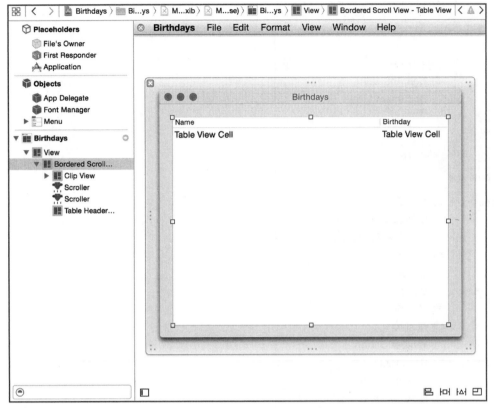

FIGURE 6-7

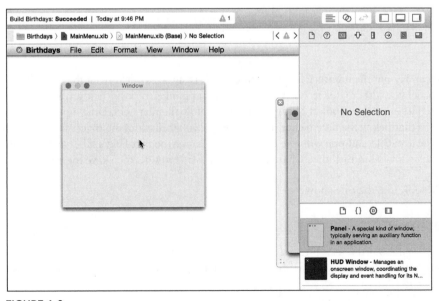

FIGURE 6-8

FIGURE 6-9

15.   **Now you can lay out the interface for the dialog sheet.** Drag a text field from the object library onto the panel you just created it. Use the editor's layout guides to position it properly. Then, drag a date picker from the object library, placing it below the text field. Drag a push button and position that below the date picker. Finally, drag two labels from the object library, aligning one with the text field and one with the date picker. Change the text field's label to Name and the date picker's label to Birthday. Change the button's title to OK, then save the project.

Your panel should look like the one shown in Figure 6-10.

Getting User Input

Great! You're done laying out the user interface for Birthdays, which means you can move on to writing Swift code. Select `AppDelegate.swift` in the file navigator to display the app delegate's code in the editor pane.

FIGURE 6-10

Examining Xcode Files

Take a moment to examine the file that was created automatically for you by Xcode. The work of configuring a managed object context and persistent store coordinate has already been done entirely for you. Listing 6-1 shows the contents of the app delegate template provided by Xcode.

LISTING 6-1: AppDelegate.swift

```
import Cocoa

@NSApplicationMain
class AppDelegate: NSObject, NSApplicationDelegate {

    @IBOutlet weak var window: NSWindow!


    func applicationDidFinishLaunching(aNotification: NSNotification) {
        // Insert code here to initialize your application
    }

    func applicationWillTerminate(aNotification: NSNotification) {
        // Insert code here to tear down your application
    }

    // MARK: - Core Data stack

    lazy var applicationDocumentsDirectory: NSURL = {
        let urls = NSFileManager.defaultManager().URLsForDirectory(
            .ApplicationSupportDirectory, inDomains: .UserDomainMask)
        let appSupportURL = urls[urls.count - 1] as NSURL
        return appSupportURL.URLByAppendingPathComponent("com.monkey-robot
            .Birthdays")
    }()

    lazy var managedObjectModel: NSManagedObjectModel = {
```

continues

continued

```
        let modelURL = NSBundle.mainBundle().URLForResource(
            "Birthdays", withExtension: "momd")!
        return NSManagedObjectModel(contentsOfURL: modelURL)!
    }()

    lazy var persistentStoreCoordinator: NSPersistentStoreCoordinator? = {
        let fileManager = NSFileManager.defaultManager()
        var shouldFail = false
        var error: NSError? = nil
        var failureReason = "There was an error creating or loading the " +
                            "application's saved data."

        // Make sure the application files directory is there
        let propertiesOpt = self.applicationDocumentsDirectory
.resourceValuesForKeys(
            [NSURLIsDirectoryKey], error: &error)
        if let properties = propertiesOpt {
            if !properties[NSURLIsDirectoryKey]!.boolValue {
                failureReason = "Expected a folder to store application data, " +
                    "found a file \(self.applicationDocumentsDirectory.path)."
                shouldFail = true
            }
        } else if error!.code == NSFileReadNoSuchFileError {
            error = nil
            fileManager.createDirectoryAtPath(
                self.applicationDocumentsDirectory.path!,
                withIntermediateDirectories: true, attributes: nil, error: &error)
        }

        // Create the coordinator and store
        var coordinator: NSPersistentStoreCoordinator?
        if !shouldFail && (error == nil) {
            coordinator = NSPersistentStoreCoordinator(
                managedObjectModel: self.managedObjectModel)
            let url = self.applicationDocumentsDirectory
.URLByAppendingPathComponent(
                "Birthdays.storedata")
            if coordinator!.addPersistentStoreWithType(NSXMLStoreType,
                configuration: nil,
                URL: url,
                options: nil,
                error: &error) == nil {
                coordinator = nil
            }
        }

        if shouldFail || (error != nil) {
            // Report any error we got.
            let dict = NSMutableDictionary()
            dict[NSLocalizedDescriptionKey] = "Failed to initialize the " +
                                        "application's saved data"
            dict[NSLocalizedFailureReasonErrorKey] = failureReason
            if error != nil {
                dict[NSUnderlyingErrorKey] = error
```

```swift
        }
        error = NSError(domain: "YOUR_ERROR_DOMAIN",
                        code: 9999,
                        userInfo: dict)
        NSApplication.sharedApplication().presentError(error!)
        return nil
    } else {
        return coordinator
    }
}()

lazy var managedObjectContext: NSManagedObjectContext? = {
    let coordinator = self.persistentStoreCoordinator
    if coordinator == nil {
        return nil
    }
    var managedObjectContext = NSManagedObjectContext()
    managedObjectContext.persistentStoreCoordinator = coordinator
    return managedObjectContext
}()

// MARK: - Core Data Saving and Undo support

@IBAction func saveAction(sender: AnyObject!) {
    if let moc = self.managedObjectContext {
        if !moc.commitEditing() {
            NSLog("\(NSStringFromClass(self.dynamicType)) " +
                "unable to commit editing before saving")
        }
        var error: NSError? = nil
        if moc.hasChanges && !moc.save(&error) {
            NSApplication.sharedApplication().presentError(error!)
        }
    }
}

func windowWillReturnUndoManager(window: NSWindow) -> NSUndoManager? {
    if let moc = self.managedObjectContext {
        return moc.undoManager
    } else {
        return nil
    }
}

func applicationShouldTerminate(
    sender: NSApplication) -> NSApplicationTerminateReply {
    if let moc = managedObjectContext {
        if !moc.commitEditing() {
            NSLog("\(NSStringFromClass(self.dynamicType)) unable to " +
                "commit editing to terminate")
            return .TerminateCancel
        }

        if !moc.hasChanges {
            return .TerminateNow
```

continues

continued

```
                }

                var error: NSError? = nil
                if !moc.save(&error) {
                    // Customize this code block to include application-specific
recovery steps.
                    let result = sender.presentError(error!)
                    if (result) {
                        return .TerminateCancel
                    }

                    let question = NSLocalizedString(
                        "Could not save changes while quitting. Quit anyway?",
                        comment: "Quit without saves error question message")
                    let info = NSLocalizedString(
                        "Quitting now will lose any changes you have made since " +
                        "the last successful save",
                        comment: "Quit without saves error question info");
                    let quitButton = NSLocalizedString("Quit anyway",
                        comment: "Quit anyway button title")
                    let cancelButton = NSLocalizedString("Cancel",
                        comment: "Cancel button title")
                    let alert = NSAlert()
                    alert.messageText = question
                    alert.informativeText = info
                    alert.addButtonWithTitle(quitButton)
                    alert.addButtonWithTitle(cancelButton)

                    let answer = alert.runModal()
                    if answer == NSAlertFirstButtonReturn {
                        return .TerminateCancel
                    }
                }
            }
            // If we got here, it is time to quit.
            return .TerminateNow
        }

    }
```

The template already provides a number of properties and methods for working with the various objects in the Core Data stack. These are all defined under the comment `// MARK: - Core Data stack`. The template provides four properties—all lazily generated—for working with Core Data.

`managedObjectModel` loads the `Birthdays.momd` file. (`.momd` files are the compiled output of `.xcdatamodeld` files.)

The `persistentStoreCoordinator` property creates and returns a default persistent store coordinator for your application. Crucially, it handles any errors that may arise from trying to initialize a persistent store coordinator. Because an error may occur while creating and loading a persistent store coordinator, the return type of this property is an optional value so as to be compatible with Swift's type system. This is yet another way that Swift ensures that a value has been properly initialized and that the caller must be aware of any errors that can arise during the creation of the value. If an error does occur, this property also takes care of displaying an error dialog to the user.

> **NOTE** *A production application may want to modify the* persistentStore-Coordinator *property to handle errors differently. For example, it may decide to present a friendlier error dialog to the user. For your production applications, you may find it necessary to modify this property to handle errors differently; however, for this demonstration application, the default error handling will suffice.*

Third, the managedObjectContext property creates a managed object context, using the persistent store coordinator created by its associated property. Note that this property handles the condition in which a persistent store coordinator could not be created by unpacking the optional value returned by the persistentStoreCoordinator property, returning nil if a persistent store coordinator—and thus a managed object context—cannot be created. Thus, its return value is also an optional value. A persistent store coordinator error is handled in a Swift if block:

```
let coordinator = self.persistentStoreCoordinator
if coordinator == nil {
    return nil
}
```

The template also provides another property, applicationDocumentsDirectory, for retrieving a path to the application's support directory. On OS X, this is a subdirectory of ~/Library/Application Support. This path is used by other properties—namely, persistentStoreCoordinator—to easily set the path to Core Data's backing store.

The template also provides a number of methods to facilitate undo management in conjunction with Core Data, as well as an application termination handler for automatically saving the object graph when the user quits the application. These methods are defined under the section denoted by the comment // MARK: - Core Data Saving and Undo support. Undo support is generally useful in Core Data applications, but for the purposes of this demonstration, you will not have to work directly with Core Data's undo mechanism. But the framework is provided automatically, so feel free to implement it on your own if you are looking for a challenge!

The first change you should make to the default AppDelegate class is to add Interface Builder outlets for four of the elements you added to MainMenu.xib: the table view, the panel, and the text field and date picker inside the panel. Add these four lines to the AppDelegate class definition, below the Interface Builder outlet that already exists:

```
@IBOutlet weak var tableView: NSTableView!
@IBOutlet weak var panel: NSPanel!
@IBOutlet weak var nameField: NSTextField!
@IBOutlet weak var dateField: NSDatePicker!
```

Note that these properties also make use of the Swift type system and runtime. They are declared as weak variables, which instructs the Automatic Reference Counting system that manages memory in Swift programs to not retain these variables; this is the same thing as the weak property attribute in Objective-C. You also declare types for your properties, and end them with an exclamation point, or "bang" (!). This forces the property value to be unwrapped. Because properties are not set up until the associated nib file has been loaded, Swift IB outlets are actually optional values. However, optional values are a bit more unwieldy to work with, and the outlets will be connected by the time the application is up and running, so you suffix the type with an exclamation point (or bang) to force the optional to be unwrapped, so you can work directly with the type instead.

Switch back to the MainMenu.xib file and connect the IB outlets. Start by Control-clicking on the AppDelegate instance in MainMenu.xib and dragging a connection to the table view in the main window, selecting tableView as the connection's outlet. Do the same for the NSPanel instance, as well as the text field and date picker in the panel. When you're done, switch back to AppDelegate.swift.

Adding Methods to the AppDelegate Class

In order for the Birthdays application to work properly, there are a few methods that you must add to its AppDelegate class. The first is to create a function that will be invoked when the user selects New from the File menu (or presses ⌘-N). In fact, the default main menu is already set up to invoke an action when New is selected if the corresponding method exists in the application delegate class. That method is newDocument(). Add the code in Listing 6-2 to your AppDelegate class to handle this action.

LISTING 6-2: AppDelegate.swift

```swift
@IBAction func newDocument(sender: AnyObject!) {
    nameField.stringValue = ""
    dateField.dateValue = NSDate()
    panel.makeFirstResponder(nameField)
    NSApp.beginSheet(panel,
                modalForWindow: window,
                modalDelegate: self,
                didEndSelector: nil,
                contextInfo: nil)
}
```

Let's break this method down. First, you declare it with the following signature:

```swift
@IBAction func newDocument(sender: AnyObject!)
```

The @IBAction indicates this is the target of an Interface Builder action; it is akin to the IBAction return type in Objective-C code. This function takes a single parameter: sender. sender can be of type AnyObject. AnyObject is similar to the id type in Objective-C. In plain English, it means that this target can be the result of an action sent by any type of object. Theoretically, the parameter could also be nil, but because a sender object is sent when any interface action is invoked, it is safe to unwrap that optional value; thus, we suffix the type with an exclamation point (!).

The next three lines set up the initial state of the new birthday dialog sheet by making the name field blank and the date picker initialized to the current date and by focusing on the name field:

```
nameField.stringValue = ""
dateField.dateValue = NSDate()
panel.makeFirstResponder(nameField)
```

Strictly speaking, initializing the dialog sheet is not necessary. The first time it is shown, the text field would be blank and the date picker would be set to a default value anyway. The panel is not removed from memory when the sheet closes, however, so subsequent invocations will show the data the user previously entered—a substandard experience, to be sure. Moreover, the window will be focused on the last element with which the user interacted, which is probably the date picker. These three lines initialize the sheet to a more pleasant state for the user.

Finally, the panel is invoked as a dialog sheet:

```
NSApp.beginSheet(panel,
              modalForWindow: window,
              modalDelegate: self,
              didEndSelector: nil,
              contextInfo: nil)
```

This is the Swift version of the following Objective-C invocation:

```
[NSApp beginSheet:panel
    modalForWindow:window
     modalDelegate:self
    didEndSelector:NULL,
       contextInfo:nil];
```

The Swift code is, of course, calling Objective-C code. Thanks to the niceties of Swift syntax, you call the method in nearly the same way in Swift, passing named parameters for all but the first parameter—and, of course, you do it using Swift's more "traditional" method invocation syntax. Otherwise, the code is nearly the same. Once again, Swift allows you to leverage your Objective-C knowledge and experience!

Go ahead: Build and run your application. It won't save data or even create a new birthday record, but you should be able to interact with the application. Try selecting New from the File menu. A dialog sheet should pop up. Of course, its handler has not been written yet, so you won't be able to dismiss the sheet yet. You can quit the application by force-quitting it or by pressing the Stop button in Xcode.

Handling the Dialog Sheet

Obviously, a dialog sheet that doesn't do anything—even close—is not useful, so you should write a method to handle the closing of the dialog sheet. This method should take the data the user input in the name and date fields, and create a birthday record using Core Data. Add the code in Listing 6-3 to your AppDelegate class.

LISTING 6-3: AppDelegate.swift

```
@IBAction func createBirthday(sender: AnyObject!) {
    let ctx = managedObjectContext!
    let entity = NSEntityDescription.entityForName("Birthday",
```

continues

continued

```
                                              inManagedObjectContext: ctx)!
    let birthday = NSManagedObject(entity: entity,
                              insertIntoManagedObjectContext: ctx)
    birthday.setValue(nameField.stringValue, forKey: "name")
    birthday.setValue(dateField.dateValue, forKey: "birthday")

    var error: NSError?
    if !ctx.save(&error) {
        NSLog("Could not save \(error): \(error?.userInfo)")
    }

    NSApp.endSheet(panel)
    panel.orderOut(sender)
    tableView.reloadData()
}
```

This method is a bit more complex than the last one you created, so let's take a closer look at it.

The `createBirthday()` method is an Interface Builder action, so it has the same signature as `newDocument()`. Its first line retrieves the managed object context from the application delegate. Recall that the `managedObjectContext` property returns an optional value, so the first line also forces it to be unwrapped:

```
let ctx = managedObjectContext!
```

The second line creates an `NSEntityDescription` that represents the `Birthday` entity you defined earlier:

```
let entity = NSEntityDescription.entityForName("Birthday",
                                    inManagedObjectContext: ctx)!
```

An `NSEntityDescription` can be thought of as the "type" of an entity; it is to an `NSManagedObject` what an Objective-C `Class` type is to an `id` type. An `NSEntityDescription` is a factory that produces `NSManagedObject` classes—in this case, a `Birthday`—rather than *instances* of `NSManagedObject`. You create the entity description by passing the name of the desired instance, "Birthday," and the context in which it should be created. As with most Core Data classes, initialization can fail, so `NSEntityDescription.entityForName()` actually returns an optional value, which you force to be unwrapped.

> **NOTE** *A production application may want to handle* `nil` *return values from methods like* `NSEntityDescription.entityForName()`, *but for brevity, such error handling has been left out of this demo application.*

The third line creates an instance of the `Birthday` entity. This is similar to an instance of a class—it gives you a unique piece of data with which to work. An instance of an entity is created by passing the entity description and object context to `NSManagedObject`:

```
let birthday = NSManagedObject(entity: entity,
                        insertIntoManagedObjectContext: ctx)
```

The next two lines after that set the `name` and `birthday` attributes in your new Birthday entity instance. Unlike standard objects, these values cannot be set directly through properties. Rather, they are set using Cocoa's key-value coding mechanism, which is accessed through the `setValue()` method on `NSManageObject` (and its subclasses).

Following that is the crucial part of the method: instructing Core Data to persist the new object to disk. This is accomplished with four simple lines of code that demonstrate Swift's type system and error handling in action:

```
var error: NSError?
if !ctx.save(&error) {
    NSLog("Could not save \(error): \(error?.userInfo)")
}
```

In this code:

➤ You declare an optional `NSError` value. You don't know if an error will be created—hopefully not!—but you have to be able to handle the worst scenario, just in case.

➤ The managed object context is saved by invoking its `save()` method, which instructs Core Data to persist the object to disk. The error variable, `error`, is passed as a reference to this function by prefixing it with the ampersand (`&`).

➤ If `save()` fails—signified by a return value of `false`—a log message with the details of the failure is written.

Finally, the method closes with three lines of code that dismiss the dialog sheet, so users won't have to force-quit the application. These three lines of code also reload the table view so new data will appear immediately:

```
NSApp.endSheet(panel)
panel.orderOut(sender)
tableView.reloadData()
```

These lines are identical to what you would find in an Objective-C application, save for being written in Swift's, instead of Objective-C's, syntax.

Hooking Up the Dialog Sheet

Now, you have to hook up the dialog sheet's OK button to this action. Switch back to `MainMenu` `.xib` and Control-drag a connection from the panel's OK button to the `createBirthday()` outlet you just created in your `AppDelegate` class.

Build and run the Birthdays application again. You should now have a fully functional dialog sheet. You can invoke it by selecting New from the File menu and enter a new birthday. This time, clicking OK will actually dismiss the sheet!

Displaying Data

Now, you only have one problem: You can't see the data you've entered in the main window. To fix the display issue, you'll have to set up the application delegate as a data source for the main window's table view and implement the appropriate methods for passing data back to the table view.

Implementing the Table View's Behavior

First, go to `MainMenu.xib` and Control-drag a connection from the table view to the application delegate, setting `dataSource` as the connection. Now, switch back to `AppDelegate.swift`. It's time to implement the methods that will allow the table view to interact with the Core Data object graph you've created.

> **NOTE** *In larger production applications, you may find it desirable to create another class specifically to act as a table view's data source. Otherwise, the application delegate class can quickly become cluttered with unrelated behaviors. However, in this simple demonstration application, it is fine to use the application delegate as a data source for your table view.*

Add the three methods in Listing 6-4 to your `AppDelegate` class.

LISTING 6-4: AppDelegate.swift

```
private func fetchBirthdays() -> [AnyObject]? {
    let ctx = managedObjectContext!
    let req = NSFetchRequest(entityName: "Birthday")

    var error: NSError?

    if let results = ctx.executeFetchRequest(req, error: &error) {
        return results
    } else {
        NSLog("Could not fetch \(error): \(error?.userInfo)")
        return nil
    }
}

func numberOfRowsInTableView(tableView: NSTableView) -> Int {
    if let birthdays = fetchBirthdays() {
        return birthdays.count
    } else {
        return 0
    }
}

func tableView(tableView: NSTableView,
            objectValueForTableColumn tableColumn: NSTableColumn?,
            row: Int) -> AnyObject? {
    let col = tableColumn!.identifier
    if let birthdays = fetchBirthdays() {
        return birthdays[row].valueForKey(col)
    } else {
        return nil;
    }
}
```

These three methods work together to retrieve saved data from Core Data's backing store and display it to the user. The real work is done in the `fetchBirthdays()` method. Take a look at the method's signature:

```
private func fetchBirthdays() -> [AnyObject]?
```

This method is private. It returns an optional array of `AnyObject`—that is, it *may* return an array containing any type of object, *or* it may return `nil`.

The second line of `fetchBirthdays()` again retrieves and unwraps the `managedObjectContext` to make it easier to work with. The third line creates a fetch request object, specifying the `Birthday` entity as the target of the fetch request. You can think of this as analogous to a query in a relational database; the specified entity is the "table" you are querying.

Finally, the remainder of the function performs the actual fetch request. First, an optional error object is created to potentially hold an error result, in case the fetch request fails. The remaining lines execute the request:

```
if let results = ctx.executeFetchRequest(req, error: &error) {
    return results
} else {
    NSLog("Could not fetch \(error): \(error?.userInfo)")
    return nil
}
```

The first line of the `if` statement performs the request using the managed object context. `executeFetchRequest()` returns an optional array of any object type (again, it may return an array containing any object, or it may return `nil`). A reference to the error object declared previously is passed in so that `executeFetchRequest()` can return additional information if the request fails.

The first line of the `if` statement also unpacks the return value of `executeFetchRequest()` into the `results` variable. This works neatly with Swift's robust type system; if the value can be unwrapped, a non-nil value was returned, and that value can be returned from `fetchBirthdays()` in the next line. On the other hand, if `executeFetchRequest()` failed, it will return `nil`, and instead execution will jump to the `else` branch of the `if` statement, where the error is logged and `nil` is returned from `fetchBirthdays()`.

> **NOTE** *Swift's type system helps you a great deal here by requiring you to handle error cases. In Objective-C, it would be entirely possible to ignore the error condition and possibly return an unexpected value (or type of value) from the* `fetchBirthdays()` *method. In Swift, this is not possible.*

The next two methods implement behavior necessary for the application delegate to act as a data source. The first, `numberOfRowsInTableView()`, simply fetches the list of birthdays from Core Data and returns the count; or, if the list of birthdays cannot be fetched (`fetchBirthdays()` returns `nil`), a count of 0 is returned instead. Again, Swift's ability to unwrap optional types is used in the `if` statement to determine if an error occurred while fetching birthdays and respond appropriately:

```
if let birthdays = fetchBirthdays() {
```

```
      return birthdays.count
} else {
      return 0
}
```

The final method you implemented is passed a table view, column, and row, and returns an appropriate value for the table view cell that is being created. The return type of this method is `AnyObject?`; that is, it can return any type of object, or even `nil`. This corresponds to a return type of `id` in Objective-C.

First, the column's identifier, which corresponds to an attribute in the `Birthday` entity, is retrieved:

```
    let col = tableColumn!.identifier
```

Note that `tableColumn` can theoretically be `nil`, although, because you can reasonably expect it won't be (because you can assume the Cocoa runtime is working properly), it is first unwrapped (using the `!` operator), and its identifier property is retrieved.

Next, you have the standard `if` statement you saw previously: A list of birthdays is retrieved from Core Data using the `fetchBirthdays()` method, and if that succeeds, control jumps into the `if` branch; otherwise, control jumps to the `else` branch, where `nil` is returned.

The list of birthdays, if successfully fetched, is returned as an array. Each element of the array represents another row in our table view, so the appropriate record is fetched by getting the record at the index that corresponds to the `row` parameter passed to this method. Technically `fetchBirthdays()` returns an array of any object type, but because this is coming from Core Data, it *should* be an array of `NSManagedObject` instances. In order to get the label needed for the table view cell that is being created, the value for the key specified by the table column's identifier is retrieved from the `NSManagedObject` instance, as shown in the following line:

```
    return birthdays[row].valueForKey(col)
```

You may have noticed that this method has a fairly strange name, `tableView`. In Objective-C, the complete name of the method would be `tableView:objectValueForTableColumn:row:`. This method makes it more obvious how Objective-C method names are mapped to Swift method signatures: The first part becomes the "name" of the method, and the subsequent parts are named parameters to the method. (The finer details of how this mapping is achieved is covered in Chapter 9.)

The Completed Application Delegate

The completed form of the `AppDelegate` class, including the modifications you made from the template, is shown in Listing 6-5.

LISTING 6-5: AppDelegate.swift

```
//
//  AppDelegate.swift
//  Birthdays
//
//  Created by Michael Dippery on 12/3/14.
//  Copyright (c) 2014 Michael Dippery. All rights reserved.
//
```

```swift
import Cocoa

@NSApplicationMain
class AppDelegate: NSObject, NSApplicationDelegate, NSTableViewDataSource {

    @IBOutlet weak var window: NSWindow!
    @IBOutlet weak var tableView: NSTableView!
    @IBOutlet weak var panel: NSPanel!
    @IBOutlet weak var nameField: NSTextField!
    @IBOutlet weak var dateField: NSDatePicker!


    func applicationDidFinishLaunching(aNotification: NSNotification) {
        // Insert code here to initialize your application
    }

    func applicationWillTerminate(aNotification: NSNotification) {
        // Insert code here to tear down your application
    }

    // MARK: - UI Elements

    @IBAction func newDocument(sender: AnyObject!) {
        nameField.stringValue = ""
        dateField.dateValue = NSDate()
        panel.makeFirstResponder(nameField)
        NSApp.beginSheet(panel, modalForWindow: window, modalDelegate: self,
didEndSelector: nil, contextInfo: nil)
    }

    @IBAction func createBirthday(sender: AnyObject!) {
        let ctx = managedObjectContext!
        let entity = NSEntityDescription.entityForName("Birthday",
inManagedObjectContext: ctx)!
        let birthday = NSManagedObject(
            entity: entity,
            insertIntoManagedObjectContext: ctx)
        birthday.setValue(nameField.stringValue, forKey: "name")
        birthday.setValue(dateField.dateValue, forKey: "birthday")

        var error: NSError?
        if !ctx.save(&error) {
            NSLog("Could not save \(error): \(error?.userInfo)")
        }

        NSApp.endSheet(panel)
        panel.orderOut(sender)
        tableView.reloadData()
    }

    // MARK: - Table View Data Source

    private func fetchBirthdays() -> [AnyObject]? {
        let ctx = managedObjectContext!
        let req = NSFetchRequest(entityName: "Birthday")
```

continues

continued

```swift
        var error: NSError?

        if let results = ctx.executeFetchRequest(req, error: &error) {
            return results
        } else {
            NSLog("Could not fetch \(error): \(error?.userInfo)")
            return nil
        }
    }

    func numberOfRowsInTableView(tableView: NSTableView) -> Int {
        if let birthdays = fetchBirthdays() {
            return birthdays.count
        } else {
            return 0
        }
    }

    func tableView(tableView: NSTableView,
                   objectValueForTableColumn tableColumn: NSTableColumn?,
                   row: Int) -> AnyObject? {
        let col = tableColumn!.identifier
        if let birthdays = fetchBirthdays() {
            return birthdays[row].valueForKey(col)
        } else {
            return nil;
        }
    }

    // MARK: - Core Data stack

    lazy var applicationDocumentsDirectory: NSURL = {
        let urls = NSFileManager.defaultManager().URLsForDirectory(
            .ApplicationSupportDirectory, inDomains: .UserDomainMask)
        let appSupportURL = urls[urls.count - 1] as NSURL
        return appSupportURL.URLByAppendingPathComponent("com.monkey-robot
.Birthdays")
    }()

    lazy var managedObjectModel: NSManagedObjectModel = {
        let modelURL = NSBundle.mainBundle().URLForResource(
            "Birthdays", withExtension: "momd")!
        return NSManagedObjectModel(contentsOfURL: modelURL)!
    }()

    lazy var persistentStoreCoordinator: NSPersistentStoreCoordinator? = {
        let fileManager = NSFileManager.defaultManager()
        var shouldFail = false
        var error: NSError? = nil
        var failureReason = "There was an error creating or loading the " +
                            "application's saved data."

        // Make sure the application files directory is there
```

```
        let propertiesOpt = self.applicationDocumentsDirectory
.resourceValuesForKeys(
            [NSURLIsDirectoryKey], error: &error)
        if let properties = propertiesOpt {
            if !properties[NSURLIsDirectoryKey]!.boolValue {
                failureReason = "Expected a folder to store application data, " +
                    "found a file \(self.applicationDocumentsDirectory.path)."
                shouldFail = true
            }
        } else if error!.code == NSFileReadNoSuchFileError {
            error = nil
            fileManager.createDirectoryAtPath(self.applicationDocumentsDirectory
.path!, withIntermediateDirectories: true, attributes: nil, error: &error)
        }

        // Create the coordinator and store
        var coordinator: NSPersistentStoreCoordinator?
        if !shouldFail && (error == nil) {
            coordinator = NSPersistentStoreCoordinator(
                managedObjectModel: self.managedObjectModel)
            let url = self.applicationDocumentsDirectory
.URLByAppendingPathComponent(
                "Birthdays.storedata")
            if coordinator!.addPersistentStoreWithType(
                NSXMLStoreType,
                configuration: nil,
                URL: url,
                options: nil,
                error: &error) == nil {
                coordinator = nil
            }
        }

        if shouldFail || (error != nil) {
            // Report any error we got.
            let dict = NSMutableDictionary()
            dict[NSLocalizedDescriptionKey] = "Failed to initialize the " +
                                              "application's saved data"
            dict[NSLocalizedFailureReasonErrorKey] = failureReason
            if error != nil {
                dict[NSUnderlyingErrorKey] = error
            }
            error = NSError(domain: "YOUR_ERROR_DOMAIN", code: 9999, userInfo: dict)
            NSApplication.sharedApplication().presentError(error!)
            return nil
        } else {
            return coordinator
        }
    }()

    lazy var managedObjectContext: NSManagedObjectContext? = {
        let coordinator = self.persistentStoreCoordinator
        if coordinator == nil {
            return nil
        }
```

continues

continued

```
            var managedObjectContext = NSManagedObjectContext()
            managedObjectContext.persistentStoreCoordinator = coordinator
            return managedObjectContext
        }()

        // MARK: - Core Data Saving and Undo support

        @IBAction func saveAction(sender: AnyObject!) {
            if let moc = self.managedObjectContext {
                if !moc.commitEditing() {
                    NSLog("\(NSStringFromClass(self.dynamicType)) " +
                            "unable to commit editing before saving")
                }
                var error: NSError? = nil
                if moc.hasChanges && !moc.save(&error) {
                    NSApplication.sharedApplication().presentError(error!)
                }
            }
        }

        func windowWillReturnUndoManager(window: NSWindow) -> NSUndoManager? {
            if let moc = self.managedObjectContext {
                return moc.undoManager
            } else {
                return nil
            }
        }

        func applicationShouldTerminate(sender: NSApplication) ->
    NSApplicationTerminateReply {
            if let moc = managedObjectContext {
                if !moc.commitEditing() {
                    NSLog("\(NSStringFromClass(self.dynamicType)) " +
                            "unable to commit editing to terminate")
                    return .TerminateCancel
                }

                if !moc.hasChanges {
                    return .TerminateNow
                }

                var error: NSError? = nil
                if !moc.save(&error) {
                    // Customize this code block to include
                    // application-specific recovery steps.
                    let result = sender.presentError(error!)
                    if (result) {
                        return .TerminateCancel
                    }

                    let question = NSLocalizedString("Could not save changes " +
                        "while quitting. Quit anyway?",
```

```
                comment: "Quit without saves error question message")
        let info = NSLocalizedString("Quitting now will lose any " +
            "changes you have made since the last successful save",
            comment: "Quit without saves error question info");
        let quitButton = NSLocalizedString("Quit anyway",
            comment: "Quit anyway button title")
        let cancelButton = NSLocalizedString("Cancel",
            comment: "Cancel button title")
        let alert = NSAlert()
        alert.messageText = question
        alert.informativeText = info
        alert.addButtonWithTitle(quitButton)
        alert.addButtonWithTitle(cancelButton)

        let answer = alert.runModal()
        if answer == NSAlertFirstButtonReturn {
            return .TerminateCancel
        }
      }
    }
    // If we got here, it is time to quit.
    return .TerminateNow
  }

}
```

Go ahead and build and run your program. Your Birthdays application should be fully functional. You can add new birthdays and see the new birthdays appear in the table view.

SUMMARY

This chapter demonstrated the use of Core Data from Swift code. As is commonly the case with Swift programs, very little has changed, with the exception of syntax and some modifications to work with Swift's type system. Prior familiarity with Core Data can easily be leveraged when creating a Swift program. Apple has designed Swift to work nearly seamlessly with existing Objective-C APIs, and you should encounter few if any problems when using Core Data with Swift.

PART II
Advanced Swift Concepts

7

Extending Classes

WHAT'S IN THIS CHAPTER?

➤ Adding new methods and properties to existing classes

➤ Ensuring that classes implement desired behavior using protocols

➤ Adopting new protocols in existing classes

➤ Composing protocols to create rich new data types

➤ Creating generic functions that can work with many different data types

WROX.COM CODE DOWNLOADS FOR THIS CHAPTER

You can find the wrox.com downloads for this chapter at http://www.wrox.com/go/proswift on the Download Code tab. The code for this chapter is contained in the following files:

➤ Colors.playground

➤ Protocols.playground

➤ Queue.playground

➤ Squares.playground

Classes, structs, and enumerations are essential parts of Swift programming. Swift's type system ensures that types are always used in an expected, safe way, minimizing bugs in programs written in the language. While it may seem like this makes code inflexible and tedious to write, it turns out that Swift's type system is so powerful that the opposite is true: Using features of the language, you can easily write flexible code that still takes advantage of the safety offered by Swift.

WORKING WITH CLASS EXTENSIONS

One of the most visible features of Objective-C was *categories*. Categories allow Objective-C programmers to "open up" existing classes—including classes they don't control (or even have the source code for)—and to add new methods and properties to those classes. Objective-C's categories were originally conceived as a way to group related methods together in source code (and annotate the purpose and general usage of those classes), but in doing so, they opened up the possibility of adding new methods to existing classes. Categories are an essential feature that adds a great deal of flexibility for object-oriented programming in Objective-C.

Objective-C's categories are also a widely misunderstood feature of the language. Many Objective-C programmers do not understand how categories work. In particular, many novice and even intermediate programmers do not realize that categories are compiled into a binary and are thus available to any part of the program's codebase; instead, they believe that categories are used only when the header file that declares the category is imported into a source code file. This has led to countless misunderstandings and questions about categories on mailing lists and web forums, not to mention a great deal of errors in programs that make use of categories.

Furthermore, in adding flexibility to the language, categories are also brittle and can add complexity to Objective-C programs that can easily result in programming errors. Categories can re-declare and re-implement methods found in other categories, or even the class's implementation itself. If a category defines an existing method, the exact method implementation used by the program is undefined. It is also possible to declare a method in a category but never implement it, leading to bugs that will only appear at runtime if an object tries to invoke that unimplemented method. Both of these situations were allowed by the compiler and, depending on the compiler and settings used, may not even result in warnings at compilation time.

Even so, categories added such a great deal of flexibility to object-oriented programming in Objective-C that they became an essential feature of the language. In fact, the Cocoa and Cocoa Touch frameworks make great use of categories. The feature is so cherished that it was not dropped completely in Swift, appearing as a feature of the Swift language known as *class extensions*.

As a language with much more rigorous type safety, Swift's class extensions solve many of the problems inherent in Objective-C's categories while still retaining the flexibility expected of the language feature. Using class extensions, Swift programmers can add both properties and methods to an existing class (even one they don't control). You can also use class extensions to adopt a protocol in an existing class. (Protocols are covered in more detail later in this chapter.) Best of all, the compiler ensures that class extensions are implemented correctly, preventing the kind of errors found in the use of categories in Objective-C.

Adding Methods to Classes

Class extensions are most commonly used to add methods to an existing class, including classes from Apple's own frameworks (such as Foundation, AppKit, and UIKit). They are often used as an alternative to subclassing. In fact, if you only want to add methods to a class (as opposed to overriding behavior), class extensions both allow you to avoid the complexities of subclassing *and* add those methods to *all* instances of a class (not just instances of its subclass). Programmers often use class extensions to implement new convenience initializers, or add methods to allow for additional behavior specific to their own applications.

For instance, let's say you were writing an application that made heavy use of CSS color codes. A CSS color code is made up of three bytes: one for the amount of red in the color, one for the amount of green, and one for the amount of blue. These three bytes are encoded in a hexadecimal string. For example, the color red is encoded as FF0000—a value of 255 for red, and 0 bytes for both green and blue. In CSS code, this string is prefixed with a # symbol so it appears as #FF0000 (or #ff0000, as the hexadecimal string is case-insensitive) in source code.

In your hypothetical CSS-centric application, you may find it necessary to convert these color codes into an NSColor (or UIColor) object. Doing so is fairly straightforward, but it would be simplest if NSColor simply offered an initializer into which you could pass a CSS color code and get back a color object. Alas, out of the box, NSColor does not offer such functionality. But thanks to class extensions, you can easily add it.

> **NOTE** *This specific example demonstrates the addition of a convenience initializer to* NSColor. NSColor *and* UIColor *are very similar, however, so the same code should also work for* UIColor.

Listing 7-1 shows the code for adding such a convenience initializer to NSColor. (The NSColor class only exists in Cocoa, not Cocoa Touch, so the following playground is for OS X. The same idea applies for the UIColor class in the UIKit framework on iOS, though.)

LISTING 7-1: Colors.playground

```
import Cocoa

extension NSColor {
    convenience init(fromCSSString css: String) {
        var cssCode = css
        if css.hasPrefix("#") {
            cssCode = css.substringFromIndex(advance(css.startIndex, 1))
        }
        let scanner = NSScanner(string: cssCode)
        var colorCode: CUnsignedLongLong = 0
        if scanner.scanHexLongLong(&colorCode) {
            let red = CGFloat((colorCode & 0xff0000) >> 16) / 255.0
            let blue = CGFloat((colorCode & 0x00ff00) >> 8) / 255.0
            let green = CGFloat(colorCode & 0x0000ff) / 255.0
            self.init(red: red, green: green, blue: blue, alpha: 1.0)
        } else {
            NSLog("Could not scan CSS string: \(css)")
            self.init(red: 0.0, green: 0.0, blue: 0.0, alpha: 1.0)
        }
    }
}
```

Let's break the example shown in Listing 7-1 down, piece by piece, to highlight the important parts. Class extensions are introduced by the `extension` keyword, followed by the name of the class being extended. What follows is the body of the extension in curly braces; these are implementations of the methods and properties to be added to the class. The class extension in Listing 7-1 adds only one method: a convenience initializer that takes a string representing a CSS color code and turns it into a color object.

Most of the initializer's block simply parses the CSS string (removing the leading # character if necessary) and converts the hexadecimal components into actual integers using `NSScanner`. The parts most applicable to class extensions are the last lines of each part of the if/else statement:

```
self.init(red: red, green: green, blue: blue, alpha: 1.0)
```

As you can see, a class extension has access to *all* of the methods of the class it extends, including initializers. As a convenience initializer, the `init()` method in Listing 7-1 has to ultimately call one of `NSColor`'s designated initializers, which it does after parsing the CSS string.

There's not much more than that to a basic class extension, although there are more advanced use cases for class extensions.

Adding Properties to Classes

You can also add computed properties to classes using class extensions. For example, after adding the convenience initializer in Listing 7-1, you may realize that it would be helpful to add a property to `NSColor` to return a CSS string representing the color, too. You can easily add such a property using class extensions, as shown in Listing 7-2.

LISTING 7-2: Colors.playground

```
import Cocoa

extension NSColor {
    var CSSString: String {
        let red = Int(redComponent * 255.0)
        let green = Int(greenComponent * 255.0)
        let blue = Int(blueComponent * 255.0)
        return NSString(format: "#%02x%02x%02x", red, green, blue)
    }
}
```

As before, you declare an extension to `NSColor` using the `extension` keyword. Instead of creating a method, however, you declare a new computed property to add to the class and then define the type of that property as well as its body.

Extensions may only add computed properties. You cannot add stored properties, nor can you add property observers. You can, however, provide both a getter and a setter for a computed property; properties added in a class extension need not be read-only (as the property in Listing 7-2 is).

Mutating Classes in Extensions

The method and property added in Listings 7-1 and 7-2 do not alter the internal state of an NSColor object at all. This is not a requirement of class extensions, however. Methods (and properties) added in an extension are free to change the internal state of a class as needed. However, methods that alter the internal state of an object must be marked with the mutating keyword; otherwise, the compiler issues an error. Listing 7-3 shows a Square class and accompanying extension that mutates the class.

LISTING 7-3: Squares.playground

```
import Foundation

struct Square {
    var side: Double

    func area() -> Double {
        return side * side
    }
}

extension Square {
    mutating func updateArea(area: Double) {
        side = sqrt(area)
    }
}

var square = Square(side: 10)
square.area()
square.updateArea(1000)
square.area()
square.side

let square2 = Square(side: 100)
square2.updateArea(50)
```

> **NOTE** *It is important to remember that even if an extension provides a mutating method, the rules for* let *versus* var *still apply: If you create a constant (using* let, *instead of* var), *you cannot change that object's values, even if you call a mutating method. The compiler issues an error on line 24 of Listing 7-3, preventing you from calling the* updateArea() *method on a constant.*

SPECIFYING BEHAVIOR WITH PROTOCOLS

In addition to extensions, you can also use protocols to specify additional functionality for a class (including classes you don't control). You can think of a protocol as a contract. By adopting a protocol, a class ensures that it provides the interface and behavior specified as part of the protocol.

Protocols are an integral part of Objective-C programming and should be familiar to Objective-C programmers. Protocols in Swift are not much different, although they have some additional features. Most important, a protocol creates a new *type* in Swift, making protocols a full-fledged element of Swift's robust type system. Just as a class or struct called `Rectangle` introduces a new `Rectangle` type to a program, a protocol named, for example, `Random` also introduces a new type called `Random`. This means that you can specify constants, variables, properties, and function and method parameters as being of type `Random`, just as they could be of type `String` or `Int` (or any of the other multitude of types available in Swift).

Unlike classes and structs, protocols do not provide an implementation of a behavior, only a specification. It is up to classes that adopt the protocol to provide the actual implementation of the method or property specified in a protocol. Simply put, protocols are a way of telling code what methods and properties a variable provides, without forcing it to be a specific class.

Adopting Protocols

Protocols may be adopted by classes, structs, and even enumerations. A class, struct, or enumeration adopts a protocol by adding the protocol name after a colon, just as though it would a superclass:

```
class MyClass: MyProtocol {
```

A class (or struct or enum) may specify multiple protocols that it adopts. Each protocol name is separated by a comma. If a class adopts multiple protocols, it must implement all of the methods and properties from each protocol it adopts:

```
class MyClass: MyProtocol, MyOtherProtocol {
```

If a class also inherits from another class, its superclass should be listed first, before protocols:

```
class MyClass: MySuperclass, MyProtocol, MyOtherProtocol {
```

Declaring Properties and Methods

Protocols declare a list of properties or methods that a conforming class must implement, without providing an implementation. It is up to each adopting class to define the implementation of the protocol's methods or properties. Classes that adopt a method *must* implement the protocol's methods or properties (except in the case of optional methods and properties, as noted later in this chapter).

The properties and methods required by a protocol are listed in the body of the protocol just as they are with classes, except that no body is provided. Listing 7-4 shows an example of a protocol, `Shape`, and one conforming method, `Square`.

LISTING 7-4: Protocols.playground

```
protocol Shape {
    var isSquare: Bool { get }
    func area() -> Int
}

struct Square: Shape {
```

```
        let side: Int

        var isSquare: Bool { return true }

        func area() -> Int {
            return side * side
        }
    }

    let square = Square(side: 10)
    square.isSquare
    square.area()
```

The Shape protocol in Listing 7-4 specifies one method, area(), and one property, isSquare. Protocols do not (and cannot) specify whether a property is a stored or computed property; that implementation detail is left up to each individual class that implements the protocol. Properties specified by protocols *must* be declared as var properties. However, the protocol can specify whether the property has only a getter, or both a getter and a setter, by putting the keywords get or set in braces after the property declaration. Shape specifies that the isSquare property is read-only (it only has a getter). A setter could also be required by the addition of the set keyword, as shown here:

```
    var isSquare: Bool { get, set }
```

Had a setter been required, the Square property would have had to implement a setter as well as a getter.

Both the properties and methods specified in a protocol may alter the internal state of instances of classes that conform to them. If a method changes the internal state of an object, however, it must be marked with the mutating keyword. Listing 7-5 shows how the Shape protocol may be altered to change the visibility of a shape.

LISTING 7-5: Protocols.playground

```
protocol Shape {
    var isSquare: Bool { get }
    func area() -> Int
    mutating func makeVisible()
    mutating func makeInvisible()
}

struct Square: Shape {
    let side: Int
    var isVisible: Bool

    var isSquare: Bool { return true }

    func area() -> Int {
        return side * side
    }

    mutating func makeVisible() {
```

continues

continued

```
        isVisible = true
    }

    mutating func makeInvisible() {
        isVisible = false
    }
}

var square = Square(side: 10, isVisible: true)
square.isSquare
square.area()
square.isVisible
square.makeInvisible()
square.isVisible
```

Protocols may also specify initializers that must be implemented by conforming classes. As with classes, these initializers may also be marked as `required` (meaning that a class and all of its subclasses must implement that initializer) or `convenience` (to make them a convenience initializer). As with regular classes, initializers in protocols may also be failable. Initializers in protocols do not provide an implementation.

> **NOTE** *For more information on the various types of initializers available to classes, refer to Chapter 3.*

Working with Optional Methods and Properties

Protocols may also specify *optional* methods and properties. These are methods that an adopting class may or may not elect to implement. Optional methods *must* be called using optional chaining, and they return an optional value (in other words, if an optional method specifies a `String` as its return type, it actually returns a `String?`) to indicate that the method may or may not be called, so it may or may not return a value. Methods that are optional are prefixed with the `optional` keyword. Listing 7-6 shows a protocol with an optional method.

LISTING 7-6: Protocols.playground

```
import Cocoa

@objc protocol Transaction {
    func commit() -> Bool
    optional func isComplete() -> Bool
}

class DatabaseTransaction: Transaction {
    func commit() -> Bool {
        println("Commiting")
        return true
```

```
    }
}

let db: Transaction = DatabaseTransaction()
db.commit()
db.isComplete?()
```

Note that the call to `db.isComplete` is suffixed with a question mark (?). Because the method may not exist, you can call it optionally. As a result, `isComplete()` also returns an optional value. Because `DatabaseTransaction` does not implement `isComplete()`, `nil` is returned when that method is invoked.

> **NOTE** *In the example given in Listing 7-6, it is necessary to specify the db constant's type as* `Transaction` *instead of letting Swift infer it to be a* `DatabaseTransaction`. *If the Swift compiler is allowed to infer the type instead, it will emit an error on the last line,* `db.isComplete?()`, *because the compiler knows that* `DatabaseTransaction` *does not implement the* `isComplete()` *method. Swift's type inference is so robust that occasionally you must use a couple tricks so code examples actually demonstrate something useful.*

Note, too, that the protocol is marked with the `@objc` attribute, making it compatible with Objective-C code. This is required if a protocol has optional methods or properties because Swift will use the Objective-C runtime to check for the presence of optional methods on an adopting class. Unfortunately, this means that protocols with optional methods can *only* be adopted by classes; structs and enumerations cannot adopt protocols that include optional methods.

Protocols generally don't include optional methods or properties because they are designed to specify a strict interface for classes. However, optional methods and properties can occasionally be useful, and are pervasive in the Cocoa and Cocoa Touch frameworks, so even if you don't use them yourself, you'll likely run into them at some point.

PROTOCOLS AND OPTIONAL METHODS

Optional protocol methods did not become available in Objective-C until the release of version 2.0 of the language. Optional methods are mostly defined in protocols that are used in conjunction with delegates. Prior to Objective-C 2.0, delegates were generally typed simply as `id`, and you were required to read their documentation to figure out what methods they were expected to implement. Furthermore, classes that made use of a delegate had to check to see if their delegates implemented a specific method, as there was no way to tell the compiler that a given method was required to be implemented by a delegate class.

continues

continued

With the introduction of Objective-C 2.0, delegate classes could now be typed using protocols. However, classes that make use of delegates often have both required and optional methods for their delegates (and sometimes only optional methods). Optional methods are used as a way for delegates to extend or enhance functionality. Because of this constraint, Objective-C 2.0 added optional methods to protocols, allowing delegates to adopt a protocol, thus making programming with delegates slightly less cumbersome.

Protocols Are Types

Protocols are types, just like classes, structs, and enumerations. As such, you can use them anywhere you can use other types: variables, constants, properties, method and function arguments, and return types. You can even use them with the same operators that work with classes, structs, and enums, and you can use them to constrain a collection type (such as a list or dictionary) to a particular type as well.

Checking for Protocol Conformance

Because protocols are types on the same level as classes and structs, you can use the `is` operator to check to see if a constant or variable conforms to a given protocol. You can also use the `as` or `as?` operators to cast a variable to a protocol type. Listing 7-7 shows how you can use these operators in conjunction with a protocol. Here, `items` is an array of several different types of variables (`Ints`, `Strings`, and `Rectangles`, to be specific). A `for` loop iterates through the items, only printing them if they are serializable.

LISTING 7-7: Protocols.playground

```
import Cocoa

@objc protocol Serializable {
    func serialize() -> String
}

class Rectangle: Serializable {
    let length: Int
    let width: Int

    init(length: Int, width: Int) {
        self.length = length
        self.width = width
    }

    func serialize() -> String {
        return "{length: \(length), width:\(width)}"
    }
```

```
    }

    let items = [1, 2, 3, Rectangle(length: 4, width: 4), "5",
                Rectangle(length: 6, width: 6)]

    for item in items {
        if let it = item as? Serializable {
            println(it.serialize())
        }
    }
```

> **NOTE** *The protocol is marked with the @objc attribute, meaning that it is compatible with Objective-C code. You can check for protocol conformance only if the protocol is marked as @objc because Swift uses the Objective-C runtime to do protocol conformance checks. Likewise, because only classes (not structs or enumerations) are compatible with Objective-C, such protocols can only be adopted by classes.*

Using Protocol Types in Collections

You can use protocols as the type specifier for collections such as lists and dictionaries, too. Listing 7-8 demonstrates the use of a protocol as a type specifier in an array.

LISTING 7-8: Protocols.playground

```
import Cocoa

@objc protocol Serializable {
    func serialize() -> String
}

class Rectangle: Serializable {
    let length: Int
    let width: Int

    init(length: Int, width: Int) {
        self.length = length
        self.width = width
    }

    func serialize() -> String {
        return "{length: \(length), width:\(width)}"
    }
}

class Triangle: Serializable {
    let sideA: Int
    let sideB: Int
    let sideC: Int
```

continues

continued

```
    init(sideA: Int, sideB: Int, sideC: Int) {
        self.sideA = sideA
        self.sideB = sideB
        self.sideC = sideC
    }

    func serialize() -> String {
        return "{sides: (\(sideA), \(sideB), \(sideC)}"
    }
}

let items2: [Serializable] = [Rectangle(length: 10, width: 10),
                              Triangle(sideA: 4, sideB: 8, sideC: 16),
                              Rectangle(length: 15, width: 25)]
let reps = items2.map({ $0.serialize() })
reps
```

> **NOTE** `items2` *is not "an array of rectangles and triangles." It is, instead, "an array of serializables." Therefore, while you can call any methods specified in the protocol (in this case,* `serialize()`*), you cannot invoke methods that are specified in the class but not in the protocol.*

Composing Protocols

There may be times when you want to specify that a variable, constant, function parameter, or return type conforms to a set of protocols, but you don't want to specify a particular type. You can *compose* a set of protocols together to specify a type. A variable of such a type must conform to all protocols in the composition. For example, you can write a function, `hideIfSquare()`, that hides a given object if it is both able to hide and a square:

```
func hideIfSquare(var quad: protocol<Disappearing, RegularQuadrilateral>) {
    if quad.isSquare {
        quad.makeInvisible()
    }
}
```

Protocol composition can give you a powerful, yet very flexible, way to declare types in your program.

Inheriting from Other Protocols

Like classes and structs, protocols can also inherit from one or more other protocols. Protocol inheritance is specified similarly to class inheritance: The parent protocol is specified after a colon at the end of the protocol's name. If the protocol inherits from multiple protocols, the parent protocol names are separated by commas. If a protocol inherits from another protocol, then adopters of that protocol must implement the methods required by both protocols.

In Listing 7-9, the previous Shape protocol is modified so that it inherits from two new protocols, Disappearing and RegularQuadrilateral. Square only adopts Shape, but because of protocol inheritance, it must adopt the methods specified in the Disappearing and RegularQuadrilateral protocols, as well.

LISTING 7-9: Protocols.playground

```swift
protocol Disappearing {
    mutating func makeVisible()
    mutating func makeInvisible()
}

protocol RegularQuadrilateral {
    var isSquare: Bool { get }
}

protocol Shape: Disappearing, RegularQuadrilateral {
    func area() -> Int
}

struct Square: Shape {
    let side: Int
    var isVisible: Bool

    var isSquare: Bool { return true }

    func area() -> Int {
        return side * side
    }

    mutating func makeVisible() {
        isVisible = true
    }

    mutating func makeInvisible() {
        isVisible = false
    }
}

var square = Square(side: 10, isVisible: true)
square.isSquare
square.area()
square.isVisible
square.makeInvisible()
square.isVisible
```

Adopting Protocols in Class Extensions

You can also use class extensions to adopt protocols in classes you don't control. This powerful mechanism allows you to define a protocol and then add it to existing classes, making them conform to that protocol so you can use them wherever that protocol type is expected.

You can adopt a protocol in an extension by placing the protocol name after the extension's class, preceded by a colon, just as you would with a class definition. You should then implement all the required methods of the protocol in the body of the class extension, along with any optional methods you wish to implement. Listing 7-10 demonstrates how you can make Swing's `String` class conform to the `RegularQuadrilateral` protocol you wrote earlier.

LISTING 7-10: Protocols.playground

```
extension String: RegularQuadrilateral {
    var isSquare: Bool { return false }
}

let s = "string"
s.isSquare
```

The extension effectively makes instances of `String` also instances of `RegularQuadrilateral`. You can pass a `String` instance to any function or method that expects a `RegularQuadrilateral`.

Sometimes you may also be working with a third-party class that already has the methods required by a protocol you wrote. Even though instances of that third-party class implement the required method, they are not considered to be of the same type as the protocol because the third-party class definition has not explicitly declared them to be as such. You can use class extensions to declare that the third-party class does, in fact, conform to your protocol. Because the class already provides the required methods, however, the class extension's body can simply be empty.

Listing 7-11 shows a case in which you define a protocol, `LowercaseString`, that requires a single property, `lowercaseString()`. Swift's `String` class already provides such a property, but it does not conform to `LowercaseString` because the class's definition does not declare that it does. Using a class extension, you can inform the `Swift` compiler that instances of `Strings` are, in fact, also instances of `LowercaseString`. The extension has an empty body because `String` already implements the required property.

LISTING 7-11: Protocols.playground

```
import Foundation

protocol LowercaseString {
    var lowercaseString: String { get }
}

extension String: LowercaseString {}

let t = "The String"
t.lowercaseString
```

Together, protocols and class extensions work within Swift's type system to give you an immense amount of power and flexibility in implementing new types and even making existing types conform to the specifications of your new types. They can make a program easy to read, and functions and methods more generic, all without sacrificing the safety of the Swift type system.

WORKING WITH GENERICS

Consider a case in which you are tasked with writing a function that returns the maximum of two integers. For your first pass, it would make sense to write a simple function that takes two integers and returns the greater of the two, like this:

```
func max(a: Int, b: Int) -> Int {
    return a > b ? a : b
}
```

Later on, you need a function that returns the larger of two floating-point values, so you write another max function:

```
func max(a: Double, b: Double) -> Double {
    return a > b ? a : b
}
```

You write a bit more code and create your own class that also has an ordering, and find you need a function to return the larger of two instances of that class, so you add another max function:

```
func max(a: CustomClass, b: CustomClass) -> CustomClass {
    return a > b ? a : b
}
```

At this point, you start to realize that you've essentially written the same function three times, albeit for different types, and you realize you're going to go crazy if you have to write a separate max function for every orderable type in your program. There must be a better way!

Luckily, Swift has a better way: generics. *Generics* are a way to specify that a function takes certain types as arguments and returns certain types, but you don't specify what those types are. Instead, you use a placeholder name to indicate types that should be identical, but can be of *any* type. Such a function or method is said to be generic.

Consider your max function. Each implementation takes two arguments of the same type (because it generally doesn't make sense to compare objects of different types) and then returns an object of the same type. You can probably envision a single function that may look something like this:

```
func max(a: Type, b: Type) -> Type {
    return a > b ? a : b
}
```

Of course, that would be a function that takes objects of type Type and returns an object of type Type!

Swift allows you to specify generic types in a similar way, but the syntax is slightly different. You specify an arbitrary *placeholder* name for the types of arguments your function or method expects and use them in place of an actual type. The placeholder name is specified after the function name in angled brackets, as shown here:

```
func max<T>(a: T, b: T) -> T {
    return a > b ? a : b
}
```

This new function definition says that it takes two objects, each of the same type, and returns an object of the same type. That type is referred to as T within the body of the function. The function can accept *any* type, although the parameters must be of the same type. The following function call would be valid:

```
max(10, 100)
```

However, you could not pass two objects of different types:

```
max(10, "string")    // This results in a compiler error
```

> **NOTE** *You can use any valid identifier for the placeholder name in generic functions and methods. However, it is considered best practice to use single-character names, such as* T, E, K, *or* V, *unless your specific situation calls for something more meaningful.*

Thanks to Swift's generics, you can specify a single function that can work with many different types of objects. As with all of Swift's other type-related features, generics fit neatly into its type system, giving you all of its safety while still allowing you to write flexible code.

Generic Classes

Often, you may want a class to work with any data type, so long as the class works with a consistent type. One such case is Swift arrays. You can put any object in a Swift array, but all the objects in the array must be of the same type. Dictionaries are another example: Keys and values may be of different types, but *all* keys are of the same type, and *all* values are of the same type.

You can use generics with classes, structs, and enumerations similarly to how they are used in functions and methods (as shown in the previous section). For instance, consider the case of a simple Queue data structure. While you can put any type in the queue, all items contained in the queue should be of the same type. Using generics, you can design the class so it works with any types, but ensure that those types are consistent (and that the compiler prevents misuse). Listing 7-12 shows a simple implementation of this queue data structure. Notice that the underlying array, items, is parameterized by the generic type of the Queue. Likewise, insert() takes an object of the same type, and remove() and peek() return items of the same type. When initialized, the Queue is parameterized to only work with Ints, so the final line, which attempts to insert a String, results in a compiler error.

LISTING 7-12: Queue.playground

```
class Queue<T> {
    var items = [T]()

    func insert(item: T) {
        items.append(item)
    }

    func remove() -> T? {
        if items.isEmpty {
```

```
            return nil
        } else {
            return items.removeAtIndex(0)
        }
    }
}

var queue = Queue<Int>()
queue.insert(10)
queue.insert(20)
queue.remove()
queue.insert("string")      // This will not work!
```

There is one caveat when using class extensions with generic classes: When extending a generic class, you do not specify the type placeholder in the extension, although you can use the type placeholder in the body of the extension. Queue would be extended as shown in Listing 7-13.

LISTING 7-13: Queue.playground

```
extension Queue {
    func peek() -> T? {
        if items.isEmpty {
            return nil
        } else {
            return items[0]
        }
    }
}
```

Working with Type Constraints

It's often useful to specify that a generic type extend from a certain class or adopt a certain protocol to ensure that the type implements the methods expected by the function, method, or class that makes use of the generic type. For example, you may want to specify that any type of item managed by the Queue class can be compared using the == operator, so that you can implement a method such as hasItem() to determine if an item is already in the queue. You can specify a class from which a generic type must inherit, or a protocol it must adopt, by specifying it after the generic placeholder, preceded by a colon. Listing 7-14 shows a modification to the Queue class that requires that it only take Equatable objects (Equatable objects can be compared using the == operator). It also adds a method, hasItem(), in an extension that checks to see if an item is already in the queue.

LISTING 7-14: Queue.playground

```
class Queue<T: Equatable> {
    var items = [T]()

    func insert(item: T) {
        items.append(item)
    }
```

continues

continued

```swift
    func remove() -> T? {
        if items.isEmpty {
            return nil
        } else {
            return items.removeAtIndex(0)
        }
    }
}

extension Queue {
    func peek() -> T? {
        if items.isEmpty {
            return nil
        } else {
            return items[0]
        }
    }
}

extension Queue {
    func hasItem(obj: T) -> Bool {
        for item in items {
            if item == obj {
                return true
            }
        }
        return false
    }
}

var queue = Queue<Int>()
queue.insert(10)
queue.insert(20)
queue.peek()
queue.remove()
queue.hasItem(20)
queue.hasItem(10)
```

SUMMARY

Swift offers programmers a rich type system combined with the flexibility that experienced Objective-C programmers have come to expect in iOS and OS X programming. In this chapter, you have learned how you can ensure that classes implement a set of methods or properties using protocols. You have also learned how you can extend classes to add new methods to existing classes, including ones you don't have control over, and even adopt protocols in existing classes. You have also learned how you can use generics to avoid the tediousness of implementing the same function for different data types. Most importantly, you have seen how all of these capabilities fit neatly into Swift's type system, allowing you to work with classes in powerful new ways without sacrificing any of the safety provided by the Swift compiler.

Advanced Data Types

WHAT'S IN THIS CHAPTER?

➤   Modeling data using algebraic data types

➤   Improving code quality with optional types

➤   Overloading existing operators for new data types

➤   Creating custom operators to express the intent of your code

➤   Understanding how closures work

WROX.COM CODE DOWNLOADS FOR THIS CHAPTER

You can find the wrox.com downloads for this chapter at http://www.wrox.com/go/ proswift on the Download Code tab. The code for this chapter is contained in the following files:

➤   `Casting.playground`

➤   `Closures.playground`

➤   `Custom Operators.playground`

➤   `Dimension.playground`

➤   `JSON.playground`

➤   `Operators.playground`

➤   `Some.playground`

➤   `Tuples.playground`

Swift draws inspiration from many languages, especially functional programming languages. While you can certainly get by with the more basic features discussed previously in this book, you will no doubt encounter some of Swift's more advanced features as you become more experienced and proficient in Swift programming. This chapter introduces you to Swift's more advanced concepts, particularly enumerations, optional types, and closures. When you are done, you will have many more tools in your Swift toolbox to help you improve the quality of your code.

WORKING WITH ENUMS AND ALGEBRAIC DATA TYPES

Although Swift is heavily geared toward object-oriented programming, it draws elements and inspiration from many functional programming languages. You've already seen some of these elements, including Swift's use of closures and functions as first-class data types that can be passed around as parameters to other functions and returned as values from functions. Another idea that Swift borrows from functional programming languages is *algebraic data types*, as you can see in Swift's enum type.

Algebraic data types are central to many functional programming languages, including Haskell and Standard ML. Simply put, *algebraic data types* are a composite data type. That is, they may contain multiple values (such as a data type with multiple integer fields), or they may consist of *variants*, or multiple finite different values.

For example, consider a simple algebraic data type: the Boolean type that exists in most, if not all, programming languages. A Boolean is a single type that may take on one of two values: true or false. Each instance of a Boolean type must be either true or false, but the instance cannot be both at once—it has to be one or the other.

Algebraic data types can also be a composite type. For example, a 2-tuple of two integers is a fairly simple algebraic data type. Such a tuple could be expressed as having type `(Int, Int)`, and a possible value for the type could be `(2, 2)`.

Algebraic data types can get even more complex. They can, for example, be a composite type with variants. You could create an enum, `Dimension`, for holding the length and width of a room. You can express this enum in both U.S. feet and metric meters. In Swift, you could define such an enum like this:

```
enum Dimension {
    case US(Double, Double)
    case Metric(Double, Double)
}
```

The `Dimension` enum could be created like this:

```
let roomSizeMetric = Dimension.Metric(5.0, 4.0)
```

You will see how to create more complex enums in Swift shortly. (The syntax for working with enumerations is also covered in Chapter 1.)

Matching Patterns

Languages that support algebraic data types often support a number of features that allow programmers to easily work with individual fields of composite types or different variants of a given type. These features are particularly relevant when writing functions to act on the different fields or variants in a type-safe way. One such feature is called *pattern matching*. Pattern matching allows programmers to define functions that operate differently on each of a type's variants, as well as to easily pull out individual fields from a given type—all while maintaining the language's type safety guarantees. In fact, the compilers of many languages with pattern matching will issue warnings or errors if you do not properly handle all of a type's fields or variants. These warnings help you write safer, more robust code.

Take another look at the `Dimension` enum defined earlier. With pattern matching, it's fairly easy to write a function, `convertDimension`, that will take a `Dimension` as a parameter and convert it to the other variant (U.S. measurements to metric and vice-versa):

```
func convertDimension(dimension: Dimension) -> Dimension {
    switch dimension {
    case let .US(length, width):
        return .Metric(length * 0.3048, width * 0.3048)
    case let .Metric(length, width):
        return .US(length * 3.28084, width * 3.28048)
    }
}
```

Swift's pattern matching syntax is a bit cumbersome, so let's break down the `convertDimension` function into its constituent parts.

First, notice the `switch` statement. The `switch` is the basic way of working with Swift's enumerated types. It allows you to match on each case of a Swift enum, handling each one possibly differently. If you use enumerations a lot, the `switch` statement will become your bread and butter.

The body of the `switch` has a case statement matching each case of the enum. In the preceding example, the `.US` variant is first matched. Note that because the Swift compiler knows you are working with a `Dimension` type, you don't have to use the full `Dimension.US` type name—`.US` will suffice. (This is generally true when working with enums—if the compiler can figure out the type, you can leave off the type name when working with one of its variants.)

In this case statement, you also pull out the individual fields of the `Dimension` type and bind them to the variable names `length` and `width`. Note that the keyword `let` is used (before the variant name) in order to allow the fields to be matched and bound to the `length` and `width` variables. This is shorthand for this line of code:

```
case .US(let length, let width):
```

You can use this shorthand whenever you are pulling out *all* of the fields of an enumerated type. (If you only want a subset, you must use the longer syntax.)

Finally, in the body of the case statement, a `Dimension.Metric` object is created by multiplying the `length` and `width` variables by 0.3048 (thus converting feet to meters) and returning the newly created object.

The second case statement handles dimensions expressed in metric meters. It's nearly the same as the previous case statement, although it returns a `Dimension.US` object instead.

Although the syntax is a bit unwieldy, you've probably seen that it's pretty easy to handle all of the cases of an enumerated type. Note that Swift does, in fact, require you to handle *all* cases. You can, of course, use a `default` statement in the `switch` statement's body as a catch-all, as noted in Chapter 1, but either way, if you leave out a case, the compiler will issue a warning. This feature is, in fact, quite powerful, as it prevents you from introducing runtime errors in your program if you forget to handle a case. Swift's advanced type system once again prevents you from shooting yourself in the foot.

Listing 8-1 shows the code for handling the `Dimension` type, including a function for printing out the individual fields of an enum. This function, `printDimensions`, also uses a switch statement in the same vein as `convertDimension`.

LISTING 8-1: Dimension.playground

```
enum Dimension {
    case US(Double, Double)
    case Metric(Double, Double)
}

let roomSizeMetric = Dimension.Metric(5.0, 4.0)

func convertDimension(dimension: Dimension) -> Dimension {
    switch dimension {
    case let .US(length, width):
        return .Metric(length * 0.3048, width * 0.3048)
    case let .Metric(length, width):
        return .US(length * 3.28084, width * 3.28048)
    }
}

let roomSizeUS = convertDimension(roomSizeMetric)

func printDimensions(dimension: Dimension) {
    switch dimension {
    case let .US(length, width):
        println("US measurements are: \(length) x \(width)")
    case let .Metric(length, width):
        println("Metric measurements are: \(length) x \(width)")
    }
}

printDimensions(roomSizeMetric)
printDimensions(roomSizeUS)
```

Putting It All Together with JSON

One common operation that makes exemplary use of Swift's enumerations is the parsing of JSON data. Many web services return data in JSON format, and parsing and processing JSON have become a staple of most applications, particularly on iOS (which is much more reliant on web services than OS X apps). While Apple provides a JSON parser in the Foundation framework in the form of the `NSJSONSerialization` class, that parser is much more geared to Objective-C than it is to Swift. With the power provided by enumerations, you can potentially model JSON data in a much more Swift-centric manner.

JSON values can consist of six different data types: dictionaries (also referred to as "objects" in JavaScript parlance), arrays, strings, numbers (which are always floating-point values in JSON), Booleans, and null. Each JSON value is one and only one of these types. Furthermore, a JSON dictionary may contain any of these types as values (although its keys are always strings), and an array may contain any of these types of values.

It's clear at this point that the structure of JSON data lends itself nicely to being modeled using algebraic data types. You can define a `JSONValue` enumeration that encompasses all possible types and represent each JSON type as a variant within that enumeration. The following code shows one possible definition of a `JSONValue` enumeration in Swift:

```
enum JSONValue {
    case JObject([String: JSONValue])
    case JArray([JSONValue])
    case JString(String)
    case JNumber(Double)
    case JBoolean(Bool)
    case JNull
}
```

In order to handle a JSON value, you could simply write a function (or method) with a `switch` statement that could handle each individual type appropriately. Listing 8-2 shows a sample implementation of a JSON enumeration with a function for turning a JSON object into a string.

LISTING 8-2: JSON.playground

```
enum JSONValue {
    case JObject([String: JSONValue])
    case JArray([JSONValue])
    case JString(String)
    case JNumber(Double)
    case JBoolean(Bool)
    case JNull
}

func JSONToString(object: JSONValue) -> String {
    switch object {
    case let .JObject(obj):
        var elements: [String] = []
        for (key, val) in obj {
            let jval = JSONToString(val)
            elements.append("\(key): \(jval)")
        }
        return "{" + ", ".join(elements) + "}"
    case let .JArray(vals):
        let strings = vals.map { JSONToString($0) }
        return ", ".join(strings)
    case let .JString(val):
        return val
    case let .JNumber(val):
        return "\(val)"
    case let .JBoolean(val):
        return val ? "true" : "false"
    case .JNull:
        return "null"
    }
}
```

continues

continued

```
let jsonPerson = JSONValue.JObject([
    "firstName": JSONValue.JString("Jane"),
    "lastName": JSONValue.JString("Doe"),
    "age": JSONValue.JNumber(39),
    "isAwesomeSwiftProgrammer": JSONValue.JBoolean(true),
    "address": JSONValue.JNull,
    "favoriteColors": JSONValue.JArray([
        JSONValue.JString("red"), JSONValue.JString("purple")]),
])

JSONToString(jsonPerson)
```

Thanks to enums, processing JSON is not just easy (and certainly easier than the cumbersome method using NSJONSerialization demonstrated in Chapter 5)—it's type-safe, too!

WORKING WITH OPTIONAL TYPES

When writing software, it is necessary to represent the notion of an unknown value. While variables can often be initialized to a known value, frequently a value cannot be known or determined at initialization time. Programming languages have various ways of representing an unknown value. Setting a value to null is the most common way to set a variable to an unknown value.

Working with Null Values

The null value takes various names and forms depending on the programming language. In Objective-C, this value is known as nil. C represents an unknown value using the NULL pointer value. Java uses null, Python uses the None object, and Ruby, like Objective-C, uses nil. In all of these languages, however, the specific value is used for the general concept of a value that is unknown.

Null values are not without their problems. The biggest issue is that in many languages, including C, Objective-C, and Java, they are not type-safe: Null values can be assigned to a variable of *any* type, so the compiler cannot determine if a variable has an actual value or the null value. In most languages that have the concept of a null value, attempting to resolve the value of a variable set to null, or call a method on such a value, results in an error at runtime that usually causes a program to crash. For example, attempting to dereference a NULL value in C results in a segmentation fault; in Java, calling a method on a null value results in a NullPointerException. Python throws a TypeError if a method is called on None.

Objective-C, on the other hand, famously allows methods to be called on nil. However, such method calls are conceptually a no-op, as the nil object will not act on them. While this will not result in a runtime error as it does in many other languages, it leads to unexpected program behavior if the programmer was not expecting a value to be nil.

Most crucially, compilers in these languages cannot determine *a priori* if a value is null or not, and so they cannot issue compiler errors if a null value is used in a way that is not allowed.

Because of these issues, programmers in such languages must be conscious of improperly using null values. Often such code is littered with checks for null values. Of course, the compiler cannot guarantee that such checks were made, so programming errors often make their way into production code. Crashes are not the only problem with such code; improper use of null values can also lead to major security vulnerabilities. These issues have led the computer scientist Tony Hoare to describe the introduction of null values as "my billion-dollar mistake."

Excluding Null Values

Given the pervasiveness of the concept in modern programming languages, many programmers may be led to believe that null values are a necessary wart, and it is impossible to create a programming language without them. They may be surprised to learn that many languages get along just fine without null values. As it turns out, null is *not* a necessary component of a programming language.

The functional programming language Haskell, for example, does not have null values. Instead, it uses a data type called `Maybe` to represent unknown values. Haskell's `Maybe` type is an algebraic data type. It has two variants, `Nothing` and `Just`. `Nothing` acts similarly to null in other languages (without the inherent problems, as I will discuss shortly). `Just`, on the other hand, represents a value that *does* exist.

In Haskell, variables that may have an unknown value are represented using the `Maybe` type. Thus, a variable that *might* be an integer or might be "null" would not be an `Int`, but rather a `Maybe Int`. That variable could have the value `Nothing`, or it could, for example, have the value `Just 10`.

At first glance, it may seem like this is no better than a simple null value like `nil`. However, because of Haskell's robust type system, the compiler can issue warnings and errors if possibly null values are used incorrectly. For example, if you write a function that takes a `Maybe Int` as a parameter, but do not handle the case in which it is `Nothing`, the compiler will inform you of this error. Likewise, if you write a function that takes an `Int`, and you pass it a `Maybe Int`, the compiler will issue an error. Haskell is able to use the power of the language's type system and compiler to prevent errors that otherwise might go unnoticed until runtime.

Understanding Swift's Version of Null

Swift's concept of null is similar to that of Haskell's. On the surface, Swift seems to have a `nil` value just like Objective-C: Constants and variables can be set to `nil` without any problem. However, it is important to note this is just syntactic sugar around Swift's `Some` enumeration, which is actually used to encapsulate possibly null values. Take a look at the variable declaration here:

```
var x: String? = nil
```

In the preceding example, the variable *x* is *not* a `String`. Rather, it is of type `Optional<String>`, signified in the shorthand syntax by a question mark at the end of the type name.

Understanding Swift enumerations is integral to understanding its optional types. Swift uses optional types to represent unknown values. Specifically, it uses an enumeration called `Optional`. `Optional` has roughly this structure:

```
enum Optional<T> {
    case Some(T)
    case None
}
```

In the earlier example, the variable *x* is of type `Optional<String>`. Specifically, because it is set to nil, it is the `None` variant. `nil` is just a handy shorthand for setting a value to that variant. *x* can later be set to an actual value, as shown in the following example:

```
var x: String? = nil
x = "string"
```

Now *x* appears to have the value `"string"`. In reality, however, it has the value `Some("string")`. This is a crucial distinction from `nil` as used in Objective-C, as the compiler can now prevent you from using *x* as though it were a simple string. This means that if *x is* nil, you are prevented from using it as though it has a value, which prevents many of the runtime errors commonly found in Objective-C programs.

But how do you make use of *x* in a safe way?

Chaining Optional Values

In languages whose null values are not well-integrated into the type system (such as C, Objective-C, and Java), code is often littered with checks to ensure that values are not null. In C, for example, it would not be uncommon to see code like this:

```
if (x->some_field && x->some_field->another_field) {
    do_something_with_field(x->some_field->another_field);
}
```

Similar constructs can often be seen in Objective-C.

Aside from being clunky, such code is not type-safe by any means. In the preceding example, there is nothing preventing the programming from passing x->some_field->another_field to the do_something_with_field() function, even if it *is* null. In fact, such errors are not uncommon, either because programmers forget to check values or because they find such checking to be too unwieldy.

Thanks to Swift's language features, laboriously checking for `null` values is not required. Swift provides a convenient shorthand that makes working with optional values easy. This shorthand is referred to as *optional chaining*.

Optional chaining allows you to call methods on an optional type. If the type exists (it is a `Some`), the method call proceeds as normal; if it does not exist (it is `None`, or `nil`), then the resulting value will also be `nil`. Listing 8-3 shows this chaining in action.

LISTING 8-3: Some.playground

```
import Foundation

var s: String? = nil
s = "string"
s?.uppercaseString    // Some("STRING")

var t: String? = nil
t?.uppercaseString    // nil
```

In this sense, Swift's `None` (or `nil`) acts very similarly to nil to Objective-C. The key here is that it works within Swift's type system. You could not simply call `s.uppercaseString`; the compiler would issue an error because `uppercaseString` is not a method defined for the `Option` type. You *must* deal with the possible nil value.

As demonstrated in Chapter 5, you have several ways to circumvent this feature. For example, you can use the exclamation point (`!`) to *force* an optional value to be unwrapped. However, if you force a `nil` value to be unwrapped, a runtime error will occur. The following line of code would result in a runtime error:

```
t!.uppercaseString
```

In general, forcing a value to be unwrapped should be done with caution. Frequently, you know a type is technically an optional value, but you also know it will never be `nil`. However, these occasions are rare, and you should avoid forcibly unwrapping a value whenever possible.

You can also unwrap values as part of an `if` statement and take different actions depending on whether the optional value exists or not. For example, the following code will print "`t is nil`" to the console:

```
if let val = t {
    println("t is not nil")
} else {
    println("t is nil")
}
```

Swift's `Option` is a powerful way to encapsulate unknown values in a type-safe way. You will find a lot of Swift code that makes use of this feature, particularly when interfacing with C and Objective-C code (which is discussed in more detail in the next chapter).

UNDERSTANDING TYPE CASTING

In Swift, type casting refers to two separate but related operations: checking the type of a variable, and forcing a variable to be of a certain type. The first operation, checking the type of a variable, can simply be done with the `is` keyword. It is most commonly used in `if` statements, as shown here:

```
let s = "string"

if s is String {
    println("s is a string")
} else {
    println("s is not a string")
}
```

However, while the preceding sample is syntactically correct Swift code, the compiler actually issues an error because it knows that the test is always true because it can infer that s is a String. This highlights a question you may have about type checking: Why is it useful if Swift has type inferencing?

Type checking is useful when dealing with classes that have subclasses. A variable may be typed to the base class but may actually be an instance of a subclass. Type checking allows you to determine which class the object is an instance of.

Consider the program in Listing 8-4. It has a base class, `Animal`, with two subclasses, `Bird` and `Mammal`. An array, `zoo`, is created to hold a few objects. This array is of type `Array<Animal>` because all the items in the array are of type `Animal` (even though they're actually subclasses of

Animal). When iterating through the array, you use the `is` operator to determine if the item is of type `Bird` or `Mammal`, printing out an appropriate message for each animal.

The `is` operator often comes in handy when working with classes with many subclasses. It is especially common when interfacing with Objective-C code, which often returns something of type `AnyObject`—the base class of all Objective-C classes in Swift. Unfortunately, `AnyObject` is a fairly vague type, so you can use the `is` operator to find out the instance's *exact* type. You may recall that this technique was used when parsing JSON data in Chapter 5.

LISTING 8-4: Casting.playground

```
class Animal {
    let species: String

    init(species: String) {
        self.species = species
    }
}

class Bird: Animal {
    let wingspan: Int

    init(species: String, wingspan: Int) {
        self.wingspan = wingspan
        super.init(species: species)
    }
}

class Mammal: Animal {
    let numberOfLegs: Int

    init(species: String, numberOfLegs: Int) {
        self.numberOfLegs = numberOfLegs
        super.init(species: species)
    }
}

let zoo: [Animal] = [Mammal(species: "monkey", numberOfLegs: 2),
                     Bird(species: "golden eagle", wingspan: 78),
                     Mammal(species: "polar bear", numberOfLegs: 4)]

for animal in zoo {
    if animal is Bird {
        println("Saw a \(animal.species) flying")
    } else {
        println("Saw a \(animal.species) walking")
    }
}
```

Similarly, you can use Swift's `as` operator to actually coerce an object to another type than what the compiler has inferred it to be. The `as` operator comes in two flavors: the plain `as` operator, and `as?`. The former coerces the object into the desired type without asking. If the object cannot be coerced to that type, a runtime error is thrown. The `as?` operator is more polite: It asks an object if it can be coerced to a given type. If the object can be, then a `Some` is returned; otherwise, `nil` is returned. `as?` is most often used as part of an `if` statement. For example, you could add the following `for` loop to Listing 8-4 to coerce an animal in the array to a given type, and then print out an appropriate message:

```
for zooAnimal in zoo {
    if let animal = zooAnimal as? Bird {
        println("Saw a bird with a \(animal.wingspan)-inch wingspan")
    } else if let animal = zooAnimal as? Mammal {
        println("Saw an mammal walking on \(animal.numberOfLegs) legs")
    }
}
```

Note that in the first `for` loop in Listing 8-4, you did not have access to the fields of the `Bird` and `Mammal` subclasses because the code treated the animal variable as an object of type `Animal` so it did not know about `wingspan` or `numberOfLegs`. However, in the second `for` loop shown in the preceding code, you have actually coerced `zooAnimal` into a specific subclass, so the `animal` variable is aware of its subclass's properties—meaning you can use them in code.

You can use the `as` operator to forcefully coerce an object to a certain class, but if the object cannot be coerced to that class (it's not an instance of that class or a subclass), a runtime error will occur. If you added the `for` loop that follows to the code in Listing 8-4, you'd get a runtime error:

```
for zooAnimal in zoo {
    let animal = zooAnimal as Bird
    println("Saw a bird with a \(animal.wingspan)-inch wingspan")
}
```

Obviously it's best to use `as?` whenever possible. You should use `as` only if you *know* it will not result in a runtime error (unless you're happy with your program crashing, of course).

GROUPING VALUES WITH TUPLES

Apple introduced a new data structure with Swift: the tuple. Far from being advanced, however, this data type is actually quite simple. A composite type, it can be used to group multiple values together. In this sense, it is much like an array. It differs from an array in two significant ways, however: A tuple's size cannot be changed, and it can contain items of different types.

Tuples are most commonly used when you need a fairly simple way to group multiple different types of data together but don't really need to create a list or a struct. For example, you can use it to represent a point in 3D space, as shown here:

```
let point = (0, 10, 5)
```

You can also use a tuple to represent an HTTP status code along with a human-readable representation of the status:

```
let res = (200, "OK")
```

You should only use tuples as a simple group of values. If you need a more complex structure, a class or struct is more appropriate.

However, thanks to their simplicity (as well as their rigid structure), Swift has support for easily decomposing a tuple into its constituent parts. It's easy to assign variables to the individual elements of a tuple:

```
let point = (0, 10, 5)
let res = (200, "OK")
let (x, y, z) = point
let (statusCode, statusString) = res
```

You can also access the individual elements of a tuple:

```
let point = (0, 10, 5)
let y = point.1
```

Like arrays, tuples are zero-indexed.

Tuples are also frequently used to return multiple values from a function. Listing 8-5 shows a function that takes two integers and returns the quotient, as well as the remainder left over from division. These values are returned in the form of a tuple.

LISTING 8-5: Tuples.playground

```
func divide(num: Int, denom: Int) -> (quotient: Int, remainder: Int) {
    return (num / denom, num % denom)
}

divide(10, 4)
divide(100, 50)
```

Functions that return tuples can also return optional tuples, meaning that the return value can be a tuple, or `nil`. You could modify the function shown in Listing 8-5 to return `nil` if the denominator is 0, as shown in Listing 8-6.

LISTING 8-6: Tuples.playground

```
func divideSafe(num: Int, denom: Int) -> (quotient: Int, remainder: Int)? {
    if denom == 0 { return nil }
    return (num / denom, num % denom)
}

divideSafe(10, 4)
divideSafe(100, 50)
divideSafe(20, 0)
```

Optional tuples follow the same rules as other optional types. You can chain them or unwrap them the same way you would an `Option` of any other type.

Returning multiple values from a function can be very useful, but you should be careful using this technique. If a function is returning multiple values, it may be combining multiple operations that would best be suited for separate functions, or you may be returning a data structure that would best be modeled using a class or struct. As always, you should use your best judgment. Regardless of your choice, it's helpful to know that the functionality exists, should you decide you need it.

CUSTOM OPERATORS

One new feature in Swift that may be unfamiliar to programmers with an Objective-C or C background is the ability to overload existing operators (+, −, *, /, and the like) for their custom data types, as well as the capability to create new operators. C and Objective-C define a static set of operators that only work on data types defined in the language, such as integers and floating-point numbers. Swift extends operators to custom data types and even allows programmers to define new operators and add them to existing or new data types. This feature can allow Swift programmers to write more compact, more readable code.

First, consider a simple `Fraction` struct:

```
struct Fraction {
    let numerator: Int
    let denominator: Int
}
```

It would be nice if `Fraction` structs could be multiplied together, wouldn't it? Multiplying fractions is a pretty common operation. In Objective-C, you would have to define a method that would take in another `Fraction` instance and perform the arithmetic; in C, you'd write a function. You could do the same in Swift, but it would be even nicer if Swift's multiplication operator, *, could be used instead.

Luckily, Swift allows you to overload * for use with your custom data types, such as this `Fraction` struct. You can define * on `Fraction` instances with a simple function definition:

```
func * (left: Fraction, right: Fraction) -> Fraction {
    return Fraction(numerator: left.numerator * right.numerator,
                    denominator: left.denominator * right.denominator)
}
```

Let's take a look at the preceding function definition. First, you declare a function named *. This indicates that you are overloading the * operator. * is a binary operator, meaning it takes two arguments, so your function should take two arguments, too. You can name the arguments anything you want, although `left` and `right` are common choices to indicate which side of the operator the arguments appear on. (* is an *infix* operator, meaning it appears *between* its two arguments.) The result of the multiplication will also be a `Fraction`, so that is the return type of the function. Finally, the body of the function is the arithmetic that needs to be performed on the `Fractions`.

> **NOTE** *Operators are overloaded using functions, not methods defined on a class or struct.*

When you are done, you can multiply two `Fractions` together:

```
let f1 = Fraction(numerator: 3, denominator: 4)
let f2 = Fraction(numerator: 1, denominator: 2)
let f3 = f1 * f2
```

You can also define the * operator on other data types. For example, it would also be nice to multiply a Fraction by a whole number. You can simply define your * function again, but this time take a Fraction and an Int as arguments:

```
func * (left: Fraction, right: Int) -> Fraction {
    return Fraction(numerator: left.numerator * right,
                    denominator: left.denominator)
}
```

Now you can multiply a Fraction by an integer:

```
let f4 = f1 * 10
```

Of course, this won't let you multiply an integer by a Fraction. To do that, you'll have to define a function that flips the arguments. However, you can still make use of the function you defined earlier:

```
func * (left: Int, right: Fraction) -> Fraction {
    return right * left
}
```

Multiplying an integer by a Fraction works as expected:

```
let f5 = 10 * f1
```

As you can see, overloading operators for your own types is easy. You can even overload operators for your own types so they work with existing types.

Now that you can multiply Fractions together, you realize that it may make sense to divide Fractions as well. You probably remember from elementary school that when you divide two fractions, you multiply the first by the *inverse* of the second. It makes sense, then, to have an operator that returns the inverse of a fraction.

After a careful analysis, you decide to overload the ~ operator on Fractions. ~, however, is a *unary* operator: It only takes a single argument. Swift has two unary operator types: prefix and postfix. Prefix unary operators go *before* their arguments, and postfix go *after*. Defining them works much like defining binary operators, but you must specify whether the unary operator is prefix or postfix by putting the prefix or postfix keyword before func. You can overload ~ to invert a Fraction with this function definition:

```
prefix func - (fraction: Fraction) -> Fraction {
    return Fraction(numerator: fraction.denominator,
                    denominator: fraction.numerator)
}
```

Once you have the invert operator defined, writing a function to overload / on Fractions is trivial:

```
func / (left: Fraction, right: Fraction) -> Fraction {
    return left * -right
}
```

It is also easy to overload / so it can work with Ints, as you did for the * operator. Feel free to give this a try on your own.

Now that you have * and / defined, it would also be nice to overload their *compound assignment* operators: *= and /=. That is easy to do, too, and can even be done in terms of the * and / operators you have already overloaded. The key difference is that the first parameter for overloaded compound assignment operators should be an inout parameter, and you should do the assignment inside the body of the function instead of returning a value. (The functions for overloaded compound assignment operators do not ever return a value.) Here are the definitions for `*=` and `/=`:

```
func *= (inout left: Fraction, right: Fraction) {
    left = left * right
}

func /= (inout left: Fraction, right: Fraction) {
    left = left / right
}
```

Again, you could also define compound assignment operators that work with Ints as well. Those examples aren't shown here, but if you're feeling adventurous, feel free to try implementing them yourself.

The final operators you may wish to implement are the equivalence operators `==` and `!=`. These are defined the same way as arithmetic operators, except that they always return a Bool:

```
func == (left: Fraction, right: Fraction) -> Bool {
    return left.numerator == right.numerator &&
            left.denominator == right.denominator
}

func != (left: Fraction, right: Fraction) -> Bool {
    return !(left == right)
}
```

Note that both `==` and `!=` are overloaded. Swift does not automatically infer `!=` from `==` or vice-versa; you must define both. However, it is common for `!=` to be defined in terms of `==` by simply negating the return value of `==`.

> **NOTE** *The implementation of* `==` *for* Fraction *is pretty naïve. Right now,* Fraction *does not represent fractions in their reduced form, so* `==` *may return* false *for* Fractions *that, mathematically, are equal. For example,*
>
> $\frac{3}{4}$ *and* $\frac{6}{8}$ *are the same value mathematically, but because of the way in*
>
> *which* `==` *is implemented,* Fraction(numerator: 3, denominator: 4) `==` Fraction(numerator: 6, denominator: 8) *will return* false. *A similar issue occurs in the multiplication operator, which does not reduce its resulting value. A more robust form of this class would probably want to represent fractions in their reduced form.*

A complete listing of the operator implementations for the Fraction class, as well as some examples of their use, is shown in Listing 8-7.

LISTING 8-7: Operators.playground

```
struct Fraction {
    let numerator: Int
    let denominator: Int
```

continues

continued

```
}

prefix func - (fraction: Fraction) -> Fraction {
    return Fraction(numerator: fraction.denominator,
                    denominator: fraction.numerator)
}

func * (left: Fraction, right: Fraction) -> Fraction {
    return Fraction(numerator: left.numerator * right.numerator,
                    denominator: left.denominator * right.denominator)
}

func * (left: Fraction, right: Int) -> Fraction {
    return Fraction(numerator: left.numerator * right,
                    denominator: left.denominator)
}

func * (left: Int, right: Fraction) -> Fraction {
    return right * left
}

func / (left: Fraction, right: Fraction) -> Fraction {
    return left * ~right
}

func *= (inout left: Fraction, right: Fraction) {
    left = left * right
}

func /= (inout left: Fraction, right: Fraction) {
    left = left / right
}

func == (left: Fraction, right: Fraction) -> Bool {
    return left.numerator == right.numerator &&
           left.denominator == right.denominator
}

func != (left: Fraction, right: Fraction) -> Bool {
    return !(left == right)
}

let f1 = Fraction(numerator: 3, denominator: 4)
let f2 = Fraction(numerator: 1, denominator: 2)
let f3 = f1 * f2
let f4 = f1 * 10
let f5 = 10 * f1
let f6 = ~f1
let f7 = f1 / f2
var f8 = Fraction(numerator: 3, denominator: 4)
f8 *= f2
f8 /= f2
f4 == f5
f4 == f8
```

Defining Custom Operators

Sometimes Swift's predefined operators are not enough to capture an operation you wish to define on one of your own classes (or even an existing class). Take, for example, raising an integer by a certain power. The Python programming language provides the operator ** for raising a number by a value. Out of the box, Swift does not provide such an operator. However, Swift *does* allow you to define your own operators, and defining a ** operator is a simple exercise.

First, you have to declare that you are introducing a new operator. You declare this in the global scope by using the operator keyword followed by the name of the operator (that is, the symbols that make up the operator) and a set of empty braces. The operator is prefixed by the keyword infix, postfix, or prefix, depending on how you intend to use the operator. In the case of the new ** operator you are defining, it is an infix operator, so you would declare it like so:

```
infix operator ** {}
```

Now you can define operator functions as you would any other operator, as shown earlier in this chapter. For example, defining the ** to operate on Ints is easy:

```
func ** (left: Int, right: Int) -> Int {
    return Int(pow(Double(left), Double(right)))
}
```

You could go ahead and define it on Doubles as well:

```
func ** (left: Double, right: Int) -> Double {
    return pow(left, Double(right))
}

func ** (left: Int, right: Double) -> Double {
    return pow(Double(left), right)
}

func ** (left: Double, right: Double) -> Double {
    return pow(left, right)
}
```

Defining Precedence and Associativity

But what about that set of empty braces you typed when declaring the operator? Those seem unnecessary. As it turns out, you can define a custom operator's precedence and associativity within those braces, if you want to change them from the defaults.

Associativity defines how the operator is grouped when combined with other operators of the same precedence. In Swift, operators can have an associativity of left, right, or none. For example, if your new ** had an associativity of left, then 2 ** 3 ** 4 would be parsed as (2 ** 3) ** 4, resulting in 4096. If it has an associativity of right, it would be parsed as 2 ** (3 ** 4), resulting in . . . well, an extremely large number that actually causes the Swift playground to crash when evaluated. If it has an associativity of none, then the expression 2 ** 3 ** 4 cannot be written at all.

Precedence describes the priority that an operator should be given when used as part of a mixed expression. For example, given the expression 4 + 2 * 4, you no doubt know that the result is 12 because the multiplication happens before the addition. In other words, the expression is parsed as

`4 + (2 * 4)`. Swift's predefined operators have a precedence defined, and you can define precedence for your own operators as well.

Try some complicated expressions out with the `**` operator you just defined. You'll see, for example, that `2 * 10 ** 2` results in the value of 400. However, according to what you learned in mathematics, the `**` operator should be applied first, so the result of that expression is 200. Therefore, the precedence of `**` should be higher than Swift's `*` operator, which has a precedence of 150. (The precedence and associativity of Swift's built-in operators are shown in Table 8-1.)

TABLE 8-1 Swift Operator Associativities and Precedences

OPERATOR	ASSOCIATIVITY	PRECEDENCE
<<	None	160
>>	None	160
*	Left	150
/	Left	150
%	Left	150
&*	Left	150
&/	Left	150
&%	Left	150
&	Left	150
+	Left	140
-	Left	140
&+	Left	140
&-	Left	140
|	Left	140
^	Left	140
..<	None	135
...	None	135
is	None	132
as	None	132
<	None	130
<=	None	130

OPERATOR	ASSOCIATIVITY	PRECEDENCE
>	None	130
>=	None	130
==	None	130
!=	None	130
===	None	130
!==	None	130
~=	None	130
&&	Left	120
||	Left	110
??	Right	110
?:	Right	100
=	Right	90
*=	Right	90
/=	Right	90
%=	Right	90
+=	Right	90
-=	Right	90
<<=	Right	90
>>=	Right	90
&=	Right	90
^=	Right	90
|=	Right	90
&&=	Right	90
||=	Right	90

You can set the associativity and precedence in the empty set of braces in the operator definition. To do so, use the keyword associativity followed by one of right, left, or none, then the keyword precedence followed by a number (higher numbers indicate a higher precedence). For example, you can define your ** operator as being right-associative and having a precedence of 200 by declaring it like this:

```
infix operator ** { associativity left precedence 200 }
```

Listing 8-8 shows the completed implementation of the ** operator.

LISTING 8-8: Custom Operators.playground

```
import Foundation

infix operator ** { associativity left precedence 200 }

func ** (left: Int, right: Int) -> Int {
    return Int(pow(Double(left), Double(right)))
}

func ** (left: Double, right: Int) -> Double {
    return pow(left, Double(right))
}

func ** (left: Double, right: Double) -> Double {
    return pow(left, right)
}

2 ** 2
10 ** 2
10 ** 10

2.5 ** 2
10.4 ** 2
11.3 ** 10

2.5 ** 2.1
10.4 ** 2.6
11.3 ** 12.3

2 * 10 ** 2
2 * 10 ** 2 ** 2

2 ** 3 ** 4
```

With the associativity and precedence set, your ** operator should now behave as expected. Go ahead and try it out!

A Final Word about Operators

Many programmers have differing opinions about the extent to which you should use overloaded and custom operators. Some believe that their use can greatly improve the readability of code. Others believe that their use greatly obscures code, particularly when existing operators are overloaded to mean completely different things (for example, how C++ overloads << to print a string to cout).

As with many of Swift's more advanced features, you should use discretion when overloading or creating custom operators. As you work with Swift, you should develop a sense of when the use of these features is appropriate, and when they're more confusing than helpful. Overloaded and custom operators can make code more concise and understandable, but if you overload an operator to do something completely different than expected, it can cause a lot of surprises—and headaches—for yourself and other programmers. Always write code as though your colleagues are angry people who know where you live.

USING FUNCTIONS AND CLOSURES

Functions are a fundamental part of the Swift language. Throughout this book, you've seen many ways in which functions are used in Swift programming. *Closures* are another feature of Swift that has been mentioned, although not discussed in great detail. Closures are analogous to blocks in Objective-C: They are bits of code that you can assign to variables and pass around to functions or methods, or even pass to functions and methods that accept them. Closures can be found in many languages, particularly functional programming languages and languages that draw inspiration from functional programming (like Swift).

But what are closures exactly? Closures encapsulate a bit of code, just like a function. They also encapsulate the surrounding scope of the closure. In fact, that is where closures get their name: They are said to *close over* a bit of code and its environment. A closure still has access to that environment, even when passed to other parts of code.

Listing 8-9 shows closures in action.

LISTING 8-9: Closures.playground

```
var x = 10

let doubleX = { x * 2 }

doubleX()
x = 50
doubleX()

let adder = { y in x + y }

adder(10)
x = 100
adder(25)

func printComputedValue(fn: (Int -> Int)) {
    println(fn(10))
}

printComputedValue(adder)
x = 1000
printComputedValue(adder)
```

In Listing 8-9, you initially create a variable x with a value of 10. A simple closure that takes no parameters and multiplies x by 2 is defined. Note that x is not passed into the closure; rather, the closure draws x from its surrounding scope. When the closure doubleX is first called (just as you'd call a function), it returns a value of 10. Then, you change the value of x to 50. Observe that when you call doubleX again, it now returns a value of 100.

Why is this? `doubleX` has "closed over" the scope that contained x. Whenever you call it, it will use the *current* value of x in its computation. Hence, once you changed x to the value 50, `doubleX` returned 100.

You can also create closures that take parameters and operate on them. Such a closure is created in Listing 8-9 and assigned to `adder`. `adder` simply adds the value passed into it to the *current* value of x. Observe again how the return value of `adder` changes as you change the value of x.

Because closures are objects, they can also be passed to other functions. You can define a function, `printComputedValue`, that takes a function as an argument. In this case, its argument, `fn`, is a function that takes one `Int` parameter and returns an `Int`. `printComputedValue()`, calls that function with the argument 10, and prints out the resulting value.

The closure `adder` is passed into that function. Remember that `adder` closes over the scope, which contains x. Watch how the behavior of `printComputedValue()` changes whenever x is changed.

Closures are powerful data types that are used pervasively in Swift. It's trivial to implement a sort function, for example, that can work with many different data types using closures.

Closures are so powerful, in fact, that functions are essentially closures that are bound to a name in a global scope. Just like closures, you can treat functions as objects, passing them to other functions (or methods) that take functions as parameters. Functions that take other functions as arguments and/or return functions are known as *higher-order functions*.

Closures are integral to functional programming. Many Swift programmers are aficionados of the functional programming paradigm, so it is likely that you will see many third-party APIs making extensive use of closures and higher-order functions in the future.

SUMMARY

Swift, like Objective-C, is a simple language to learn, but mastering its full feature set is no easy task. The language makes use of many advanced features seen in many other high-level modern languages. In this chapter, you learned about many ideas from functional programming that have made their way into Swift, particularly algebraic data types and closures. You also learned how to use Swift's optional types to write safer, more robust code, and how to use overloaded and custom operators to express the intent of your code in a clearer, more concise manner. Objective-C programmers may initially find these tools and features to be unfamiliar, but once you have started using them in your code, you will no doubt see their power and wonder how you lived without them for so long.

Bridging Swift and Objective-C

Swift incorporates a lot of modern language features, bringing both the iOS and OS X platforms into the twenty-first century and alleviating some of the headaches programmers had when working with Objective-C. However, because both operating systems have a strong heritage rooted in C and Objective-C, it is likely that you will have to work with code written in these languages at some point. This chapter shows some of the key features that allow Swift to interoperate with C and Objective-C, including namespaces, modules, and the functionality that bridges Swift to these older languages.

THE SUCCESSOR TO OBJECTIVE-C

Apple's release of Swift in June 2014 came as a surprise to many iOS and OS X programmers. For years, there had been speculation that Apple would release a successor to Objective-C. In 2008, development on MacRuby, an implementation of Ruby that offered near-seamless bridging between Ruby and Objective-C, ramped up. Many programmers believed that Apple would eventually bless Ruby as the next language for application development on both OS X and iOS. Ruby was a popular language among many Mac developers, and many were excited about using Ruby instead of Objective-C in the future. Moreover, Ruby and Objective-C share many common language concepts, and it seemed that transitioning from Objective-C to Ruby would be an easy process.

Development on MacRuby stalled around 2010; the project became more and more moribund until its final release in 2012, after which it was effectively canceled. The primary developer of MacRuby spun it off into a commercial project called RubyMotion that offered support for Ruby programming on iOS. That project continues to be developed and has seen some success in the marketplace.

As it turned out, in 2010, development efforts shifted from Ruby to a new project that eventually became Swift, headed by the lead developer of the LLVM project used by Apple to build its compiler toolchain. Four years later, Apple announced beta versions of Swift, with the language being officially released in the fall of 2014 alongside iOS 8 and OS X 10.10.

Swift, of course, is much different from either Objective-C or Ruby. It draws ideas and inspiration from a variety of languages, including Rust, Haskell, Ruby, Python, and C#. Unlike Objective-C and Ruby, however, it is a statically typed language, and thus represents a paradigm shift from "traditional" OS X and iOS programming.

With the introduction of Swift, many programmers have speculated about the future of Objective-C on Apple's platforms. Apple has clearly stated that Swift is designed not only as a high-level applications language, but also as a lower-level systems programming language that could eventually replace C and C++. The potential exists for Swift to eventually become the primary language for development on these platforms, and it is expected that newer frameworks and libraries will be written in Swift (and thus expose a Swift-centric API), with the possibility that older libraries and frameworks will eventually be rewritten in Swift, too.

This is, of course, just speculation right now. Objective-C is an old language, and most of the frameworks on both OS X and iOS, as well as the lower-level parts, are written in Objective-C or C. NeXTSTEP, the operating system that provided the foundation for OS X (and, by extension, iOS), has been using Objective-C since the mid-1980s. Simply put, there is so much code written in Objective-C and C in Apple's operating systems that it is not going to be removed completely anytime soon, if ever.

Even if your applications are written completely in Swift, you will still need to interface with Objective-C code, and it is likely you will also work with lower-level system services written in C. You may even find yourself making use of C++ in your Swift applications. Luckily, Apple has made it easy to call C and Objective-C code from Swift (calling C++ code is a bit trickier). Swift's syntax makes calling C and Objective-C code a bit clunky at times, and because of Objective-C's dynamic nature, many of the features of Swift, particularly its type system, are, for all intents and purposes, ignored when working with Objective-C. In practice, however, the integration is almost as seamless as working with C code in Objective-C.

The introduction of Swift has not nullified Objective-C, and it's still important for Swift programmers to understand and know how to work with existing libraries and frameworks written in Objective-C. While a thorough understanding of Objective-C is not necessary (although it *is* helpful), understanding how Swift bridges to C and Objective-C is still important. An examination of these features and tools is crucial for any Swift programmer.

INTRODUCING NAMESPACES AND MODULES

Swift introduces two key features that are not native to either Objective-C or C: namespaces and modules. Namespaces are a way to logically group related functionality together. Most other languages make use of namespaces or an equivalent feature, including C++, Java, Python, and Ruby.

Modules are a way to package Swift code for distribution or use in other projects. They combine compiled Swift code with metadata on the classes, structs, enumerations, functions, and other entities that Swift code exports (or makes available). Swift modules also include a header file that allows Objective-C code to make use of Swift modules (as shown later in this chapter) and may optionally include documentation about the Swift code contained in the module.

> **NOTE** *Swift modules should not be confused with Ruby modules. Ruby's modules are more like namespaces in Swift, whereas modules in Swift are more like Ruby's gems.*

Organizing Code with Namespaces

Namespaces are a way to group related functions and classes together. Often, a library or application groups all its own functions and classes together into a common namespace. Sometimes, programmers will further group certain parts of their library or framework in smaller nested namespaces to further improve the organization of their code.

Namespaces are not merely a means of organizing code, however. They also provide a way to identify different functions and classes. Most crucially, they can help to prevent *name clashes*, which occur when two or more libraries used by an application define a function or class with the same name. Namespaces also allow programmers to easily import specific functions or classes they want to use from a third-party library, without having to import all the functions and classes provided by that library.

Most modern programming languages have some form of namespacing. In C++, for example, you can group related functions and classes together under a namespace. Java has *packages*, which allow classes to be grouped together. Ruby and Python both have modules.

Objective-C famously does not have namespaces. This is partly due to its age (Objective-C is, after all, nearly thirty years old) and partly due to the fact that C does not have namespaces either, and Objective-C has always strived to maintain backward compatibility with C. Instead, Objective-C programmers are encouraged to prefix their classes, structs, and functions with two or three letters in order to create a name that will hopefully be unique. For example, the classes from the

Foundation and AppKit frameworks are conspicuously prefixed with the letters *NS*, and the classes from iOS's UIKit framework are prefixed with *UI*.

THE NS PREFIX

There is some dispute as to where the famous NS prefix comes from. Most of these classes were a part of the Foundation framework in the NeXTSTEP operating system, which forms the basis of OS X. NeXTSTEP's programmers used the NX prefix on their classes and functions. This prefix was changed to NS after NeXT and Sun collaborated to create OpenStep, an object-oriented framework that offered a NeXTSTEP-like environment on other platforms. Depending on whom you ask, some will say that NS refers to NeXTSTEP, and others will say that NS refers to NeXT/Sun.

These prefixes are most commonly used to avoid name conflicts with multiple libraries or frameworks. For example, what if two libraries both created a class called String? A name conflict would occur if an application linked to both of these libraries because the compiler would not be able to tell which String class the application code was referring to. Prefixes help alleviate this problem. The Foundation framework can call its string class NSString, and the third-party library can use a different prefix, say MPD, and call its string class MPDString. Now you can link both libraries to the application, and have no ambiguity in class names—the application code will either refer to NSString or MPDString.

This system is, of course, a bit fragile. There is no compiler support for enforcing these mechanisms. Classes are not required to use a two-or three-letter prefix in their names. Furthermore, if two libraries happen to use the same prefix *and* export classes or functions with the same name, there will still be conflicts.

In order to deal with this problem, namespaces were introduced in Swift. As in other languages, Swift's namespaces allow you to group related items, such as classes and functions, together. Most interesting, however, is that Swift's namespaces are not explicit. You do not declare a namespace as you do in languages like C++ or Java. Instead, namespaces are created automatically based on your application's targets. For example, if you are creating an application, everything within that application target in Xcode is part of a common namespace. Frameworks and libraries create their own namespaces as well. You do not have to explicitly create a namespace for your code.

Namespaces are closely related to Swift *modules*, which are discussed in more detail in the next section.

In practice, Swift namespaces are nearly invisible to you. You'll find working with namespaces to be natural, and not much different from working with Objective-C code. Furthermore, while namespaces and modules are not in and of themselves an explicit part of the bridge between Swift and Objective-C, both features come into play when working with code in other libraries and frameworks (including those written in C and Objective-C), so understanding how namespaces and modules work is helpful when understanding how to interface with other code.

Distributing Code with Modules

Modules are Swift's way of grouping and distributing code together. Conceptually, they are very similar to the notion of libraries and frameworks that you are used to from Objective-C and C. Essentially, Swift combines a library (either static or dynamic) with metadata that describes what names and symbols are exported, and possibly documentation about the code contained in the module. You can think of them as a library, header files, and documentation all rolled into one.

In fact, system libraries and frameworks, such as Foundation, AppKit, and UIKit, have essentially been exported as a module to make them available to Swift code. Many of the core C libraries are available as importable Swift modules, too.

You can group your own code into Swift modules as well. Creating your own modules can be especially useful if you have code that you wish to reuse across multiple projects. Xcode does not provide a target type of a Swift module, however; instead, you create a framework or static library target written in Swift, just as you would for an Objective-C framework or static library. Xcode's compiler toolchain will take care of packaging your code into a framework or static library that can be imported by other projects.

In fact, for the most part, modules are fairly invisible to you, the end user. The only thing you really have to keep in mind is that you must import a module (i.e., a framework or library) if you wish to use it in your application—whether it is a module you created, or a third-party module used by your application. This is done with Swift's `import` keyword, followed by the name of the module you are targeting. You have already seen this in use with `import Foundation`, `import AppKit`, and `import UIKit`, which are part of the Swift source code templates provided by Xcode.

Using Access Modifiers

Swift provides *access modifiers* that are useful when developing code that you intend to package as a framework or library and reuse in other projects. There are three levels of access modifiers in Swift:

➤ `internal` designates a function, global variable, class, struct, or enumeration that is usable only within its own target (an application if you are developing an application, or a library or framework if you are packaging your code for reuse).

➤ `private` designates an entity that is usable only within the source code file in which it is defined (similar to the static keyword in C and Objective-C).

➤ `public` designates an entity that is available outside of its target. For applications, this does not mean much, but for frameworks and libraries, it means that the symbol can be used by code that imports the framework or library.

By default, all entities are `internal`. In practice, when developing applications, this does not matter much because `public` does not have much meaning for application targets. Simply put, it means any class, function, and so on, that you create in your application is available *anywhere* in your application, without the need for an `import` statement.

`internal` has a slightly different meaning in the context of frameworks and libraries. As with application targets, it means that the entity can be used by *any* code in your framework or library, without an `import` statement. However, the entities is not available outside of your library or framework. Other projects that make use of your library or framework cannot use these entities, even if they import your module.

`private` entities are only available in the source code file in which they are defined—they cannot be imported and used anywhere else, even by other code in the same target. `private` entities are strictly implementation details, and other code may as well pretend like they don't exist.

`public` entities are really only useful for libraries and frameworks. These functions, classes, and so on, actually become available to other projects that explicitly use your library or framework by including an `import` statement. They are not useful in application targets because application targets are not typically imported by other projects.

These access modifiers are especially useful when generating a bridging header that allows your Swift code to be used by Objective-C (which will be discussed in more detail later in this section): Only `public` entities will be included in the header file for libraries and frameworks, and only `public` and `internal` entities will be included in the header file generated for application targets.

Specifying an Access Level

Specifying an access level for an entity is simple: You just have to write `public`, `private`, or `internal` before the definition of the entity. Here is an example of how you could define a private class and a public function:

```
private class Widget {
    let name: String

    init(name: String) {
        self.name = name
    }
}

public func doubleIt(x: Int) -> Int {
    return x * 2
}
```

Swift's access modifiers are simple and straightforward to use, but you only *have* to think about them if you're writing a library or framework. Of course, even when writing an application, `private` is useful if you want to hide the implementation details of certain classes or parts of your code.

Strictly speaking, Swift's access modifiers are only tangentially related to the mixing of Swift code with Objective-C and C, but as you'll see later in this chapter, they do have some ramifications when automatically generating headers to be used by Objective-C and C code.

HOW SWIFT AND OBJECTIVE-C INTERACT

Despite the impact Swift has already made on the iOS and OS X development communities, applications and frameworks written entirely in Swift are not likely to appear en masse immediately. There will still be a great need for iOS and OS X applications to interface with Objective-C code (if only because so many existing frameworks shipped with those platforms are written in Objective-C), and it's likely that many developers will even have a need to call out to C code from time to time. It's also likely that, as developers migrate, you will find a need to call Swift code from Objective-C.

Luckily, it's fairly easy to call Swift classes from Objective-C code. In fact, you don't have to make many changes to your Swift code for it to be available from Objective-C. There are only a few key things you need to know.

Using Swift Classes in Objective-C

Swift classes that you intend to use from Objective-C must inherit from an Objective-C class. If your Swift class inherits from an existing Objective-C class (for example, UIColor), then it is automatically available in your Objective-C code. Swift's base class, however, is *not* an Objective-C class. If your Swift class does not inherit from an Objective-C class, then you can mark it with the @objc attribute, as shown in the code snippet that follows:

```
@objc class MyObjectiveCCompatibleClass {
}
```

By marking a class as @objc, the entirety of the class is available from Objective-C code. You can also mark specific elements of the class, such as methods or properties, with @objc, to make only those elements available from Objective-C.

The @objc also takes an optional name argument that exports the marked entity to Objective-C using that name:

```
@objc class Person {
    let name: String

    @objc(initWithName:)
    init(data: String) {
        self.name = data
    }
}
```

The preceding code makes a class called Person available in Objective-C with the initialization initWithName:.

If you don't specify a custom name, the compiler derives an Objective-C interface from the Swift names. For example, this block of code exposes the same interface as the one before to Objective-C:

```
@objc class Person {
    let name: String

    init(name: String) {
        self.name = name
    }
}
```

You can also mark entities such as functions with the @objc modifier in order to make those functions available from Objective-C as well.

Generating an Objective-C Header

If you want to call Swift code from Objective-C, you must generate a *bridging header.* The bridging header declares your Swift module's Objective-C interface. That header can be imported into Objective-C source files and used by your Objective-C classes.

The compiler takes care of creating a bridging header for you. This header file is called YourModule-Swift.h, where YourModule, of course, is the name of your module (by default, the name of your application or framework). This file will not appear in Xcode, but you can add an #import statement to the top of your Objective-C source code files to make use of it. (You can Command-click on the file to see what it looks like, although it's not terribly elegant.)

> **NOTE** *When you add a Swift file to an Objective-C project, Xcode asks if you want to create a bridging header. This allows you to also use Objective-C code in Swift. Details on using Objective-C code in Swift are described in the next section.*

That's all there is to it. You can now import that bridging header into your Objective-C files, just like a normal header file, and your Swift code—classes, structs, enums, functions, and the like—will be available.

Objective-C and Swift-Only Features

While Swift classes map cleanly to Objective-C, there are some Swift features that do not map to Objective-C. The following features are not available to Objective-C code that calls Swift code:

➤ Generics

➤ Tuples

➤ Enumerations

➤ Structs

➤ Global (top-level) functions

➤ Global variables

➤ Type aliases

➤ Variadics

➤ Nested types

➤ Curried functions

Using Swift Code in an Objective-C Application

Working with Swift code from Objective-C can best be illustrated with a quick example project. The CircleTool project is an Objective-C command-line tool that uses a Swift class to calculate the circumference of a circle. After building this simple application, you will more clearly be able to see how to work with Swift code from Objective-C.

Creating the project is easy.

1. **Create a command-line tool project in Xcode.** Launch Xcode and select the Create a new Xcode project option. From the OS X Application templates, select Command Line Tool and click Next. Name the program **CircleTool**. Make sure Objective-C is selected

from the Language drop-down menu, as shown in Figure 9-1. Click Next and save your project.

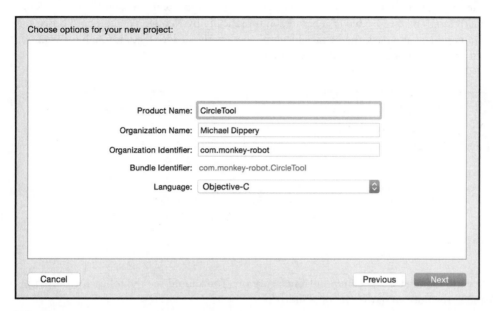

Choose options for your new project:

Product Name:	CircleTool
Organization Name:	Michael Dippery
Organization Identifier:	com.monkey-robot
Bundle Identifier:	com.monkey-robot.CircleTool
Language:	Objective-C

Cancel   Previous   Next

FIGURE 9-1

2. **Add a Swift file to the project.** Right-click the CircleTool group in the file navigator pane and select New File. Select the Swift File template and click Next. Save the file as `Circle.swift`. You will be asked if you want to create a bridging header file. This is only necessary if you intend to use your own Objective-C classes in your Swift code. Because you're not going to do that, you may select No.

3. **Create the `Circle` class.** Copy the code from Listing 9-1 into your `Circle.swift` file. Note that the `Circle` class inherits from `NSObject`. This is important! It allows your class to be used from Objective-C.

LISTING 9-1: Circle.swift

```swift
import Foundation


public class Circle: NSObject {
    public let radius: Int
    public var circumference: Double {
        return Double(radius * 2) * 3.14159
    }

    public init(radius: Int) {
        self.radius = radius
    }
}
```

4. **Finish the command-line tool.** The main executable portion of the program will be written in Objective-C. Replace the code in the existing `main.m` file with the code in Listing 9-2. Take special note of the second line of `main.m`, which imports the header file for the Swift Circle class. This header file is generated automatically by Xcode. You can hold down the Command key and click the header filename to view the header file, although it won't be pretty because it is automatically generated.

LISTING 9-2: main.m

```
#import <Foundation/Foundation.h>
#import "CircleTool-Swift.h"

int main(int argc, const char * argv[]) {
    @autoreleasepool {
        Circle *circle = [[Circle alloc] initWithRadius:10];
        NSLog(@"Circle's circumference is %.2f", [circle circumference]);
    }
    return 0;
}
```

You can now build and run this command-line program. You should see the following output in the console pane at the bottom of the Xcode window:

```
Circle's circumference is 62.83
```

And that's it! You have written an application that combines both Swift and Objective-C code. It's pretty simple—so painless, in fact, that you should now be comfortable mixing Objective-C and Swift in your own projects.

Using Objective-C in Swift

Until Swift has gained longevity comparable to that of Objective-C, it is likely you will be making use of Objective-C code in your Swift projects. Luckily, frameworks that ship with OS X and iOS can be used in your Swift code with nothing more than a simple `import` statement (as shown earlier in this chapter). However, if you wish to use your own Objective-C code in your Swift projects, you must generate a bridging header file.

Generating a Bridging Header

Luckily, generating a bridging header is easy. In fact, if you add an Objective-C file to your Swift project, Xcode offers to create a bridging header for you, as shown in Figure 9-2.

Xcode creates a file called `YourModule-Bridging-Header.h` (where `YourModule` is replaced by the name of your module—the name of your application or framework, by default). The header file that Xcode creates is blank. You must fill in the header files that you want to make available for Swift code. For instance, if you have an Objective-C class called `Rectangle`, declared in a file called `Rectangle.h` and implemented in `Rectangle.m`, you would enter the line `#import "Rectangle.h"` in the bridging header file created by Xcode. You can now use your Objective-C classes in Swift without the need to import anything into the Swift source code files.

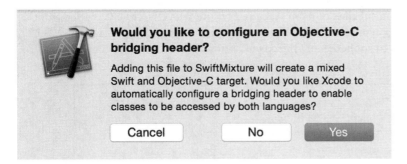

FIGURE 9-2

Calling Objective-C Code from Swift

To demonstrate how to make use of Objective-C code in Swift, you'll create a simple command-line application called SwiftMixture. You write the main executable code of SwiftMixture in Swift, but you will call code in an Objective-C class to do some of its calculations.

1.   **Create a new command-line tool in Xcode.** Launch Xcode and click Create a new Xcode project. From the OS X Application templates, select Command Line Tool and click Next. Name the program SwiftMixture. Make sure Swift is selected in the Language drop-down, as shown in Figure 9-3. Click Next and save your project.

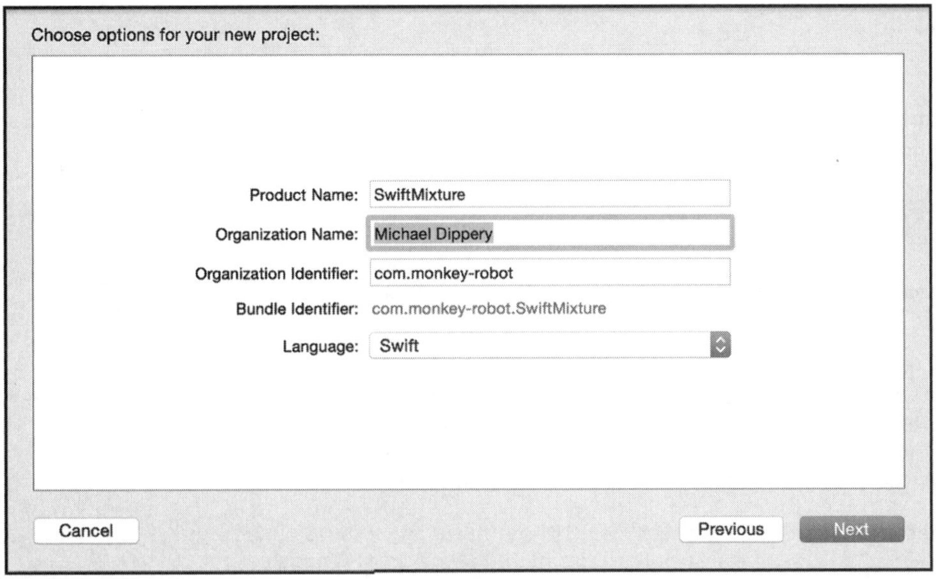

Choose options for your new project:

Product Name: SwiftMixture

Organization Name: Michael Dippery

Organization Identifier: com.monkey-robot

Bundle Identifier: com.monkey-robot.SwiftMixture

Language: Swift

Cancel   Previous   Next

FIGURE 9-3

2.   **Add an Objective-C class.** Right-click on the SwiftMixture group in the file navigator and select New File. Select Cocoa Class from the templates and click Next. Name the class

Rectangle. Make it a subclass of NSObject, and ensure that Objective-C is selected in the Language drop-down, as shown in Figure 9-4. Click Next and save your file. When prompted, click Yes to configure an Objective-C bridging header file.

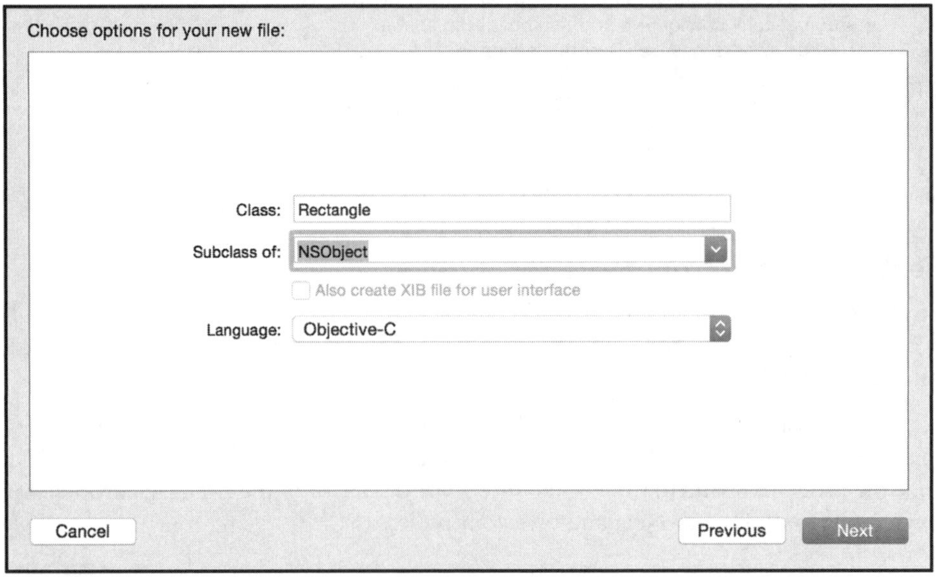

Choose options for your new file:

Class: Rectangle

Subclass of: NSObject

☐ Also create XIB file for user interface

Language: Objective-C

Cancel   Previous   Next

FIGURE 9-4

3. **Write the Rectangle class's header file.** Replace the code in Rectangle.h with the code in Listing 9-3.

LISTING 9-3: Rectangle.h

```objc
#import <Foundation/Foundation.h>


@interface Rectangle : NSObject

@property (copy, nonatomic) NSString *identifier;
@property (strong, nonatomic) NSNumber *length;
@property (strong, nonatomic) NSNumber *width;

+ (instancetype)rectangleWithIdentifier:(NSString *)anIdentifier
                                  length:(NSNumber *)aLength
                                   width:(NSNumber *)aWidth;
- (instancetype)initWithIdentifier:(NSString *)anIdentifier
                            length:(NSNumber *)aLength
                             width:(NSNumber *)aWidth;

@end
```

4. **Write the `Rectangle` implementation.** Replace the code in `Rectangle.m` with the code in Listing 9-4.

LISTING 9-4: Rectangle.m

```objc
#import "Rectangle.h"


@implementation Rectangle

@synthesize identifier, length, width;

+ (instancetype)rectangleWithIdentifier:(NSString *)anIdentifier
                                  length:(NSNumber *)aLength
                                   width:(NSNumber *)aWidth
{
    return [[self alloc] initWithIdentifier:anIdentifier
                                     length:aLength
                                      width:aWidth];
}

- (instancetype)initWithIdentifier:(NSString *)anIdentifier
                            length:(NSNumber *)aLength
                             width:(NSNumber *)aWidth
{
    if ((self = [super init])) {
        identifier = [anIdentifier copy];
        length = aLength;
        width = aWidth;
    }
    return self;
}

- (NSString *)description
{
    return [NSString stringWithFormat:
        @"%@ <identifier=%@, length=%@, width=%@>",
        self.class, self.identifier, self.length, self.width];
}

@end
```

5. **Configure the bridging header.** The bridging header lists the Objective-C code that should be made available to Swift code. You're going to be using only one Objective-C class, `Rectangle`, so the bridging header is fairly simple. Copy the following code into `SwiftMixture-Bridging-Header.h`:

```objc
#import "Rectangle.h"
```

6. **Implement the executable code.** The main executable code of the program is written in Swift. Copy the code from Listing 9-5 into your `main.swift` file. Notice that you don't have to import anything but Foundation—your Objective-C code is imported automatically because it exists in the same target.

LISTING 9-5: main.swift

```
import Foundation

let rectangle = Rectangle(identifier: "My Rectangle", length: 40, width: 20)
println(rectangle)
```

7.   **Build and run your program.** You should see the following output printed to the console:

```
Rectangle <identifier=My Rectangle, length=40, width=20>
```

And you're done! Calling Objective-C code from Swift is amazingly simple—nearly as simple as calling Swift code from Objective-C.

USING C AND C++ CODE WITH SWIFT

Calling C code from Swift is as easy as incorporating Objective-C code in Swift projects. When you add a C source code file to your Swift project, Swift prompts you to add a bridging header file as it does when adding an Objective-C source code file, as shown in Figure 9-1. You declare functions in the C code's header file and implement them in the .c file. As with Objective-C, you should add the header file for any C code that you want to use from Swift to the bridging header file. For example, if you create C code in a file called exponents.c, with an accompanying exponents.h header file, you would add the line #import "exponents.h" to the bridging header file.

Working with C Scalar Types

You should remember some caveats when working with C, particularly when dealing with C's types. C has numerous types for scalars such as numbers, Booleans, and characters. These types can be of different widths; for instance, C offers 32- and 64-bit integers. Unfortunately, Swift's scalar types cannot automatically be converted to C's types. For example, if a C function takes an int, Swift's Int is not automatically converted to an integer. Instead, you must declare a variable of type CInt, or a more specific type such as Int32, when passing that variable to a C function. Table 9-1 shows the mapping of C types to Swift types.

TABLE 9-1: C Types and Equivalent Swift Types

C TYPE	SWIFT TYPE
bool	CBool
char, signed char	CChar
char, unsigned char	CUnsignedChar
short	CShort
unsigned sign	CUnsignedShort

C TYPE	SWIFT TYPE
int	CInt
unsigned int	CUnsignedInt
long	CLong
unsigned long	CUnsignedLong
long long	CLongLong
unsigned long long	CUnsignedLongLong
float	CFloag
double	CDouble
wchar_t	CWideChar
char16_t	CChar16
char32_t	CChar32

Accessing Memory with C Pointers

C also has pointers. Pointers allow you to access specific areas of memory. Because pointers are one of the greatest sources of bugs (and confusion), they have been eliminated from Swift. However, when you work with C code, you may have to work with pointers. Swift provides a mapping of C pointers to Swift types. Swift's mapped pointer types are generics to provide greater type safety to Swift programs. Table 9-2 shows a mapping of C's pointer types to Swift.

TABLE 9-2: C Pointer Types and Swift Equivalents

C TYPE	SWIFT TYPE
const T *	UnsafePointer<T>
T *	UnsafeMutablePointer<T>
T * const *	UnsafePointer<T>
T * __strong *	UnsafeMutablePointer<T>
Type **	AutoreleasingUnsafeMutablePointer<T>

You can convert some of the Swift types into other types. For example, if a C function takes an argument of type UnsafePointer<T>, you can pass an UnsafeMutablePointer<T> or an AutoreleasingUnsafeMutablePointer<T> instead. You can also pass an array of type [T]; the C function will receive a pointer to the first element in memory. You can also pass an inout parameter of type T. If you do not have a value to pass, you can also simply pass nil; this will be received as NULL in the C function.

> **NOTE** *Not all C functions expect to receive* NULL *as an argument. While the type system allows you to pass* nil *for any pointer argument in a C function, you may experience a runtime error if the C function is not equipped to deal with* NULL *pointers.*

Similarly, if you have a C function that takes an argument of type `UnsafeMutablePointer<T>`, you may pass an `inout` parameter of type `T` or an array of type `[T]` instead. You may also pass `nil` if you have no value to pass.

C not only has pointers to data types like `int`s and `float`s, but also to functions themselves. These can also be used from Swift. In Swift, C function pointers have the type `CFunctionPointer<T>`, where T is a closure type. For example, consider the following C function:

```
int cube(int x);
```

In C, a pointer to that function would have the type `int (*)(int)`. This would translate to the type `CFunctionPointer<(Int32) -> Int32>` in Swift.

One other important thing to note about C: C has the notion of *void pointers*, typed as `void *`, which are pointers of *any* type. If you have a C function that takes a void pointer, then the generic type `T` can be of *any* Swift type.

Working with Global Constants and Defines and Swift

C global constants are imported into Swift code, with C types mapped to Swift types appropriately. For example, if you had the following constant declared in a C header file, it would be mapped to a constant with name `MyGlobalValue` with the type `Int32` in your Swift source code files:

```
extern int MyGlobalValue;
```

Likewise, constants defined using C's `#define` compiler directive are also mapped to constants of the same name in Swift. These `#define` directives are referred to as *macros* in C. The following example macro would be available as `MY_GLOBAL_VALUE` in Swift, with the type `Int32`:

```
#define MY_GLOBAL_VALUE 32
```

C's macros can take arguments as parameters, much like functions. Unfortunately, C macros that take arguments are not available in Swift.

Calling C Code from Swift

The SwiftC project demonstrates a simple Swift command-line program that makes use of C code. In SwiftC, you'll write some C code to calculate the square and cube of a given value and then write a Swift command-line tool that will print out the square and cube of 10.

1. **Create a Swift command-line tool project.** Launch Xcode. Click the Create a new Xcode project. From the OS X Application templates, select Command Line Tool and click Next. Name the project SwiftC. Ensure that Swift is selected from the Language drop-down. Click Next and save the project.

2. **Add C files.** Right-click on the SwiftC group in the file navigator and select New File. In the templates selection window, select C File and click Next. Name the file `exponents.c`. Ensure that "Also create a header file" is selected. Click Next and save the file. When prompted, click Yes to create a bridging header file. This will be necessary to use your C code from Swift.

3. **Create the C header file.** The C header file declares the functions you will be implementing in C. Replace the default template code in `exponents.h` with the code in Listing 9-6.

LISTING 9-6: exponents.h

```c
#ifndef __SwiftC__exponents__
#define __SwiftC__exponents__

#include <stdio.h>

extern int square(int x);
extern int cube(int x);

#endif
```

4. **Implement your C functions.** Replace the default template code in `exponents.c` with the code in Listing 9-7. This code is fairly straightforward and calculates the square and cube of a given integer using the `pow()` function provided by the C standard library.

LISTING 9-7: exponents.c

```c
#include "exponents.h"
#include "math.h"

int square(int x)
{
    return (int) pow(x, 2);
}

int cube(int x)
{
    return (int) pow(x, 3);
}
```

5. **Configure the bridging header.** In the case of this project, the bridging header is pretty simple: It only needs to import `exponents.h`. In general, you will import the header files of any code you want to use in Swift in the bridging header. Copy the following code into `SwiftC-Bridging-Header.h`:

   ```c
   #include "exponents.h"
   ```

6. **Implement the executable code.** The executable code is written in Swift and makes use of the C code you wrote. Replace the contents of `main.swift` with the code in Listing 9-8.

LISTING 9-8: main.swift

```swift
import Foundation

let x: Int32 = 10
let xSquared = square(x)
let xCubed = cube(x)
println("x is \(x)")
println("x^2 is \(xSquared)")
println("x^3 is \(xCubed)")
```

Compile and run your program. You should see the following output in the console:

```
x is 10
x^2 is 100
x^3 is 1000
```

That's it! Together, Swift and Xcode make it that easy to call C code from your code written in Swift.

Using C++ Code in Swift

OS X and iOS projects most commonly are written in Objective-C or C. Almost all of the libraries and frameworks that are distributed with these platforms expose an Objective-C or C interface. However, some projects make use of C++ code. Unfortunately, you have no way to bridge C++ code to Swift. C++ code cannot be imported and used in Swift, nor can C++ code import and use Swift classes.

Using C++ code from Swift is a bit complex, and certainly more work than using C or Objective-C from Swift. If you have to use C++ code in your Swift projects, you must first write a wrapper for the C++ code in either C or Objective-C++ (a hybrid language that allows Objective-C code to use C++ code), and then create bridging header files for those wrappers and use them in Swift.

SUMMARY

Although Swift has rapidly gained traction in the iOS and OS X development communities, it is likely that programmers will have to continue interfacing with C and Objective-C code for a while. Luckily, Apple has made such integration nearly seamless. In this chapter, you learned how you can easily make use of Swift classes in Objective-C code, as well as make use of C and Objective-C code in your Swift projects. When dealing with C, the mapping between Swift and C types is not always elegant, but it is easily understood and relatively painless. You also learned about Swift namespaces and modules. While these features do not directly deal with C and Objective-C interoperability—you may need to understand namespaces and modules even when dealing with projects implemented purely in Swift—they are vital to understanding how Swift interoperates with C and Objective-C. With this knowledge, you can continue to interface with legacy code until you can create projects purely in Swift.

10

Debugging Swift Applications

WHAT'S IN THIS CHAPTER?

➤ Developing techniques for debugging

➤ Learning about debugging tools

➤ Understanding how a debugger helps diagnose and track down bugs in programs

➤ Interfacing with the debugger

➤ Investigating code at runtime

WROX.COM CODE DOWNLOADS FOR THIS CHAPTER

You can find the wrox.com downloads for this chapter at http://www.wrox.com/go/proswift on the Download Code tab. The code for this chapter is contained in the following files:

➤ CircleView.zip

➤ DebuggerExplorer.zip

In a perfect world, debugging software would not be necessary. Everything programmers created would be perfect. Unfortunately, the world is not perfect, and occasionally you will write buggy software. However, with the right tools at your disposal, even the most challenging of bugs can be detected with ease. Xcode includes a very important tool, the debugger that you can use to track down problems in your code, helping you to detect and diagnose bugs and, more importantly, fix them with a minimal amount of effort. This chapter introduces you to debugging concepts and the use of lldb, the debugger that ships with Xcode as part of its LLVM compilation suite.

THE ART OF DEBUGGING

Even the best of programmers write buggy software. Often, bugs are fairly obvious. In the worst case, they cause programs to crash, or to behave improperly, or to not work at all. These bugs are often easy to re-create and track down, and merely having some knowledge of how the software is written makes it easy to fix them. Other bugs are more subtle, only manifesting themselves in very specific situations. Such bugs are often much more time-consuming to track down and may be difficult for the tester or programmer to re-create. They often rely on knowledge not only of the code itself but of the internal state of an application at the time of the crash. Figuring out how a specific program state causes a bug can be difficult.

One of the goals of Swift is to reduce the number of bugs that programmers can inadvertently introduce into a software program. Swift achieves this goal by its use of strong typing, coupled with its advanced type inference engine. The language also limits how easily programmers can manipulate individual areas of memory (as opposed to C and Objective-C, which intentionally allow fine-grained access to a program's memory). Swift's advanced features also allow programmers to organize their program's code and approach problems in a more flexible, straightforward way. Together, these help prevent many of the errors and bugs that were common in Objective-C programs.

Unfortunately, no language can prevent *all* bugs. An entire class of bugs can occur when a programmer simply misunderstands a problem domain and writes a solution that does not actually solve the problem. Even outside of these higher-level logic bugs, Swift programs can still have errors that will cause program crashes or erroneous behavior. This is especially true when Swift programs are interfacing with C and Objective-C code, as shown in the previous chapter, because neither of these languages make the same type and memory guarantees as Swift. Therefore, as a Swift programmer, it is of utmost importance that you understand and learn how to use the tools provided by Apple through the Xcode suite to debug your programs when problems *do* occur.

Debugging is as much an art as it is a science. As with any skill, your ability to quickly and correctly diagnose and fix problems in your code will improve the more often you have to do it. Of course, like any skill, you can learn certain techniques and tools that will aid you in your debugging endeavors, making the skill easier to learn and hone. These techniques and tools are demonstrated through the creation of a simple application, CircleView. After creating the initial version of CircleView, you will see how you can use Xcode's debugging tools to gain a more thorough understanding of how your program works.

CREATING CIRCLEVIEW

CircleView is a simple iOS application. It has a single view with a circle drawn on it and a slider for controlling the size of that circle. The application itself is very simple in nature, but through it, you will gain a more complete understanding of how to use the debugging tools to get a closer look at how a program is actually executed.

You may download the source code files for CircleView from the downloads section for this chapter, or follow along in this section to build the application.

Drawing the Circle

To start, follow these steps:

1. **Create a new Xcode application.** You should select the Single View Application template from the iOS section of the new project window. Make sure that the language for the application is set to Swift and then save the project somewhere on your hard drive.

2. **Create the CircleView structure.** The structure of the CircleView is very simple. You should create a custom `UIView` subclass that becomes responsible for drawing the circle in the app's main view. Select New File from the File menu, then select the Swift File template and click Next. Save this new file in your project's directory tree with the name `CircleView`.

    The new file should now be displayed in the file editor (if it is not, select it from the file tree to display it).

3. **Create a new class called `CircleView` that is a subclass of `UIView`.** This is as shown in Listing 10-1. Don't forget to import UIKit into your new file!

`CircleView` is a relatively simple subclass of `UIView`. Because its sole responsibility is to draw the circle that the application displays, you should add three new instance variables to the class: `strokeColor`, a `UIColor` object that designates the color of the circle; `strokeWidth`, the width of the outer edge of the circle as a `CGFloat`; and `circleRadius`, which tracks the size of the circle, also as a `CGFloat`.

In order for `CircleView` to work properly, you must override two initializer methods: `init(frame:)` and `init(coder:)`. These initializers will simply set the instance variables to a default value. They will also call the associated methods in `UIView`, which will perform some initialization work as well. Listing 10-1 shows the final state of both of these initializers.

> **NOTE** *You'll notice that both of the* `CircleView` *class's initializers do the same thing. This is a result of some restrictions Swift places on initializers. Namely, the class's instance variables have to be initialized* before *calling a superclass's initializer. In actual production code,* `init(coder:)` *would probably do some more advanced work, namely unpacking values from the* `NSCoder` *object and setting them to the stored values. That's not really necessary for this simple application; as a result, both initializers are the same.*

Finally, you must override the `drawRect()` method in `CircleView` to actually draw the circle on the iPhone's screen. Drawing the circle is simple: You'll find a point roughly in the center of the iPhone's screen and then use Core Graphic's drawing methods to draw a circle with a border thickness of 5 pixels, filled with the color red. Listing 10-1 shows the complete (and fairly simple) implementation of `drawRect()`.

LISTING 10-1: CircleView.swift

```swift
import UIKit


class CircleView: UIView {
```

continues

continued

```swift
    var strokeColor: UIColor
    var strokeWidth: CGFloat
    var circleRadius: CGFloat

    override init(frame: CGRect) {
        strokeColor = UIColor.redColor()
        strokeWidth = 5.0
        circleRadius = 75.0
        super.init(frame: frame)
    }

    required init(coder aDecoder: NSCoder) {
        strokeColor = UIColor.redColor()
        strokeWidth = 5.0
        circleRadius = 75.0
        super.init(coder: aDecoder)
    }

    override func drawRect(rect: CGRect) {
        super.drawRect(rect)

        let middleX = CGRectGetMidX(rect)
        let middleY = CGRectGetMidY(rect)

        var ctx = UIGraphicsGetCurrentContext()
        CGContextSetLineWidth(ctx, strokeWidth)
        strokeColor.set()
        CGContextAddArc(ctx, middleX, middleY, circleRadius, 0.0,
                        CGFloat(M_PI * 2.0), 1)
        CGContextStrokePath(ctx)
    }
}
```

Adding Sliders

The CircleView app make use of a slider that allows the user to change the size of the circle being drawn in the main view. To work with the slider, add an IBAction method to the ViewController class that was created with the project template, as shown in Listing 10-2. This method is very simple: It accepts a UISlider instance as a parameter and grabs the UISlider object's current value. It then changes the radius of the circle in the view controller's CircleView instance to that value and asks iOS to redraw the screen.

Note that the second line of the sliderChanged() method casts the view controller's view outlet to an instance of CircleView. The view instance variable is typed as a UIView, even though it is really a CircleView, so it must be cast to a variable of type CircleView in order to change its circleRadius property. If view is *not* a CircleView, this line of code throws an exception, causing a crash at runtime. However, because you know that view is really a CircleView, it is safe to unconditionally cast it to a value of type CircleView.

The complete implementation of the `ViewController` class is shown in Listing 10-2.

LISTING 10-2: VIEWCONTROLLER.SWIFT

```swift
import UIKit

class ViewController: UIViewController {
    override func viewDidLoad() {
        super.viewDidLoad()
    }

    @IBAction func sliderChanged(sender: UISlider) {
        let val = sender.value
        let circleView = view as CircleView
        circleView.circleRadius = CGFloat(val)
        view.setNeedsDisplay()
    }
}
```

Completing the Project

To complete the project, you must make a few modifications to the application's main view:

1. **Select Main.storyboard from the file navigator to bring up the main view in the editor panel.** The first thing you must do is change the main `UIView` instance's class to that of `CircleView`, the custom `UIView` subclass you just created. Select the `UIView` object and then bring up the Identity tab in the inspector on the right-hand side of the screen. Change the class to `CircleView`, as shown in Figure 10.1.

2. **Add a `UISlider` instance to the main view.** Drag an instance of a `UISlider` from the object library to the main view. You can place it wherever you like, although centering it near the bottom is probably your best bet. Feel free to resize it as you see fit. You may need to add some auto-layout constraints to ensure that it is aligned properly on whatever device you are using to test.

3. **Control-drag a connection from the `UISlider` object you added to the `ViewController` instance in the storyboard.** Connect the `UISlider` object to the `sliderChanged()` method on the `ViewController`.

> **NOTE** *When a `UISlider` is dragged left or right, it sends a message to its outlet with itself as a parameter. In the case of the `CircleView` application, this means that whenever the slider is dragged, the `sliderChanged()` method on the `ViewController` instance is called with the `UISlider` as its argument.*

4. **Configure `UISlider` so that it knows the range of the values it should send.** In this case, you are using the value of `UISlider` as the actual radius for the circle that is being drawn. The

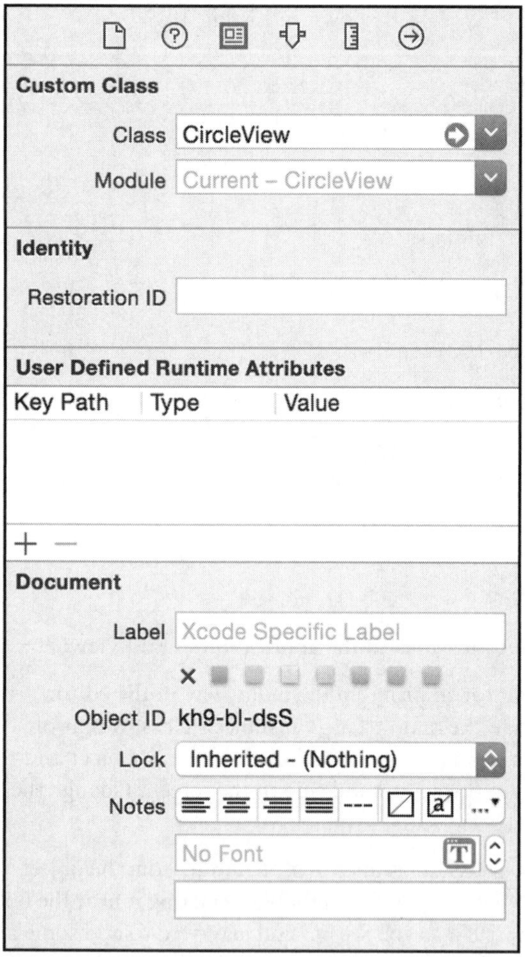

FIGURE 10-1

maximum radius of the circle that can be displayed on the iPhone's screen is about 300 pixels, so the UISlider should send values between 0 and 150.

Luckily, you can avoid doing some complicated math by changing the range of the UISlider. Select the UISlider, and then bring up the Attributes tab in the inspector on the right-hand side of the Xcode editor screen. There are three values at the top that control the range and default value of the slider: Minimum, Maximum, and Current. Set Minimum to a value of 0, Maximum to 150, and Current to 75, as shown in Figure 10-2.

5. **Build and run your application.** You should see the size of the circle change as you drag the slider left and right.

Now that your application is working, you can take a look at some debugging techniques that you can use to inspect the state of your application as it runs.

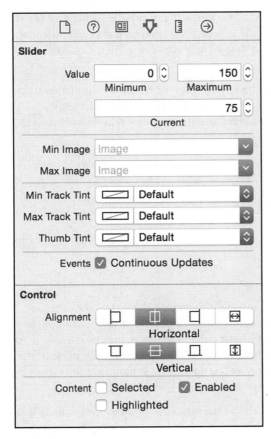

FIGURE 10-2

PRINTING VALUES

One of the simplest ways to debug an application is to simply print, or *log*, the values of different variables. This is accomplished simply by calling println() or NSLog() at various points in the application. These functions will print a string out to the console, which, when you use Xcode, appear in the console window at the bottom of the Xcode editor.

Debugging by printing values is a simple technique, but it can yield a lot of information about the state of your running program that can be helpful when debugging problems, or even investigating what happens when certain buttons are clicked—or, in the case of the CircleView app, when a slider is dragged. This insight is helpful when you are trying to figure out how some of the classes or code in Apple's frameworks, such as UIKit, are actually working underneath the hood, even without looking at the actual source code for those classes.

To illustrate how simple print statements are for investigating how a program actually runs, you can add a few NSLog() calls to the code you wrote for the CircleView app. One of the most interesting areas for study is the sliderChanged() method in the ViewController class.

Consider `sliderChanged()` for a moment. Abstractly, you know that it is called whenever the state of its connected `UISlider` changes. But how often is it called? Is it called on a timer? You know that the `UISlider` instance itself is passed as a parameter, but what is the state of that `UISlider` when the method is called?

These questions can be answered by investigating the values received by the `sliderChanged()` method. To facilitate this inquiry, add a call to `NSLog()` after the value of the `UISlider` is retrieved. Your code for the `sliderChanged()` method should look like that shown in Listing 10-3.

LISTING 10-3: ViewController.swift

```
@IBAction func sliderChanged(sender: UISlider) {
    let val = sender.value
    NSLog("slider value is \(val)")
    let circleView = view as CircleView
    circleView.circleRadius = CGFloat(val)
    view.setNeedsDisplay()
}
```

Build and run your application. Drag the slider left and right to change the size of the circle in the iPhone display. When you do, you should notice a console view pop up at the bottom of the main Xcode window. This display shows the output of any calls to `NSLog()` (or `println()`, if you have calls to `println()` as well). In this case, you should see lines showing what the value of the `UISlider` is as it is dragged left and right in the `CircleView` app. Some sample output is shown in Figure 10-3.

This output also demonstrates when and how often the `sliderChanged()` method is called. You can see that it is called whenever the state of the slider changes, not *just* when you stop sliding it. You can also see that if you stop dragging the slider, the method is no longer called (indicating that the `UISlider` instance is not *polled* for its current state).

Thanks to this simple `NSLog()` call, you've gained quite a bit of knowledge about how your application and its various UI components interact, as well as what the state of your application is while it's running. I hope you've been able to extrapolate how useful these relatively innocuous logging statements can be when you are trying to debug various aspects of your application.

Although useful and simple to add to your code, print statements (such as calls to `NSLog()` or `println()`) are not terribly powerful. Most notable, they only allow you to passively print the state of your running application, and you must designate which values should be printed before compiling and running the program. They don't allow you to interactively investigate the state of a program, print other values that you didn't anticipate needing to print, or change the value of a variable at runtime. They also require you to specify where to print data before running the program, making it so you can't automatically print data whenever a particular method or function is called. They also don't allow you to inspect the state of code that you don't have control over, such as that in Apple's frameworks or third-party modules.

After seeing both the usefulness and limitations of garden variety print statements, you may think that the preceding list of features is magic and is simply not possible to do in a running program. However, all of those features *are* possible to do in a running program. To use these features, however, you have to make use of a very special and very important tool: the debugger.

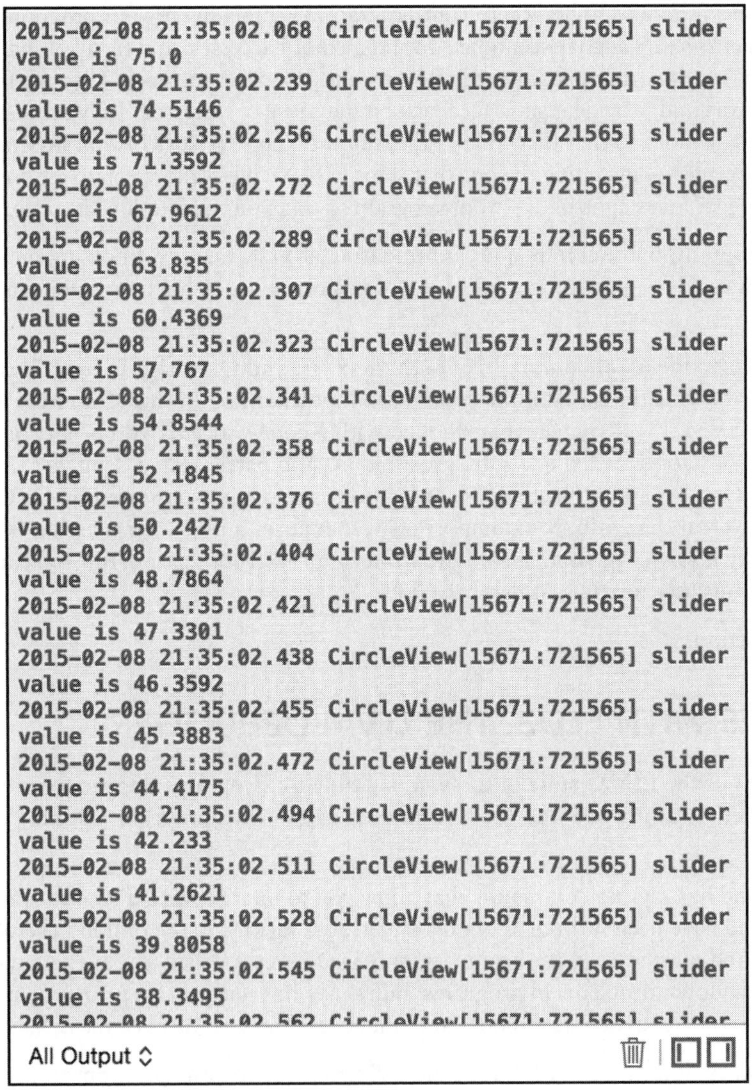

```
2015-02-08 21:35:02.068 CircleView[15671:721565] slider
value is 75.0
2015-02-08 21:35:02.239 CircleView[15671:721565] slider
value is 74.5146
2015-02-08 21:35:02.256 CircleView[15671:721565] slider
value is 71.3592
2015-02-08 21:35:02.272 CircleView[15671:721565] slider
value is 67.9612
2015-02-08 21:35:02.289 CircleView[15671:721565] slider
value is 63.835
2015-02-08 21:35:02.307 CircleView[15671:721565] slider
value is 60.4369
2015-02-08 21:35:02.323 CircleView[15671:721565] slider
value is 57.767
2015-02-08 21:35:02.341 CircleView[15671:721565] slider
value is 54.8544
2015-02-08 21:35:02.358 CircleView[15671:721565] slider
value is 52.1845
2015-02-08 21:35:02.376 CircleView[15671:721565] slider
value is 50.2427
2015-02-08 21:35:02.404 CircleView[15671:721565] slider
value is 48.7864
2015-02-08 21:35:02.421 CircleView[15671:721565] slider
value is 47.3301
2015-02-08 21:35:02.438 CircleView[15671:721565] slider
value is 46.3592
2015-02-08 21:35:02.455 CircleView[15671:721565] slider
value is 45.3883
2015-02-08 21:35:02.472 CircleView[15671:721565] slider
value is 44.4175
2015-02-08 21:35:02.494 CircleView[15671:721565] slider
value is 42.233
2015-02-08 21:35:02.511 CircleView[15671:721565] slider
value is 41.2621
2015-02-08 21:35:02.528 CircleView[15671:721565] slider
value is 39.8058
2015-02-08 21:35:02.545 CircleView[15671:721565] slider
value is 38.3495
2015-02-08 21:35:02.562 CircleView[15671:721565] slider
```

All Output ⬍

FIGURE 10-3

WORKING WITH DEBUGGERS

A debugger is a program that runs your program, allowing you to pause execution at arbitrary points in the program and inspect the state of the application at that point. As with the print debugging described in the previous section, a debugger allows you to print out values of variables and constants. However, a debugger is much more powerful. With a debugger, you can also print out the program's current stack, as well as the contents of the CPU's registers. You can also walk through your program line by line, pausing anywhere to inspect and manipulate the state of the program. You can even jump into functions and methods that you don't control (such as functions and methods in the UIKit or Foundation frameworks, as well as third-party modules you may be using).

Debuggers work by using kernel functions to hook into your program. By attaching to your program in this way, they trap various errors (uncaught exceptions, invalid memory accesses, and the like). They also access low-level details of your program, such as the state of your program's memory. Through these mechanisms, they can trap errors and provide instant feedback on the cause of the error. They are also free to modify your program's memory so that they modify the runtime characteristics of your program in some way. Finally, most debuggers—including the one that ships with Xcode—allow you to set *breakpoints*, which means the debugger takes control over your program so that you can examine its state.

A debugger is a powerful program, but it can be quite intimidating at first. Luckily, knowing only a subset of the debugger's commands can open up a lot of doors when you are debugging problems in the programs you write.

The debugger that ships with Xcode is called *lldb*. Like both the Swift and Objective-C compilers, it is part of the LLVM suite that forms the basis of the compilation toolchain on both iOS and OS X. Before Apple started using LLVM, the debugger that shipped with Xcode was *gdb*. gdb is part of the GNU Compiler Collection, commonly called *gcc*. gdb is a standard and battle-tested debugger that debugs programs written in C, C++, and Objective-C (among other languages supported by GCC). lldb is newer, but no less powerful than gdb. Most importantly, it exposes a user interface that is nearly identical to gdb, so any knowledge you have of gdb (or may glean from reading tutorials and blog posts on the Internet) translates nearly seamlessly to lldb.

Let's take a look at lldb in action.

EXAMINING ERRORS WITH LLDB, THE LLVM DEBUGGER

lldb ships with Xcode as part of the LLVM suite of tools. It is usable for programs written for any platform supported by Xcode, including iOS and OS X, and even works with programs running in the iOS Simulator.

lldb is a very powerful tool and has myriad commands that allow you to interact with a running program. Entire books can be and have been written about debuggers, but luckily, many of lldb's useful commands are easy to learn and master (even for beginners who have never touched a debugger) and are very helpful when tracking down problems in programs. lldb's user interface is also nearly identical to that of gdb, making it easy to pick up new techniques and understand new features of the debugger.

You're probably already somewhat familiar with lldb. Whenever you launch your program from Xcode and it crashes, you are automatically dumped into an lldb console. In most cases, you've probably just hit the stop button, fixed your code, and run the program again, so you may be pleasantly surprised that you can actually interact with your program whenever it crashes. Because your program has crashed, your options are somewhat limited, of course; you can print the values of some variables and view the state of the stack and CPU registers. However, you can also manually invoke lldb while your program is running and even set it to take control in response to certain activities and actions in your program. You do this by setting *breakpoints* in your program.

Basic Breakpoints

Like gdb, lldb works on the concept of a *breakpoint*. Breakpoints allow you to manually set places in your code where control of your program's execution will be turned over to the debugger. Once the debugger has taken over control of your program, you can use debugger commands to examine and even modify the state of your program. You can set breakpoints on specific lines of source code files, or whenever a particular function or method is called (even when that function or method is in a system or third-party framework outside the control of your program). You can also set *conditional breakpoints*, which are invoked whenever a particular condition is reached in a program.

The simplest way to invoke the debugger is to set a breakpoint on a specific line in a file. In Xcode, you do this graphically simply by clicking the line number on which you want to set the breakpoint when the source code file is open in the editor, as shown in Figure 10-4. Set a breakpoint at line 10.

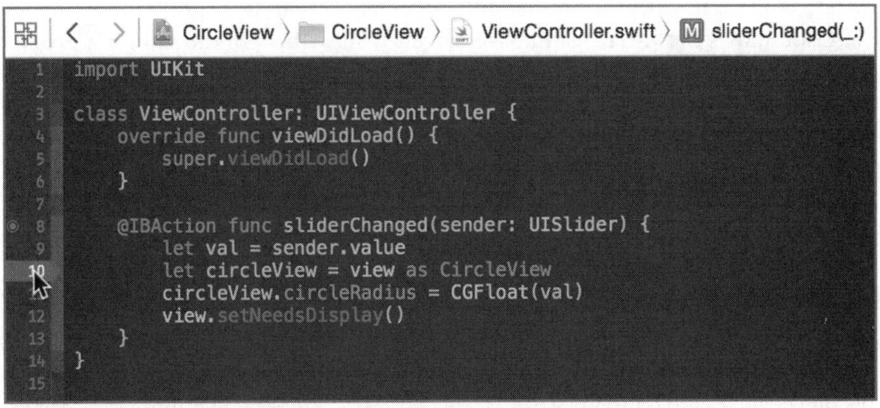

FIGURE 10-4

> **NOTE** *You may want to use the downloadable code for this chapter, to ensure that the line numbers referenced in the text match up to the proper line numbers in your code.*

A blue arrow appears on the line on which you set the breakpoint. Compile and run the CircleView app now. After it launches, drag the slider right or left. You will notice that you are returned to Xcode, where an lldb console has opened along the bottom of the main Xcode window, as shown in Figure 10-5.

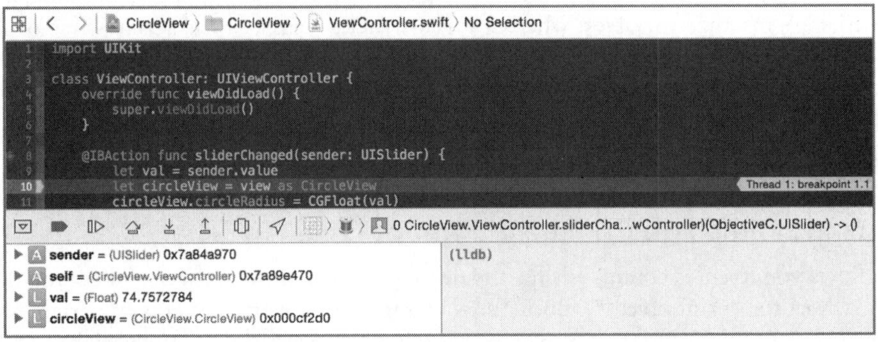

FIGURE 10-5

You should also take notice of the fact that the CircleView app has stopped responding to input. This is because execution of the program has actually paused on the breakpoint you set earlier. You cannot interact with the program because the code that handles user input cannot run until you continue execution.

But what can you do in the lldb console?

Using lldb to Inspect Programs

Take a look at the lldb console that Xcode has helpfully opened for you. It is split into two panes. The pane on the left side shows the variables that are currently in scope. On the right is a prompt, not unlike the bash command prompt you get when opening Terminal, albeit prefixed with (lldb). This, however, should not be confused with a bash shell prompt; it is instead a prompt for you to enter commands that will be interpreted by lldb.

There is also a ribbon along the top of the two debugger panes in Xcode. This, too, is split roughly in half.

Using the Variable Pane

In the left pane, arguments to the method are marked with an *A* in a square. Local variables are marked with an *L*. Next to the name of the variable is its type, as well as its location in memory. Figure 10-6 shows the variables currently in scope in the sliderChanged() method.

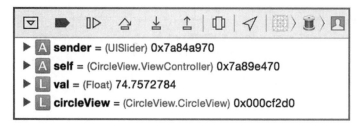

FIGURE 10-6

Each variable has a disclosure triangle next to it. Clicking a disclosure triangle shows the same data for each of the variable's instance variables: whether it is a struct or class, or the actual value of the variable if it is a scalar type such as an int or float. You can also click the disclosure triangle next to each instance variable to show *its* instance variables, ad infinitum, until you reach a point where there are no instance variables to show. Figure 10-7 shows the entire tree of instance variables for the circleView variable.

Entering Commands in the lldb Command Prompt Pane

The right pane allows you to enter commands for the debugger. Two of the most useful commands are print and po (short for "print object"). Both allow you to print out the contents of variables that are in scope. They are subtly different. print prints out a representation of any variable, including its address in memory and its constituent objects. po is most useful for Objective-C or Swift classes and prints a more human-readable representation.

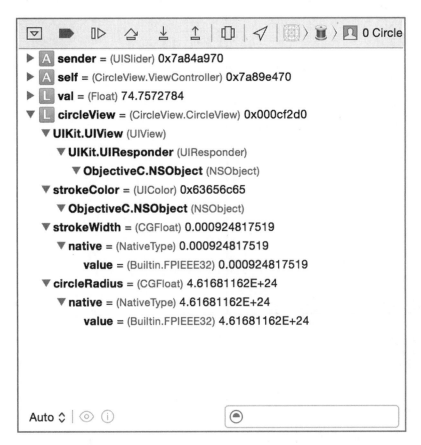

FIGURE 10-7

These commands may appear simple, but they are actually fairly powerful. Not only can they print the contents of a given variable, but they can also print the results of expressions. For example, you can enter print self.view to print the contents of the view instance variable. You can also enter things like print round(val) to see what would happen to the value of val if it were passed to the round function. If you're familiar with languages with read-eval-print loops, such as Python and Ruby, you'll quickly feel right at home in the lldb console. Figure 10-8 shows the output of some simple expressions in lldb.

Displaying Code Hierarchy with the lldb Ribbon

The right side of the lldb ribbon shows a hierarchy of your code. Specifically, it shows which thread you are currently paused in. Right now, it shows that you paused execution in the sliderChanged() method, which is running in Thread 1 (the main thread of the program), as shown in Figure 10-9.

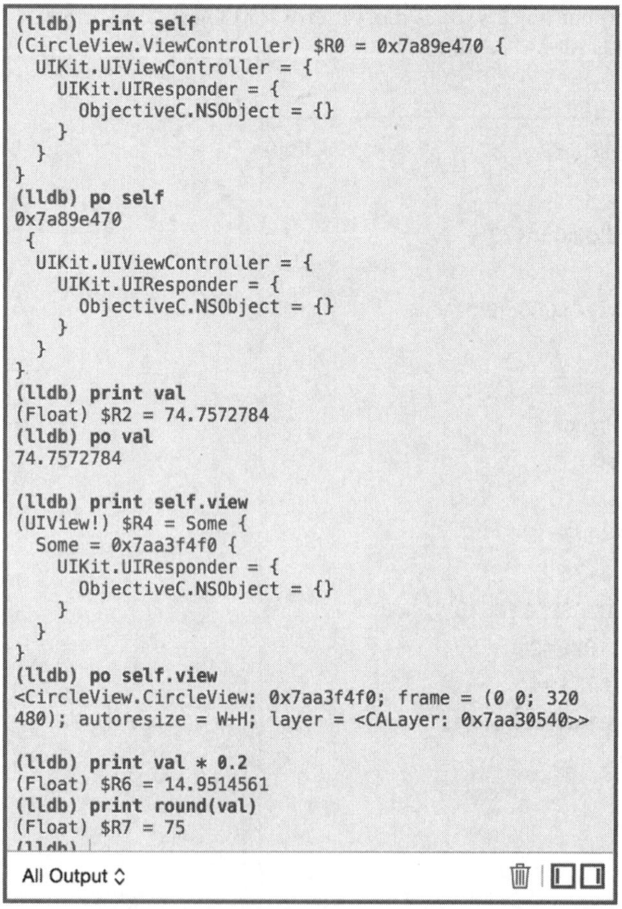

```
(lldb) print self
(CircleView.ViewController) $R0 = 0x7a89e470 {
  UIKit.UIViewController = {
    UIKit.UIResponder = {
      ObjectiveC.NSObject = {}
    }
  }
}
(lldb) po self
0x7a89e470
  {
  UIKit.UIViewController = {
    UIKit.UIResponder = {
      ObjectiveC.NSObject = {}
    }
  }
}
(lldb) print val
(Float) $R2 = 74.7572784
(lldb) po val
74.7572784

(lldb) print self.view
(UIView!) $R4 = Some {
  Some = 0x7aa3f4f0 {
    UIKit.UIResponder = {
      ObjectiveC.NSObject = {}
    }
  }
}
(lldb) po self.view
<CircleView.CircleView: 0x7aa3f4f0; frame = (0 0; 320
480); autoresize = W+H; layer = <CALayer: 0x7aa30540>>

(lldb) print val * 0.2
(Float) $R6 = 14.9514561
(lldb) print round(val)
(Float) $R7 = 75
(lldb)
```

All Output ◇   🗑 | ▢▢

FIGURE 10-8

▦ ⟩ 🗋 Thread 1 ⟩ 🔲 0 CircleView.ViewController.slide...ntroller)(ObjectiveC.UISlider) -> ()

FIGURE 10-9

Clicking the execution hierarchy displays a stack view, showing what code called the function or method of the current breakpoint. In turn, the code that called *that* frame is shown, and so on, all the way back to the beginning, as shown in Figure 10-10.

You can use this call stack navigation display to jump to other frames in your program. Doing so displays the code for that frame in the editor pane above the debugging panes, as well as the variables in the current scope on the left side of the debugger. However, if you are jumping to code that is not a part of your project (such as code in the UIKit framework), you do not get a view of the source code. Instead, the assembly code for that stack frame, and local variables and function or method arguments are not available for inspection. Use the navigation display to jump to other parts of code to get a feel for what sort of information it provides for you.

```
 0 CircleView.ViewController.sliderChanged (CircleView.ViewController)(ObjectiveC.UISlider) -> ()
 1 @objc CircleView.ViewController.sliderChanged (CircleView.ViewController)(ObjectiveC.UISlider) -> ()
 2 -[NSObject performSelector:withObject:withObject:]
 3 -[UIApplication sendAction:to:from:forEvent:]
 4 -[UIApplication sendAction:toTarget:fromSender:forEvent:]
 5 -[UIControl sendAction:to:forEvent:]
 6 -[UIControl _sendActionsForEvents:withEvent:]
 7 -[UISlider beginTrackingWithTouch:withEvent:]
 8 -[UIControl touchesBegan:withEvent:]
 9 -[UIWindow _sendTouchesForEvent:]
10 -[UIWindow sendEvent:]
11 -[UIApplication sendEvent:]
12 _UIApplicationHandleEventFromQueueEvent
13 _UIApplicationHandleEventQueue
14 __CFRUNLOOP_IS_CALLING_OUT_TO_A_SOURCE0_PERFORM_FUNCTION__
15 __CFRunLoopDoSources0
16 __CFRunLoopRun
17 CFRunLoopRunSpecific
18 CFRunLoopRunInMode
19 GSEventRunModal
20 GSEventRun
21 UIApplicationMain
22 top_level_code
23 main
24 start
```

FIGURE 10-10

Walking through a Program with the lldb Ribbon

The left half of the debugger ribbon gives you controls for walking through a program in a controlled way. Most importantly, you have four controls here, as shown in Figure 10-11. These controls may be familiar to you, as they were first introduced in Chapter 2. From left to right, they are:

➤ **Continue program execution:** Clicking this causes your program to resume execution and run until the program hits another breakpoint (which may be this breakpoint again), or terminate.

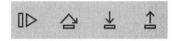

FIGURE 10-11

➤ **Step over:** Clicking this causes the program to jump to the next line of code, where it again pauses and waits for input from you.

➤ **Step into:** Clicking this causes the program to step into a function or method call on the currently paused line of code. If there is no function or method call, it jumps to the next line (as though you had pressed "Step over" instead).

➤ **Step out:** Clicking this causes the program to finish execution of the current stack and then stop when it hits the code that called the function or method with your breakpoint.

Finally, you can terminate your application by clicking the Stop button in the Xcode toolbar at the top of the Xcode window. This terminates your project and allows you to exit the debugger. (This is especially useful if you happen to set a breakpoint on a function that gets called dozens or hundreds of times—such as `sliderChanged()`!)

Removing or Disabling Breakpoints

Removing a breakpoint that you don't need or want anymore is fairly simple. All you have to do is select the file with the breakpoint to bring it up in the editor and then drag it away from the line number gutter. When you've dragged it far enough (a few pixels), an X icon appears. Releasing the drag makes the breakpoint disappear in a puff of smoke (similar to how you remove icons from the Dock) and the breakpoint no longer triggers when your program is running.

If you don't like dragging a breakpoint and turning it into smoke, you can also Control- or right-click the breakpoint and select Delete Breakpoint from the contextual menu to remove it.

You can also *disable* a breakpoint instead of removing it entirely. Right-click a breakpoint and select Disable Breakpoint to disable it. The blue icon will become translucent to indicate that it has been disabled. Disabled breakpoints will not be triggered when running your program, but you can easily re-enable them by right-clicking on a disabled breakpoint and selected Enable Breakpoint if you need to use them again. You can also disable a breakpoint by clicking on it once and re-enable it by clicking once on it again.

Go ahead and delete the breakpoint you set on line 10 of `ViewController.swift`. You won't be needing it anymore. In the next section, you'll learn a more advanced technique for triggering breakpoints only when certain conditions occur.

Setting Conditional Breakpoints

The usefulness of basic breakpoints should be fairly obvious by now, but it's also easy to see how they can actually get in the way of development. You might want to trigger a breakpoint only if a certain condition is reached—a variable falls below a certain value, for example. A basic breakpoint is triggered *every time* a line of code is executed. Luckily, however, you can add a condition to a breakpoint so that it is only invoked if that condition occurs:

1. **Set conditions on breakpoints through their edit menu.** For this example, go ahead and set a breakpoint on line 11 of `ViewController.swift`. To bring up its edit menu, right-click the breakpoint and select Edit Breakpoint, as shown in Figure 10-12.

2. **In the breakpoint editor popover, locate a field called Condition.** Here, you can set a condition that will trigger the breakpoint. You can use any valid expression and make use of any variables that are in scope for the function or method in which the breakpoint is being set.

3. **Enter val < 25 in the Condition field, as shown in Figure 10-13.** This will cause the breakpoint to trigger only when the slider's value drops below 25.

4. **Compile and run your program and drag the slider to the right.** Unlike last time, you should notice that the breakpoint is *not* triggered merely when dragging the slider.

5. **Drag the slider all the way to the left.** The breakpoint will trigger when the slider drops below 25. As before, the app's UI will stop responding (preventing you from dragging the slider any further to the left), and the debugger console will open in Xcode, allowing you to enter commands.

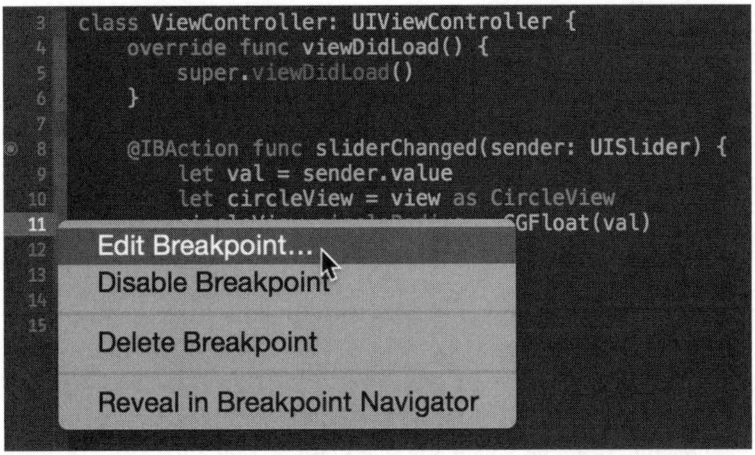

FIGURE 10-12

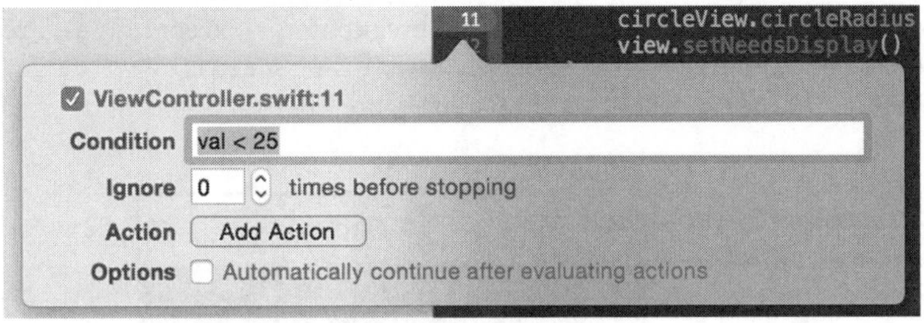

FIGURE 10-13

Aside from the trigger, conditional breakpoints are no different from regular breakpoints. You can interact with your program in exactly the same way as before. The sole difference is that these breakpoints are only triggered when the given condition happens.

When you're done investigating your breakpoint, remove it. You're about to learn about the third type of breakpoint available to you: symbolic breakpoints.

Setting Symbolic Breakpoints

Xcode offers one more type of breakpoint: the symbolic breakpoint. A symbolic breakpoint is triggered whenever a given function or method is called. The function or method need not be a part of your own source code; you can set up symbolic breakpoints to trigger for functions or methods in system or third-party frameworks, too.

Setting up a symbolic breakpoint is a bit different than setting other breakpoints. You create a symbolic breakpoint in Xcode's *breakpoint navigator*, as illustrated in the following steps:

1. **Select the breakpoint navigator from Xcode's navigator ribbon in the top left of the main Xcode window.** The breakpoint navigator is the seventh icon from the left, which looks like an arrow pointing to the right, as shown in Figure 10-14. You can also hit ⌘-7 to bring up the breakpoint navigator.

FIGURE 10-14

Right now, the breakpoint navigator should show "No Breakpoints." (If it doesn't, delete any you may have added.)

2. **Add a new breakpoint.** You can do this by clicking the plus (+) button at the bottom of the breakpoint navigator pane. Add a symbolic breakpoint by selecting Add Symbolic Breakpoint from the popup menu. This will bring up a new popover window that allows you to create a symbolic breakpoint.

3. **Create a breakpoint that will trigger whenever `sliderChanged()` is called.** You did this before when working through the section on conditional breakpoints—except now you're creating it as a symbolic breakpoint. To set it this time, enter `ViewController`
`.sliderChanged()` in the Symbol text field, as shown in Figure 10-15.

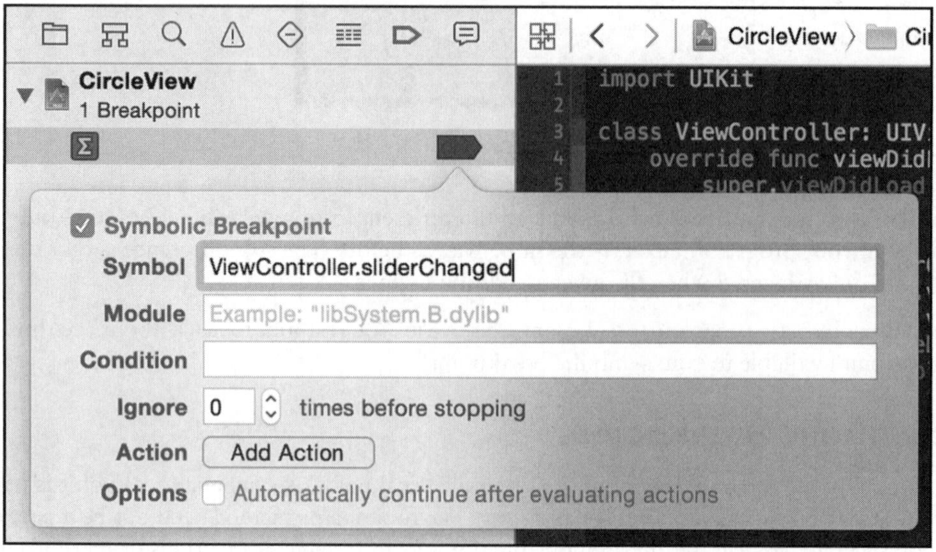

FIGURE 10-15

4. **You can edit conditions for symbolic breakpoints, just as you did for conditional breakpoints.** As with conditional breakpoints, this causes the breakpoint to trigger only when the function or method is called *and* a given condition is met. Leave the conditional fields blank for now, but be aware that they exist; they could be useful to you in the future.

5. **After creating the breakpoint, compile and run your program again.** Drag the slider left or right. As before, you'll be dumped back into the debugger console in Xcode, and you'll be able to enter commands or navigate your program as you see fit.

Symbolic breakpoints are very useful for stopping program execution within code that you don't control. For code that you *do* control, it can be much easier to set breakpoints simply by clicking on a line of code. However, symbolic breakpoints offer another, more flexible way to trigger the debugger in your application.

Exploring the Debugger

To get a better feel for how the debugger works, you'll create a simple command-line tool that will demonstrate the operations of the debugger, such as stepping into and out of code and returning from functions.

1. **Create a new Xcode project.** Launch Xcode and click the Create a new Xcode project button. Select Command Line Tool from the OS X Application templates and click Next. Name your new project **DebuggerExplorer**. Click Next and save your project.

2. **Create a simple command-line tool.** Select `main.swift` from the file navigator window. Replace the existing code with the code in Listing 10-4.

LISTING 10-4: main.swift

```swift
import Foundation

func sayHello(name: String) {
    println("Inside function sayHello()")
    println("Hello, \(name)!")
    println("Leaving function sayHello()")
}

func sayGoodbye(name: String) {
    println("Inside function sayGoodbye()")
    println("Goodbye, \(name)!")
    println("Leaving function sayGoodbye()")
}

func sayFavoriteNumber(n: Int) {
    println("My favorite number is \(n)")
}

println("Hello, world!")

var name = "Jane"

// Notice how the debugger steps over comments
```

continues

continued

```
sayHello(name)
println("Returned from function sayHello()")

sayGoodbye(name)
var x = 10
println("Returned from function sayGoodbye()")
println("Your name is \(name).")

name = "Alice"
x = 20

println("My name is \(name).")
sayFavoriteNumber(x)
println("It was nice meeting you.")
```

You can now explore the action of the debugger in a more interactive way using this program.

3. **Build and run the program.** You should see output in the console in Xcode's bottom middle pane. Observe how the program runs without any breakpoints. Your output should look like this:

    ```
    Hello, world!
    Inside function sayHello()
    Hello, Jane!
    Leaving function sayHello()
    Returned from function sayHello()
    Inside function sayGoodbye()
    Goodbye, Jane!
    Leaving function sayGoodbye()
    Returned from function sayGoodbye()
    Your name is Jane.
    My name is Alice.
    My favorite number is 20.
    It was nice meeting you.
    Program ended with exit code: 0
    ```

4. **Add a few breakpoints to your program to see how different kinds of breakpoints affect the flow of the debugger.** First, set a breakpoint on Line 19 of the program, the line with `println("Hello, world!")`, by clicking on the line number. Then add a symbolic breakpoint and set it to break on the symbol `sayFavoriteNumber`. Finally, add a conditional breakpoint that will break on Line 32—`name = "Alice"`—but edit the breakpoint so the break condition is `name == "Jane"`.

5. **Build and run your program again.** This time, you should be dropped into the debugger console as soon as your program hits Line 19 (which is immediately, because Line 19 is the first executable line of the program). Click Step Over. Notice that the debugger moves to the next line of code, 21 (because Line 20 is a blank line) and pauses execution there. In the debugger console, enter the command **po name**. You should see that an empty string has returned. This is because execution has paused *on* Line 21, but it has not been executed yet, so the variable name has not yet been initialized.

6. **Click Step Over again.** The debugger once again pauses, this time on Line 24, the first call to the `sayHello()` function. It completely skipped over Line 23 because that is just a comment, and, like the compiler, the debugger ignores commented lines of code.

> **NOTE** *Remember that you can execute code in the debugger that can have an effect on the running program. You can execute code in the debugger by entering the command* **expr**, *followed by the code that should be executed. Change the value of* name *to* Tom *by entering* **expr name = "Tom"** *in the debugger console and pressing Return. Then enter the command* **po name**. *You should see that* name *is now* "Tom" *instead of* "Jane".*

7. **Click Step Over to execute this line of code.** The function is called, and you should see the following lines of text printed to the console:

```
Inside function sayHello()
Hello, Tom!
Leaving function sayHello()
```

However, because you did not set a breakpoint in the function `sayHello()`, the debugger does not pause execution inside that function call. Instead, it *steps over* the function call, and pauses execution on Line 25, the line of code immediately after the function call. You should also note that `sayHello()` printed the modified value of the variable name, *not* its original value of "Jane".

8. **Click Step Over again.** Now the debugger pauses on the call to `sayGoodbye()`. This time, click Step Into. Notice that instead of making the function call and pausing on Line 28, the debugger drops you into the function call and pauses execution on Line 10, the first line of `sayGoodbye()`. You can click Step Over to execute Line 10 and pause the debugger on Line 11. In fact, any of the usual debugger commands will work here—stepping into a function is no different from debugging any other lines of code.

9. **Click Step Out.** Notice that the function is executed, as you see the following lines printed to the console:

```
Inside function sayGoodbye()
Goodbye, Tom!
Leaving function sayGoodbye()
```

Because you chose to step out of the function call, execution did not pause on subsequent lines of the function. The debugger only paused after the function had been executed to completion, and you are back at the original function call (Line 27).

10. **Click Continue to continue execution.** The debugger will now keep executing lines until it hits another breakpoint (including a conditional or symbolic breakpoint) or the program finishes running. Notice that the debugger does *not* pause on Line 32. This is the conditional breakpoint you set, and it is triggered *only* when the variable name has the value "Jane". This is not the case, because you modified name to have the value "Tom", so the breakpoint is not triggered.

> **NOTE** *The debugger* will *break in the first line of the function* `sayFavoriteNumber()`. *This is because you set a symbolic breakpoint for the symbol* `sayFavoriteNumber`, *so whenever the function is called, the debugger will pause execution in the first line of the function.*

11. **Click Continue to resume executing the program.** There are no more breakpoints, so the program will run to completion and exit.

SUMMARY

Debugging code is never easy, but with the help of Xcode's debugger, tracking down problems in code can be faster and more directed. In this chapter, you learned several techniques for debugging your software, ranging from the use of simple print statements to track down problems, to the use of LLVM's debugger tool to gain fine-grained control over your program's execution. With these tools and techniques at your disposal, you'll find that debugging becomes less of the chore it once was and more of a straightforward task that is a fundamental part of software construction. Who knows? Now that you know how to use advanced debugging techniques, you may even find that tracking down bugs in your program is actually fun. At the very least, it should be quick and should allow you to quickly advance to releasing your code.

11

The Swift Runtime

WHAT'S IN THIS CHAPTER?

➤ Understanding the Objective-C runtime

➤ Dispatching methods in Objective-C

➤ Investigating the Swift runtime

➤ Comparing and contrasting method dispatch in Swift

➤ Understanding how programs are assembled in Swift

WROX.COM CODE DOWNLOADS FOR THIS CHAPTER

You can find the wrox.com downloads for this chapter at http://www.wrox.com/go/proswift on the Download Code tab. The code for this chapter is contained in the following files:

➤ `Cats.playground`

➤ `hello.c`

➤ `objc-message.s`

➤ `objc-method.s`

➤ `objc-msgsend.s`

➤ `test.c`

➤ `test.c.s`

➤ `test.m`

➤ `test.m.s`

➤ `test.swift`

➤ `test.swift.s`

Programming languages are made up of many parts. The most obvious are the language's syntactic and semantic elements. The language's standard library can be considered a major part of the language's form as well. Less commonly noticed than these parts, but no less crucial, is the language's runtime. Some languages, such as Java, have enormous runtimes that include an entire virtual machine. Others, like C, have very small runtimes that are a small set of functions that support the language. Swift, on the other hand, can be said to have a two-part runtime: the specific code that allows the execution of programs written in Swift, as well as the Objective-C runtime, which Swift also makes heavy use of. Because the Objective-C runtime is also important to Swift programs, this chapter explores the Swift runtime as well as the Objective-C runtime that has supported programs since the beginning of Mac OS X.

WHAT IS A RUNTIME?

A language's *runtime* is the collection of code that supports programs written in the language. C programmers, as well as Objective-C programmers who have implemented command-line programs or examined the `main.m` file automatically included in new Xcode projects, should be familiar with the `main()` function. In C and Objective-C programs, the `main()` function is the entry point into the program; that is, when a program is launched, the operating system invokes the `main()` function to start the program. Its return value, which is an integer, is also used when exiting the program to return an exit code to the operating system (on Unix-based systems such as OS X and iOS, `main()` returns 0 to indicate it exited with no errors).

While this may initially seem like magic, behind the scenes, every C and Objective-C program actually has a bit of code that sets up the program's environment (including any command-line arguments passed to the program) and then calls the program's `main()` function. After `main()` exits, this bit of code then passes the return value of `main()` back to the operating system. It is, in fact, this bit of code, rather than `main()` itself, that the operating system invokes when launching a program.

This bit of code is part of the C language's *runtime*. Every programming language, whether compiled or interpreted, statically or dynamically typed, has a runtime. Some runtimes are very complex: For example, the runtimes for both the Java and C# languages are large bodies of code (the Java Runtime Environment and the Common Language Runtime, respectively). The runtimes for languages such as Java and C# are complex because many aspects of the language are executed when the language is running. C, on the other hand, has a relatively small runtime. The C compiler resolves many of C's language features, so only a few features of the language need be implemented in the runtime library itself.

Objective-C programs, like those written in C, are compiled to native machine code. Because Objective-C is a dynamic language, many of its features are not actually resolved until runtime. For example, the methods that an object implements are unknown until runtime, when a message passes to an object. A number of Objective-C's other language features, such as categories and method swizzling, require runtime support and are implemented as part of the Objective-C runtime.

Swift, like Objective-C, is also compiled to native machine code. As with both Objective-C and C, Swift makes use of a set of functions that enable programs written in the language to run properly—in other words, it, too, has a runtime. However, pure Swift code does not feature many of the dynamic attributes of its Objective-C cousin, while adding a host of other features (such as its type system) that are not present in Objective-C. These added features are supported at least in part by the Swift runtime (the compiler itself enables many of Swift's unique features as well). Because Swift makes heavy use of both Objective-C and the Objective-C runtime, you can think of the Objective-C runtime as a component of a Swift program as well. This mix results in a language runtime that is somewhat more complex than either C or Objective-C, although Swift's runtime doesn't have the complexity of a language like Java and the Java Virtual Machine.

As a Swift programmer, it's worth taking the time to understand both the Swift and Objective-C runtimes because your programs can make use of both. A more thorough understanding of the language runtimes not only gives you a deeper understanding of Swift as a language, but it can make troubleshooting bugs or even simply writing software in Swift easier. To start off, let's take a look at some of the features of the Objective-C runtime because that is fundamental to software development on both iOS and OS X, and then let's move on to new and different aspects of the Swift runtime itself.

UNDERSTANDING THE OBJECTIVE-C RUNTIME

Before embarking on a journey through the Swift runtime, it is wise to have an understanding of the Objective-C runtime as well as some of the concepts Objective-C embodies. While this knowledge is not, strictly speaking, necessary for programming in Swift (or in Objective-C, for that matter), it will give you a better understanding of how Swift programs are built and run and highlight some of the key differences between Objective-C and Swift, as well as their respective runtimes.

Unlike Swift, Objective-C is a dynamic language. Most crucially, method calls are not resolved until runtime, a feature known as *dynamic binding*. Objective-C is an amalgamation of concepts from both C and Smalltalk, and it models its method resolution on Smalltalk. When a message is received by an Objective-C object (that is, a method is invoked on it), the exact implementation of the associated method is looked up at runtime (using the function `objc_msgSend()`, from the Objective-C runtime), and that implementation is invoked.

The Objective-C runtime packages the name of a method being invoked (that is, a message being sent to an object) into a *selector*. When studying the Objective-C runtime, it is important to understand the concept of the selector, as well as what happens when a method is called on an object. Finally, a basic understanding of how classes are loaded and managed by the runtime is helpful to programmers working with Objective-C.

With that in mind, take a look at some of the key points of the Objective-C runtime. Afterwards, you'll have a better understanding of the OS X and iOS programming models and can see how Swift both compares and contrasts to its Objective-C counterpart.

Dispatching Methods Dynamically in Objective-C

The concept of *data encapsulation* is central to object-oriented programming languages. Instances of classes contain data members that hold the state of the instance. Classes control access to these data members and expose related behavior through the use of methods. Methods represent the manner in which outside code can interact with, and possibly control, instances of the class and thus do useful work and computations.

Many object-oriented languages, such as Swift, Java, and C++, are static languages. Classes have a consistent, well-defined set of methods, and instances of classes have a type that is known at compile time. The compiler resolves method calls at compile time, effectively turning them into function calls. As in C, these function calls have a known address in memory. The compiler changes method calls into calls to these blocks of code.

Some object-oriented programming languages, including Objective-C, are dynamic—the type of the instance is not known until the program runs. In these languages, the runtime itself, instead of a compiler, resolves the method calls, deciding what code to dispatch to (even in dynamic languages that have a compile phase, like Objective-C). This feature enables method calls to be constructed during the lifetime of the program, such as from strings, and also allows methods to be called on objects of unknown types, which may or may not respond to the message.

In languages that support such dynamic method resolution, methods can often be wrapped up as an object and passed around similarly to other data types (a feature rarely supported in static languages like Java or C++). In Objective-C, such structures are referred to as *selectors*.

An Objective-C selector (often denoted by its data type, SEL) identifies only the name of a method, not the implementation. (This differs from some languages, which wrap both the name and implementation into a single object that can be passed around as a parameter.) Selectors can be passed around as parameters to other methods (or functions); the base class has a mechanism for sending a message encapsulated in a selector to a class, and the runtime can resolve that selector into an actual method implementation.

> **METHOD IMPLEMENTATIONS**
>
> Objective-C methods are described by two data types: a selector (SEL), which represents the *name* of a method, and an implementation (IMP), which represents the actual code that is executed when a method is called (they are basically just C function pointers). Like SEL structures, IMP can be retrieved via the runtime and passed around to functions and methods as well. Most of the time, you only work with selectors. You use IMP structures when accessing some of the more advanced features of the Objective-C runtime. You can think of a SEL as an abstract representation of an Objective-C method and an IMP as the concrete implementation.

What is an Objective-C SEL? The header file for the Objective-C runtime (found at /usr/include/objc/objc.h) defines it as having the type struct objc_selector *. Unfortunately, the Objective-C header files do not make any mention, nor define the structure, of a struct objc_selector. As it turns out, the exact structure is defined internally by the compiler and depends on whether you are using the OS X or GNU runtimes. In OS X, SEL maps to a simple C string, as you can see in this simple bit of code, which outputs the word hello:

```
NSLog(@"%s", @selector(hello));
```

> **NOTE** *On the other hand, the GNU runtime maps a SEL to a C struct that contains two char * data types, one to hold the name of the method and the other to hold its parameter types.*

Selectors are an important part of Objective-C. They are fundamental to its notion of *message passing*, which describes the way methods are invoked in Objective-C.

Message Passing

Smalltalk, one of the first object-oriented programming languages and a prime inspiration for Objective-C, introduced *message passing*, a language feature in which messages are passed to a process, and the process's runtime invokes the code necessary to respond to that message. This feature differs from many object-oriented languages, in which a method is invoked directly on an object, and thus the process runs the implementation of that method. A true message passing systems allows for a great degree of flexibility, as well as improvements in areas like concurrency. While Smalltalk-76 pioneered this feature, pure message passing was eventually dropped from the language; Smalltalk-80 had a method invocation system much more similar to traditional procedure calling.

While many programmers describe Objective-C as having message passing, it is much more akin to a typical procedure-calling system as seen in languages like Java and C++, albeit with support for the dynamic nature of the language. Still, because of the dynamic nature of Objective-C, it can support features and a degree of flexibility not seen in many other object-oriented programming languages. In additional, Objective-C has a programming style and conceptual model for building software. The core OS X and iOS frameworks, and many other pieces of Objective-C code seen in the wild, take great advantage of this flexibility and power. It is hard to be an advanced Objective-C programmer without knowledge of the runtime's method invocation architecture.

> **NOTE** *Erlang, a language created by Ericsson for use in its phone switches, features a message passing system that is much more in the spirit of Smalltalk-76. Such a system becomes very powerful when implementing asynchronous programs. Whereas Objective-C is essentially a combination of C and Smalltalk, Erlang is essentially a combination of Smalltalk and Prolog. While Smalltalk is not commonly used nowadays, its influence can be felt in many modern programming languages.*

Central to Objective-C's message passing architecture are the selectors described previously. Selectors package a method call, or message, into a structure that can be passed between functions and methods. Together, SEL and IMP structures define the implementation of an Objective-C method. They enable Objective-C's *dynamic binding* (also known as *late binding*), which in turn contributes to Objective-C's flexibility. Message forwarding allows an object to catch and act on messages to which it does not explicitly respond.

Resolving Methods

The most important aspect of the Objective-C runtime is the part that manages the forwarding and dispatch of Objective-C messages to objects. Objective-C is a dynamic language, meaning that most of the decisions and functionality of the language are deferred until runtime, rather than being compiled. To understand this distinction, first consider how a simple C program is compiled. Take a look at Listing 11-1, a typical Hello World program written in C:

LISTING 11-1: hello.C

```c
#include <stdio.h>

int main (int argc, char const *argv[])
{
    printf("Hello, world!\n");
    return 0;
}
```

Listing 11-1 shows a simple C program with one function, `main()`, that calls one other function, `printf()`, that is available in the C standard library. C functions are just blocks of code that reside in memory; the function name is essentially a label for the memory address of the first instruction of the function. The compiler compiles this C code into native code, resolving the address of `printf()` and issuing an instruction for the code to jump to that address to execute the `printf()` call.

> **NOTE** *To be more precise, the linker would resolve the address of* `printf()` *because it is part of an external library. Typically, however, the linker is automatically invoked by the compiler so it is easier to describe it as part of the compiler's workflow.*

Because of their language features, object-oriented languages—even ones that are typically compiled, such as C++, Swift, and Objective-C—require a bit more work to link methods to actual code. For example, like Objective-C, C++ allows subclasses to override methods from their parent classes. Because of the polymorphic nature of the language, the compiler cannot resolve method calls to a specific memory address. Instead, C++ uses a system of *virtual method tables*, or *vtables*, to invoke the proper method at runtime. Each object has a vtable that maps method invocations to their proper implementations.

Objective-C has a system that is conceptually similar to the `vtables` of C++, although the exact implementation is different (and supports some additional language features not present in C++). The primary interface to Objective-C's method dispatching system is the function `objc_msgSend()`, found in `libobjc` and exposed via the `objc/message.h` header file.

Bear in mind that Objective-C is essentially just a set of extensions to C that allow you to use it as an object-oriented programming language. Objective-C strives to add as little overhead to C as possible; as a result, it embraces C's calling conventions throughout its runtime. Every method call is really just a call to the runtime's `objc_msgSend()` function, a dispatcher that determines what function to actually call, and then jumps into it.

> **NOTE** *In fact, the early implementations of Objective-C were simply preprocessors for C; back then, Objective-C did not have a separate compiler.*

While you do not generally call `objc_msgSend()`, every method invocation is effectively turned into a call to this function. For example, consider the simple Hello World program written in Objective-C in Listing 11-2.

LISTING 11-2: objc-method.m

```
#import <Foundation/Foundation.h>

@interface HelloWorld : NSObject
- (void)sayHello;
@end

@implementation HelloWorld

- (void)sayHello
{
    printf("Hello, world!\n");
}

@end

int main (int argc, char const *argv[])
{
    @autoreleasepool {
        HelloWorld *hello = [[HelloWorld alloc] init];
        [hello sayHello];
        [hello release];
    }
    return 0;
}
```

You can also write the program in Listing 11-2 to call `objc_msgSend()` directly, demonstrating that both these lines of code are identical:

```
[hello sayHello];
objc_msgSend(hello, @selector(sayHello));
```

Compiling and running the program in Listing 11-3 shows the same output as the program in Listing 11-2.

LISTING 11-3: objc-msgsend.m

```
#import <objc/message.h>
#import <Foundation/Foundation.h>

@interface HelloWorld : NSObject
- (void)sayHello;
@end

@implementation HelloWorld

- (void)sayHello
```

continues

continued

```
{
    printf("Hello, world!\n");
}

@end

int main (int argc, char const *argv[])
{
    @autoreleasepool {
        HelloWorld *hello = [[HelloWorld alloc] init];
        objc_msgSend(hello, @selector(sayHello));
        [hello release];
    }
    return 0;
}
```

In fact, if you examine the assembly output for the `main()` function from `objc-method.m`, you will find a number of calls to `objc_msgSend()`. You can view the assembly output by running `clang` with the `-S` flag. Running `clang -S objc-method.m` outputs a file containing the program's assembly code at `objc-method.s`. The output of `objc-method.s` is shown in Listing 11-4.

LISTING 11-4: objc-method.s

```
Ltmp9:
        .cfi_def_cfa_register %rbp
        subq    $32, %rsp
        movl    $0, -4(%rbp)
        movl    %edi, -8(%rbp)
        movq    %rsi, -16(%rbp)
        callq   _objc_autoreleasePoolPush
        movq    L_OBJC_CLASSLIST_REFERENCES_$_(%rip), %rsi
        movq    L_OBJC_SELECTOR_REFERENCES_(%rip), %rcx
        movq    %rsi, %rdi
        movq    %rcx, %rsi
        movq    %rax, -32(%rbp)         ## 8-byte Spill
        callq   _objc_msgSend
        movq    L_OBJC_SELECTOR_REFERENCES_3(%rip), %rsi
        movq    %rax, %rdi
        callq   _objc_msgSend
        movq    %rax, -24(%rbp)
        movq    -24(%rbp), %rax
        movq    L_OBJC_SELECTOR_REFERENCES_4(%rip), %rsi
        movq    %rax, %rdi
        callq   _objc_msgSend
        movq    -24(%rbp), %rax
        movq    L_OBJC_SELECTOR_REFERENCES_6(%rip), %rsi
        movq    %rax, %rdi
        callq   _objc_msgSend
        movq    -32(%rbp), %rdi         ## 8-byte Reload
        callq   _objc_autoreleasePoolPop
```

```
movl    $0, %eax
addq    $32, %rsp
popq    %rbp
ret
.cfi_endproc
```

The runtime library's `objc_msgSend()` function is the primary way through which Objective-C code interfaces with its method dispatch system, but how does it work? What exactly does `objc_msgSend()` do?

The basics of `objc_msgSend()` are fairly simple. Firstly, if you are familiar with Objective-C, you probably know that if you send a message to `nil`, the return value is `nil`. This language feature is implemented as part of `objc_msgSend()`, which first checks to see if the receiver is `nil` and returns `nil` if it is.

After this, you get into the meat and bones of `objc_msgSend()`—the part that makes the dynamic dispatch system actually work. The next thing `objc_msgSend()` does is retrieve the object's class. Every object has an instance variable called `isa` that points to its class. `objc_msgSend()` needs this object because method implementations are associated with a *class*, not individual instances of that class.

Once `objc_msgSend()` has the receiver's class, it searches the class's *method cache* to find the actual implementation of the method to invoke. Every class has a cache that associates a given selector to a method implementation. Because a method implementation is essentially just a C function, the runtime can simply jump to the start of the function (literally, by issuing an unconditional jump instruction to the CPU) to invoke the method.

Finally, the code representing the method is run, and thanks to use of an unconditional jump in `objc_msgSend()`, the return value of that method (which, again, is simply a C function) is returned to the caller.

Sometimes the method implementation is not found in the class's method cache. In such cases, the runtime must do a longer, more intensive search for the method implementation for a given selector. Because this search is so exhaustive, it is performed very rarely—generally only once per unique method because after a method implementation is found, it is added to the class's method cache (and the implementation is resolved using the previously described lookup instead).

Two conditions may occur when this exhaustive lookup is performed: A method implementation may be found, or the runtime may fail to find a method implementation (because one was never defined for the receiver's class). If a method implementation *is* found, it is added to the class's method cache, and the runtime jumps to the associated function (as described earlier). However, if the method implementation is *not* found, then the code for resolving a missing method is invoked instead.

Messages and Methods

The runtime defines several data structures for dealing with messages and method implementations. The basic data structure is a `SEL`, which represents a message in Objective-C. A `SEL` is a type definition for a `struct objc_selector *`:

```
typedef struct objc_selector *SEL;
```

> **NOTE** *Unlike a method, an Objective-C selector is not tied to a specific method implementation or class. Rather, it is an abstract representation of a message.*

A `struct objc_selector` is an opaque data type; its exact layout is not exposed. However, on OS X and iOS, a `struct objc_selector` is simply a C string internally.

On the other hand, method *implementations*, represented by an `IMP` data structure, are more clearly defined in the Objective-C runtime. While the `SEL` structure represents a message, the `IMP` structure represents an actual method implementation. It is simply a C function with the following type:

```
typedef id (*IMP)(id, SEL, ...);
```

That is, it is a pointer to a function that returns an `id` and takes an `id`, a `SEL`, and a variable number of arguments. Experienced Objective-C programmers are probably familiar with the fact that every method receives two parameters implicitly: `self`, representing the method's receiver, and `_cmd`, the `SEL` describing the method being called. The `IMP` also takes variable arguments because the arguments passed to each individual method vary and cannot be generalized.

Finally, the runtime also defines a data type for working with methods. `Method` structures are a type definition for `struct objc_method *`:

```
typedef struct objc_method *Method;
```

Again, this is an opaque data type. Conceptually, it wraps up a selector (`SEL`), a method implementation (`IMP`), and the return type and argument types of the method implementation (as returned by the `@encode` directive, described in the next section). However, as an opaque data type, its members are not used directly. The `Method` is mostly used by the runtime for passing method implementations and metadata between its own components.

EXPLORING THE SWIFT RUNTIME

Because much of Swift operates on top of or in conjunction with Objective-C code, programs written in Swift typically deal with both the Objective-C runtime and the Swift runtime. Because of the nature of Swift—namely, that it is a static language—the Swift runtime differs considerably from that of Objective-C's in some key places. One of the biggest, most important differences is in how Swift handles method dispatching at runtime.

In contrast to Objective-C, Swift does not allow for the highly dynamic method resolution that Objective-C's message passing concept allows for. Many of Objective-C's classic features, such as the ability to respond to messages not explicitly implemented by the class, its ability to "swizzle" methods (that is, replace methods in other classes at runtime), and its ability to define methods at runtime, are not possible in Swift. In exchange for the loss of these features, Swift grants superior type safety and, in theory, improved performance when dispatching methods. (Objective-C's method dispatching mechanism tends to be slower than that of languages like C++ because implementations have to be looked up in a hash table at runtime—although thanks to several tricks used by the Objective-C runtime implementation, the performance hit is generally negligible.)

Instead of using a dynamic method dispatching system like Objective-C, Swift uses *virtual method tables*, or *vtables*. Virtual method tables are also used by C++ for its method dispatching.

Understanding Virtual Method Tables

In C, a function can basically be thought of as a label for a block of code held somewhere in memory. It is easy, even trivial, for the compiler to resolve function calls to memory addresses at compile time. Once the compiler has figured out how to assemble and lay out the function blocks in memory, it can go through and rewrite function calls to be jumps to that bit of memory. (Of course, it's not *quite* that simple because the compiler also has to set up stacks and remember where to jump back to after a function returns—but the basic concept of jumping to a memory location still applies.)

Resolving function calls in object-oriented languages is a bit harder due to the fact that classes can inherit from other classes, and in doing so, can override methods in the parent class. In the case of deeply nested object hierarchies, a class may even override methods in its parent's parent class, and so on. (Things get even more complicated in languages that allow multiple inheritance, such as C++.) And an overridden method may also call its parent class's implementation as well.

Consider the simple class hierarchy in Listing 11-5. Here you have a base class, `Cat`, and two subclasses, `Housecat` and `Cougar`. Each one implements its own `speak()` method, which prints a different line. Three `Cat` variables are declared, one for each class, and `speak()` is called on each of them.

LISTING 11-5: Cats.playground

```
class Cat {
    func speak() {
        println("The cat purrs.")
    }
}

class Housecat: Cat {
    override func speak() {
        println("Meow!")
    }
}

class Cougar: Cat {
    override func speak() {
        println("Roar!")
    }
}

let cat1: Cat = Cat()
let cat2: Cat = Housecat()
let cat3: Cat = Cougar()

cat1.speak()
cat2.speak()
cat3.speak()
```

The problem here should be fairly obvious. The cat2 and cat3 constants are typed as Cat, but really they are a Housecat and a Cougar, respectively. Calls to the speak() method should invoke the method implementation in the appropriate subclass, not simply the base class's implementation.

Because of this nuance, the compiler cannot simply rewrite cat2.speak() and cat3.speak() as a jump to a specific area of memory. It won't know until runtime which implementation should *actually* be called.

One solution to this problem is virtual method tables, also known as *vtables*. Virtual method tables are simply an array of function pointers. Each item points to the implementation for a given function. Every class has one instance of a virtual table, so each instance of a given class shares a virtual table. (This means, of course, that you cannot change methods on a per-instance basis, as you can in some object-oriented languages, such as Python.)

What does a virtual method table look like conceptually, though? To answer that question, let's modify the Cat class hierarchy from Listing 11-5 to add another method, eat(), that is only defined in the Cat base class. The new implementation of this class hierarchy is shown in Listing 11-6.

LISTING 11-6: Cats.playground

```
class Cat {
    func eat() {
        println("The cat eats some food")
    }

    func speak() {
        println("The cat purrs.")
    }
}

class Housecat: Cat {
    override func speak() {
        println("Meow!")
    }
}

class Cougar: Cat {
    override func speak() {
        println("Roar!")
    }
}

let cat1: Cat = Cat()
let cat2: Cat = Housecat()
let cat3: Cat = Cougar()

cat1.speak()
cat1.eat()
cat2.speak()
cat2.eat()
cat3.speak()
cat3.eat()
```

You can think of the virtual method table for the Cat base class as being laid out like this:

```
0: pointer to Cat.eat()
1: pointer to Cat.speak()
```

Neither Housecat nor Cougar override eat(); instances essentially defer to the Cat base class for their implementations of the eat() method. (In other words, calls to cat2.eat() and cat3.eat() are calling the Cat class's eat() method.) The virtual table for the Housecat class looks like this:

```
0: pointer to Cat.eat()
1: pointer to Housecat.speak()
```

Likewise, the virtual table for the Cougar class looks like this:

```
0: pointer to Cat.eat()
1: pointer to Cougar.eat()
```

When cat2.speak() is called, for example, the runtime looks up the implementation of the Housecat class's implementation of eat() in the virtual method table. This returns a pointer to that implementation, which is then invoked, and you see "Meow!" appear in the console.

At first glance, you may wonder how this is any different from the way methods are resolved and dispatched in the Objective-C runtime. After all, both Swift and Objective-C involve looking up a method implementation at runtime and jumping to it. The key difference here is that virtual method tables are indexed by number—they're an *array*—whereas implementations are stored in a hash table in Objective-C. Because of this difference, the compiler can emit code to grab a specific implementation because both the memory location of the virtual table and the offset of a given method are known at compile time (the offset is just an index into the array). Theoretically, this is a bit faster than searching a hash table for a given implementation. Unfortunately, it also means that method implementations cannot be changed or swapped out at runtime because the virtual table is a static data structure.

Loading Swift Programs

Another aspect of the Swift runtime that is worth investigation is how programs are actually built by the compiler and loaded into memory. For the most part, the code that the Swift compiler emits is nearly identical to that of the C and Objective-C compilers, but there are a few differences that are worth taking a look at, as they shed some light on how Swift works under the hood. It's also helpful to see how to investigate the actual code that is emitted by the compiler for a given program, as this is a technique that you can use further down the road to investigate your own programs.

First, consider a simple C program that simply sets up a main() method and returns 0 immediately, as shown in Listing 11-7.

LISTING 11-7: Test.c

```c
int main(int argc, char **argv)
{
    return 0;
}
```

You can see what assembly code the compiler generates for the program by running `clang -S` `test.c` (assembly code is a human-readable representation of the code that is actually executed by the processor). This outputs a file at `test.s` containing the assembly code for the program in `test.c`. Listing 11-8 shows the assembly output for this program.

LISTING 11-8: test.c.s

```
        .section      __TEXT,__text,regular,pure_instructions
        .globl  _main
        .align  4, 0x90
_main:                                    ## @main
        .cfi_startproc
## BB#0:
        pushq   %rbp
Ltmp2:
        .cfi_def_cfa_offset 16
Ltmp3:
        .cfi_offset %rbp, -16
        movq    %rsp, %rbp
Ltmp4:
        .cfi_def_cfa_register %rbp
        movl    $0, %eax
        movl    $0, -4(%rbp)
        movl    %edi, -8(%rbp)
        movq    %rsi, -16(%rbp)
        popq    %rbp
        retq
        .cfi_endproc


    .subsections_via_symbols
```

Assembly language can be as easy to read as a foreign language if you're not familiar with it, but given the code for such a simple C program, it should be easy enough to follow along (and you shouldn't concern yourself with the particulars at this point—these samples are just here to contrast with the equivalent Swift program, shown later in this section). The most obvious part of the assembly code output should be the _main label. This is the entry point of the C program's `main()` function. The exact assembly instructions are not important for this investigation; just notice that the compiler emits several instructions to set up the function, its return value (0, in this case), and a return from the function.

Now, create an Objective-C program that is essentially the same thing, a `main()` function that simply returns 0, as shown in Listing 11-9.

LISTING 11-9: test.m

```
int main(int argc, char **argv)
{
    return 0;
}
```

Again, you can generate the assembly instructions for this program by running `clang -S test.m`; the output will be in `test.s`. The compiler will generate something like the output shown in Listing 11-10.

LISTING 11-10: test.m.s

```
        .section       __TEXT,__text,regular,pure_instructions
        .globl   main
        .align   4, 0x90
_main:                                          ## @main
        .cfi_startproc
## BB#0:
        pushq   %rbp
Ltmp2:
        .cfi_def_cfa_offset 16
Ltmp3:
        .cfi_offset %rbp, -16
        movq    %rsp, %rbp
Ltmp4:
        .cfi_def_cfa_register %rbp
        movl    $0, %eax
        movl    $0, -4(%rbp)
        movl    %edi, -8(%rbp)
        movq    %rsi, -16(%rbp)
        popq    %rbp
        retq
        .cfi_endproc

        .section       __DATA,__objc_imageinfo,regular,no_dead_strip
L_OBJC_IMAGE_INFO:
        .long   0
        .long   0


.subsections_via_symbols
```

Notice that the program is nearly the same. If you run a tool like `diff` over both files, you will see that the Objective-C version adds these four lines at the end of metadata at the end:

```
.section       __DATA,__objc_imageinfo,regular,no_dead_strip
L_OBJC_IMAGE_INFO:
        .long 0
        .long 0
```

Otherwise, the output is exactly the same as the C version.

What happens when you compile a similar version of a Swift program instead? First things first: What would a similar Swift program even look like? Because Swift programs do not require a `main()` function, but rather can have program code at the top level of the file, you really just need to create an empty Swift file named `test.swift`. Like the C and Objective-C versions, this Swift program essentially does nothing but runs and exists.

Once you have created an empty Swift file, you can run the Swift compiler on it to generate assembly instructions. This works similarly to clang, but instead, you must run `swiftc -S test.swift`

-o `test.s` to generate the assembly code. `test.s` will contain output similar to that shown in Listing 11-11.

LISTING 11-11: test.swift.s

```
        .section      __TEXT,__text,regular,pure_instructions
        .align 4, 0x90
_top_level_code:
        .cfi_startproc
        pushq   %rbp
Ltmp2:
        .cfi_def_cfa_offset 16
Ltmp3:
        .cfi_offset %rbp, -16
        movq    %rsp, %rbp
Ltmp4:
        .cfi_def_cfa_register %rbp
        popq    %rbp
        retq
        .cfi_endproc

        .globl  main
        .align 4, 0x90
_main:
        .cfi_startproc
        Pushq   %rbp
Ltmp7:
        .cfi_def_cfa_offset 16
Ltmp8:
        .cfi_offset %rbp, -16
        Movq    %rsp, %rbp
Ltmp9:
        .cfi_def_cfa_register %rbp
        subq    $16, %rsp
        movl    %edi, -4(%rbp)
        movq    %rsi, -16(%rbp)
        callq   __TFSsa6C_ARGCVSs5Int32
        movl    -4(%rbp), %edi
        movl    %edi, (%rax)
        callq   __TFSsa6C_ARGVGVSs20UnsafeMutablePointerGS_VSs4Int8__
        movq    -16(%rbp), %rsi
        movq    %rsi, (%rax)
        callq   _top_level_code
        movl    $0, %eax
        addq    $16, %rsp
        popq    %rbp
        retq
        .cfi_endproc

        .linker_option "-lswiftCore"
        .section      __DATA,__objc_imageinfo,regular,no_dead_strip
L_OBJC_IMAGE_INFO:
        .long 0
```

```
    .long 512


    .subsections_via_symbols
```

Notice that the Swift compiler generates a lot more assembly programs for this relatively simple program! In fact, the Swift assembly looks quite a bit different from the C and Objective-C assembly—although there are quite a few common elements as well. The primary difference is the introduction of a new label, _top_level_code. This is actually a function that represents the code at the top level of a Swift file—that is, executable code that does not exist as part of a function, method, or other block of code, instead running as part of a program, sort of like a main function. That's how Swift executes code written at the top level of a file: Instead of forcing you, the programmer, to encapsulate it in a main() function, it goes ahead and essentially creates a function for you. This function is labeled _top_level_code in the assembly.

The Swift compiler also creates an actual main() function, labeled as _main in the assembly output, for you as well. This adheres to the convention that the linker/loader on OS X follows: When a program is launched, some setup is performed, and then execution starts at the program's main() function. A main() function for your Swift program looks remarkably similar to the main() function for your C and Objective-C programs, with a few changes. There are a couple calls to __TFSsa6C_ARGCVSs5Int32 and __TFSsa6C_ARGVGVSs20UnsafeMutablePointerGS_VSs4Int8__. These calls perform some basic handling on the command-line arguments that pass to the main() function. Recall that every function receives a count of arguments passed to (argc) and a vector of the arguments passed to it (argv). Both of these calls are part of the Swift runtime and handle setting up those arguments and passing them to the Swift program (i.e., the _top_level_code subroutine).

Why are those names so weird? The Swift compiler performs name mangling on all of your program's symbols to avoid name clashes if, for example, two classes happen to have the same method name. The algorithm for doing so is complicated, but in the end, it ensures that your program has entirely unique symbols. You can find out what a mangled name refers to by running xcrun swift-demangle <mangled name> at the command line.

After dealing with the arguments, the main() function jumps to _top_level_code—in other words, the program *you* wrote—and executes it to completion.

As you can see, the process for assembling a Swift program is nearly the same as it is for C and Objective-C, with a few differences to deal with Swift's unique features (namely, the lack of an explicit main() function) and its type safety requirements. In the end, whether you're working with C, Objective-C, or Swift, the code is fairly similar.

SUMMARY

A language's runtime supports programs written in that language. It is an essential glue that binds the conceptual elements of the language to the concrete requirements of the platform on which programs written in that language run. While a thorough knowledge of a language's runtime is not essential to writing software in that language, it can be of great help when understanding more advanced elements of the language or troubleshooting problems. On a lighter note, it is also fun to study the component that actually executes the programs you write.

In this chapter, you saw how the Objective-C and Swift runtimes together support programs written in Swift. You also got a look at how the runtimes differ between the two languages, due to their need to support each language's unique features. You got a feel for how programs written in each language are actually assembled into something understandable by the computer and executed on the processor. With this knowledge, you have hopefully gained a deeper understanding of both Swift and Objective-C that will help you as you write programs in either language.

An Overview of C

WHAT'S IN THIS APPENDIX?

➤ Understanding the difference between procedural and object-oriented programming

➤ Using key features of the C programming language

WROX.COM CODE DOWNLOADS FOR THIS APPENDIX

You can find the wrox.com downloads for this appendix at `http://www.wrox.com/go/proswift` on the Download Code tab. The code for this appendix is contained in the following file:

➤ `boolean.c`

➤ `fnptr.c`

➤ `increment.c`

➤ `overflow.c`

This appendix covers the features and concepts introduced by the C programming language. While most Cocoa programs are written in the object-oriented style dictated by Swift (and Objective-C), C's procedural style of programming makes sense for some aspects of a program. Many system services on both OS X and iOS are also exposed only through C, and many third-party libraries and frameworks are written entirely in C, so a firm grasp of C is essential for any skilled Swift programmer.

COMPARING PROCEDURAL AND OBJECT-ORIENTED PROGRAMMING STYLES

Object-oriented programming languages are rooted in the concept of a class. An object, or instance of a class, contains data (instance variables) and defines behavior (methods) that acts on that data and interacts with other objects. This data and behavior are encapsulated in some way so that consumers of those objects can use them without knowing the details of their implementations. Classes also provide a template from which other classes may be created. Programs are modeled as a collection of objects interacting with each other to perform some useful computation or task.

> **NOTE** *Not all object-oriented programming languages use classes. In particular, JavaScript and its predecessor, Self, lack classes, and instead use prototypes in their programming models. What features are necessary for a language to be described as "object-oriented" is an open question, although most programmers agree that it is data encapsulation and polymorphism. However, the vast majority of object-oriented programming languages, including Swift, use classes and inheritance to model programs.*

Swift makes extensive use of the Objective-C runtime that is fundamental to OS X. Objective-C is built on top of the C language, a language created in the early 1970s for programming in the Unix environment on PDP minicomputers. Unlike Objective-C, C is not an object-oriented language. It has no concept of classes and no concept of data encapsulation (although both of these concepts can be mimicked to some extent). Rather than expressing programs as a collection of objects, C programmers express programs more like recipes: a step-by-step guide to performing calculations. C is also often used in systems programming because of the low-level access it gives to memory and storage devices. Both OS X and iOS are written in C, and many of their frameworks and libraries are exposed as C interfaces as well as Objective-C interfaces.

Because Objective-C is built on top of C, it is trivial to access the low-level system interfaces written in C from an Objective-C or Swift program. While many of OS X's and iOS's higher-level functionalities are written in Objective-C, and more will likely be written in Swift, some lower-level parts are only written in C. Many useful third-party libraries are also written only in C. As a Swift programmer, you are likely to encounter these C libraries at some point, so a thorough knowledge of the language is important to have in your toolbox.

OBJECTIVE-C'S ORIGINS

Objective-C traces its history back to both C and Smalltalk; it is essentially the marriage of these two languages. C provides Objective-C with its low-level programming functionality, while Smalltalk inspired the class model that allows programmers to write software with an object-oriented focus. Designed by Brad Cox and Tom Love in the early 1980s, it gained traction after being used as the primary development language for the NeXTSTEP operating system. Both the Foundation and AppKit frameworks were initially developed for NeXTSTEP, and the first web browser was written in Objective-C.

Many initially find Objective-C to be a strange combination, but it has proven effective for both OS X and NeXTSTEP developers for almost three decades, and it became the primary development language on iOS as well.

UNDERSTANDING THE IMPORTANCE OF C LANGUAGE SYNTAX

Thanks to its C lineage, there are few differences between Objective-C's and C's syntax. Most of the differences relate to Objective-C's object-oriented features, so a seasoned Objective-C or Swift programmer should have little difficulty recognizing and understanding C code. In fact, most of the differences between C and Objective-C code deal more with programming style and design, rather than syntax changes.

Defining Data with Variables and Arrays

C data types can be grouped into six categories: integral, floating-point, typedefs, enums, structs, and unions. There are also pointer and array types for each basic data type. (Pointers, structs, and unions are discussed in later sections.) Integral data types deal with integers, or whole numbers.

Integral Data Types

C defines four integral types: `char`, `short`, `int`, and `long`. Each of these may either be `signed`, meaning they can have negative values, or `unsigned`, meaning they can only have positive values. Each type also has a size, or number of bits that make up the value, although the sizes are expressed as a minimum width. `chars` are at least 8 bits wide, `shorts` and `ints` are at least 16, and `longs` are at least 64 bits. On the platforms on which OS X and iOS run, `chars` are generally 8 bits wide, `shorts` 16, and `ints` 32; `longs` may be 32 or 64, depending on whether your code is running on a 32- or 64-bit processor. However, you should not depend on these sizes always being true, and instead you should remember that a particular data type only defines a *minimum* width.

The minimum width of C's integral data types specifies the minimum range of numbers that may be contained in these variables. Unsigned types may contain values ranging from 0 to 2^n (where n is the minimum bit width of the type). Because signed types reserve one bit for the sign, they may contain values in the range $-(2^{n-1})$ to $2^{n-1}-1$.

Although integral data types may in fact be larger than the minimum width defined by C, you should not depend on them being larger, and you should treat their minimum ranges as their actual ranges.

C INTEGER WIDTHS

C is designed to be portable across many platforms. Because of its portability, it does not strictly define the bit widths of its integers, but it instead defines a minimum width and allows specific compiler implementations to use whichever size is most efficient for their target platforms. C chars represent a byte, the smallest addressable unit of a machine; almost all processors nowadays define a byte to be 8 bits wide, so chars are almost always 8 bits. Historically, C ints represent a word, the natural unit of data used by a processor. However, because 32-bit processors were very common for much of C's history, and a word on a 32-bit processor is generally 32 bits, programmers often treated ints as 32-bit data types. Even though 64-bit processors are fairly common nowadays, ints in C are still generally only 32 bits wide. Of course, this fact cannot and should not be relied upon.

Declaring integral types should be familiar:

```
char w;
short x;
int y;
long z;
```

You can also set variables to a value when declaring them:

```
char w = 'w';
short x = 1;
int y = -4200;
long z = 3000000000L;
```

Note that long values are suffixed with the letter L or l to distinguish them from integer values.

If a value is not specified when an integral variable is declared, it will have a garbage value; you should take care not to use a variable until its value has been set.

Integral types may also take the type modifier signed or unsigned. If unspecified, shorts, ints, and longs are always signed. Whether a char is signed or unsigned by default is platform-dependent, but generally they are unsigned by default.

```
signed char w = -1;
unsigned short x = 1;
unsigned int y = 4200;
unsigned long z = 3000000000L;
```

As a special case, you can simply use the type unsigned to declare an unsigned int:

```
unsigned y = 4200;
```

Perhaps surprisingly, C allows you to set an unsigned integral type to a negative value:

```
unsigned int y = -1;
```

However, the variable y actually contains the highest possible value for ints (4294967295 on most OS X platforms, which is outside of the minimum range of an int, but is the maximum *actual* possible value for ints on most platforms on which OS X runs). Why is this the case? In C, all arithmetic operations on unsigned integral types are defined according to module arithmetic modulo 2^n. Adding one to the highest possible integer value wraps that value around to 0; similarly, subtracting 1 from the lowest possible integer value (0) wraps around to the highest possible integer value. The same is not true of signed integral types: In C, overflow and underflow is undefined for signed types, and you should not rely on any platform-specific behavior.

Floating-Point Data Types

Floating-point values are those that contain a fractional component, and are commonly referred to as "decimal" values. Just as the integral types deal with integers, the floating-point data types deal with the real numbers. C defines two floating-point data types: the `float` and the `double`. C also allows a third type, the `long double`, which, as the name suggests, can hold larger values than the `double`. As with the integral types, the sizes of each data type are not strictly defined; C programmers can only assume that the values that can fit into a `float` are a subset of the values that can fit into a `double`, which in turn are a subset of the values that can fit into a `long double`. However, on most platforms you will encounter as an Objective-C programmer, `float`s are 32 bits wide, `double`s are 64 bits wide, and `long double`s are 128 bits wide.

> **NOTE** *C does not even define the exact bit structure of floating-point numbers, nor how operations may be performed on them, although today almost all C implementations use the specification defined by IEEE 754, the IEEE Standard for Floating-Point Arithmetic.*

It is important to note that C's floating-point data types are imprecise. Some real numbers simply cannot be expressed as floating-point values. Floating-point data types are finite in size, but there are infinite real numbers, so it should be fairly obvious that many (in fact, an infinite number of them) cannot be expressed as floating-point values in C. Furthermore, special techniques must be used when dealing with floating-point values, even when using simple operations such as addition and subtraction.

> **NOTE** *The "special techniques" that should be used when dealing with floating-point values are outside the scope of this chapter, and much has been written about them elsewhere. A classic article by David Goldberg, "What Every Programmer Should Know About Floating-Point Arithmetic," discusses these issues in great detail. Goldberg's article is available online at* `http://docs` `.oracle.com/cd/E19957-01/806-3568/ncg_goldberg.html`.

Doubles, `float`s, and `long double`s are declared similarly to integral types:

```
float f;
double d;
long double ld;
```

As with integers, you may assign values to them when they are declared:

```
float f = 1.24F;
double d = -99.41;
long double ld = -987.3L;
```

Note that values are suffixed with F or f to designate them floats, and with L or l to designate them long doubles.

The same initialization rules for integral types apply to floating-point types: If their values are not initialized at declaration, they will contain a garbage value, and you should not use them until they are set to a valid value.

Arrays

C also supports arrays for each of its data types. An array is a sequence of values that you can index by number. They are analogous to Swift's array type, although C's arrays, of course, are not object-oriented; they are much simpler containers for a sequence of data in memory. An array type exists for all of the basic data types, so you can have an array of ints, floats, or even structs (structs are discussed in the next section).

Declaring an array is fairly straightforward:

```
int a[32];
```

An array of 32 integers has been declared with the name a. As with scalar types (integers and floating-point values), you should not use any elements of the array until it has been initialized. You can initialize an array by designating the value of each element in curly braces:

```
int a[4] = {1, 2, 3, 4};
```

Obviously this is fairly unwieldy for large arrays, so you can also loop through the array in order to initialize it:

```
int a[32];
for (int i = 0; i < 32; i++) {
    a[i] = i * 2;
}
```

As you can see, you access an individual element of an array by specifying its index (as an integer). Take a look at the line of code that initializes an element of the array:

```
a[i] = i * 2;
```

This line of code simply says to put the value i * 2 in the array a at index i. Like NSArray, C arrays are 0-indexed, meaning that the first element is referred to with the integer 0.

> **NOTE** *Looping through the individual elements of an array is not necessary the fastest way to initialize an array. There are various functions in the C standard library, such as* memset(), *that can do the job faster. However, a for loop is a simple way to initialize an array.*

One crucial difference between C arrays and object-oriented constructs like Swift's array or Cocoa's NSArray is that C arrays do not store any information about their size. As a result, it is entirely possible to write data into memory beyond the end of the array:

```
int a[4];
for (int i = 0; i < 10; i++) {
    a[i] = i * 2;
}
```

As you can imagine, writing outside the bounds of an array is undefined behavior, and you should ensure that you only write data within the bounds of the memory allocated for the array. Writing beyond the bounds of the array can corrupt memory or cause a program crash. For example, if you compile and run the code in Listing A-1, you will see 5 printed to the screen, rather than the value of 10 as expected, because the for loop wrote beyond the bounds of a, into the memory region of x.

LISTING A-1: overflow.c

```c
#include <stdio.h>

int main (int argc, char const *argv[])
{
    int x = 10;
    int a[5];
    for (int i = 0; i < 6; i++) {
        a[i] = i;
    }
    printf("%d\n", x);
    return 0;
}
```

Typedefs

Because type annotations can often be unwieldy, C offers a solution: *type definitions*. Type definitions are also referred to as *typedefs* for short. Typedefs are not an independent type in and of themselves, but instead they offer a way to alias a type to another label. They are often referred to in C literature as *storage classes*. Typedef declarations follow the format typedef <type> <alias>.

Consider a case in which you are doing calculations with various length units. It may be easier to work with type names such as centimeters and inches, rather than int and double. You could use a typedef to declare aliases for these types:

```
typedef int centimeter;
typedef double inch;
```

Then, later in your code, you could declare variables using centimeter and inch:

```
centimeter width = 25.0;
inch height = 12;
```

The previous code declares two variables, width and height. width is actually a double and height is actually an int, but the type definitions make it clearer to know what sort of data you're actually working with.

You often use type definitions when declaring more complicated data structures, type structs, and unions (both of which you learn about in later sections of this chapter).

Enums

In C, you use enums to group a set of constant values together. They allow you to associate a constant value with a name. While they may look like a separate type, they are really just integers. Enums are simply declared as a list of constant names in braces:

```
enum { YEAR, MONTH, DAY };
```

You can then reference them in any case you would use a number—for example, when initializing variables:

```
int calendar_unit = YEAR;
```

Like structs, you can use enums in conjunction with typedefs to create a type alias, making the intent of your code more clear:

```
typedef enum { YEAR, MONTH, DAY } CalendarUnit;
CalendarUnit calendar_unit = YEAR;
```

The actual numerical values of each enum constant are set automatically by the compiler. Typically, you don't have to know the numerical values and can use the constant names instead; however, you can also set the numerical values:

```
enum { YEAR = 10, MONTH, DAY };
```

Here, YEAR has the value 10. Succeeding enum constants, if not explicitly given a value, will increase by 1; MONTH will equal 11, and DAY will equal 12.

Performing Calculations with Operators

C has a number of operators for working with and performing calculations on values and variables. Having used Swift, you should be familiar with all of them, as they are the same across both languages.

Arithmetic Operators

C has the typical arithmetic operators you'd expect coming from Swift or Objective-C. +, -, *, and / all perform the same operations as they do in Swift: addition, subtraction, multiplication, and division, respectively. These operations are valid for both integral and floating-point values. They have identical precedence in C as they do in Swift, so multiplication and division are applied before addition and subtraction. For example, in the following code, x has the value 10 because multiplication is performed first:

```
int x = 2 + 4 * 2;
```

As in Swift, you use parentheses to group arithmetic operations. In the following code, addition will be performed before multiplication, resulting in x having the value 12:

```
int x = (2 + 4) * 2;
```

C also has two additional operators, both of which are found in Swift as well: ++ and --. ++ increments a value by one, and -- decrements a value by one. In the following code, the values 11 and 9 are printed to the screen:

```
int x = 10;
int y = 10;
```

```
x++;
y--;
printf("%d\n", x);
printf("%d\n", y);
```

These operators appear in two forms: post-increment/decrement and pre-increment/decrement. In the post- form (appearing in the previous example), the value of the variable is calculated *before* the increment or decrement operation is performed; in the pre- form, the value is calculated *after* the operation. This only has ramifications when both performing the operation and evaluating its value. In Listing A-2, x holds the value 11, x2 holds the value 10 (because x is evaluated *before* it was incremented), and y and y2 both hold the value 21 (because y is evaluated *after* it was incremented).

LISTING A-2: increment.c

```c
#include <stdio.h>

int main (int argc, char const *argv[])
{
    int x = 10;
    int y = 20;
    int x2 = x++;
    int y2 = ++y;
    printf("%d\n", x);
    printf("%d\n", x2);
    printf("%d\n", y);
    printf("%d\n", y2);
    return 0;
}
```

Because it is fairly common to set a variable to a new value after evaluating an expression, C also has operators that both perform an arithmetic operation on a variable and set that variable to the result of the expression. These operators are +=, -=, *=, and /=, and are combinations of assignment with the equivalent arithmetic operator. For example, to multiply x by 2 and set x to the result, you can use this shorthand:

```c
int x = 10;
x *= 2;
```

x will now hold the value 20.

C also has a modulus operator, %, which produces the remainder from a division operation. For example, the result of the expression

```c
int rem = 22 % 10;
```

is 10, because 10 divides into 22 twice, with a remainder of 2. Like the other arithmetic operators, there is also an operator that combines the modulus with assignment:

```c
int rem = 22;
rem %= 10;
```

Finally, both - and + can operate on a single variable. When used in this fashion, they are referred to as *unary operators* or are described as being used in a *unary context*. A unary operator is an operator that takes only a single operand. When used in a unary context, - flips the sign of a value, so when you apply it to a positive value, - negates it. In the following code, x ultimately holds the value -10:

```
int x = 10;
x = -x;
```

As you would expect, if applied to a value that is already negative, - makes the value positive. In the following code, x holds the value 10:

```
int x = -10;
x = -x;
```

You can also use the + operator in a unary context, but it essentially does nothing—it exists primarily for symmetry with unary -.

Logical Operators

C has a number of operators for working with values in a Boolean context (cases in which a value is treated as true or false). These operators are ||, &&, and !, and correspond to the logical OR, AND, and NOT operations. As the name suggests, || evaluates to true if one or both operands are true, && evaluates to true if both operands are true, and ! makes a true operand false and a false operand true. (! is a unary operator.) These are most often used in if statements, or as the conditional expression in while, do while, and for loops. Listing A-3 shows an example that uses logical operators in if statements.

LISTING A-3: boolean.c

```c
#include <stdio.h>

int main (int argc, char const *argv[])
{
    int a = 0;
    int b = 1;

    if (a && b) {
        printf("a and b are both true\n");
    }

    if (a || b) {
        printf("one of a or b is true\n");
    }

    if (!a) {
        printf("a is false\n");
    }

    if (!b) {
        printf("b is false\n");
    }

    return 0;
}
```

If you compile and run the code in Listing A-3, you will see the following printed to the screen:

```
one of a or b is true
a is false
```

TRUTHINESS AND FALSINESS IN C

Unlike many programming languages such as Swift, C does not have distinct values that represent "true" and "false." Rather, expressions that evaluate to 0 are false, and all other values are true. For example, 0, '\0', and NULL are all false; 1, -10, and 'c' are all true.

The same concept applies to Objective-C, although Objective-C introduces a new type, BOOL, to explicitly denote variables that should be treated as Boolean values. Variables of type BOOL generally only take the values YES and NO. However, a BOOL is really just a signed char, and YES and NO are really just 1 and 0, respectively. However, it is considered good style to use variables of type BOOL and the values YES and NO when working with Boolean variables in Objective-C.

Swift, of course, has its own Boolean data type. To ensure the proper use of Boolean values, Swift requires that any expression used in an if statement evaluates to a Boolean type (either true or false).

C99 (the version of C standardized in 1999, and the most common version of C used in Objective-C projects) introduced its own Boolean type, _Bool, as well as the explicit values true and false. However, _Bool is really just an int, and true and false are just 1 and 0, respectively.

While you most commonly use these operators in if statements and loops, you can use them in any expression, even initialization. For example, in the code that follows, z has the value 1 (because both x and y evaluate to true):

```
int x = 10;
int y = 5;
int z = x && y;
```

This demonstrates another facet of logical operators in C: They evaluate to 1 if true, and 0 if false. When stored in a variable, that variable holds one of those values after the expression is evaluated.

C also features an operator, ?:, that takes three operands: a conditional statement, a value to yield if that conditional statement is true, and a value to yield if that conditional statement is false. This statement is often referred to simply as the *ternary operator* because it is the only C operator that takes three operands. Essentially, it combines an if/else statement into a single expression. For example, in the expression

```
int n = 10;
int x = n > 10 ? 1 : 0;
```

x will have the value 1 after the expression is evaluated.

Relational Operators

C has a number of operators for comparing two values, returning 1 if the comparison evaluates to true and 0 if the comparison evaluates to false (just as with the logical operators discussed in the previous section). Two of them test for equality: == and !=. == returns true if two values are equal to each other, and != returns true if two values are not equal to each other. Like logical operators, you most often use them in if statements or loop expressions, but you can use them in other expressions as well, such as in variable initializations.

C also has a set of operators to determine whether one value is greater than or less than another value. These operators are <, >, <=, and >=, and correspond to less than, greater than, less than or equal to, and greater than or equal to, respectively. As with the logical and equality operators, you can use them in any expression: Loops and variable initializers are the most common places you'll find them.

Bitwise Operators

The C operators that are perhaps most foreign to programmers (and probably the least commonly used, although no less important than the others) are the bitwise operators. Although they look similar to the logical operators (&& and ||), they fulfill a completely different purpose. While the logical operators work on the more abstract notions of truth and falsehood, the bitwise operators combine the actual bit patterns of values in a more concrete definition of true and false.

First, consider what is meant by a "bit pattern." Each data type in C, whether it is an int, double, or anything else, is really just a pattern of bits. Consider a variable of type char, which is 8 bits (on the platforms on which OS X and iOS run). While at a high level it may hold a value of 34, in memory it is really just the bit pattern 00100000. Because data is really just a pattern of bits, you can perform operations on the bits themselves. C provides several operators for doing so.

The building blocks of these "bitwise" operations are & (bitwise AND), | (bitwise OR), ^ (bitwise XOR), and ~ (bitwise NOT). Each takes two operands and applies the related logical operation to the bit patterns of each operand, resulting in a new value corresponding to the calculated bit pattern.

The & operator compares two values bit-by-bit, producing a new bit pattern in which a given bit position is set to 1 if both operands also had a 1 in that position, and 0 if otherwise. Let's say you supplied & with two values, 19 and 13. Their bit patterns would look like the following:

```
00010011 = 19
00001101 = 13
```

Assume you apply the & operator to them:

```
  00010011 = 19
& 00001101 = 13
  ------------
  00000001 =  1
```

The result would be 1, because 19 and 13 only share a 1 in the first bit position; all other positions differ between the two.

The | operator works similarly, but it produces a 1 in a given position if either (or both) operands have a 1 in that position, and 0 if neither of them do. Again, consider the result of the | operation on 19 and 13:

```
  00010011 = 19
| 00001101 = 13
  -------------
  00011111 = 31
```

In this case, | produces the result 31 because at least one operand has a 1 in the first 5 bit positions.

The ^ operator also takes two operands but produces a 1 in a given position if *only one* of the operands also has a 1 in that position; if both or neither do, it produces a 0. Once again, consider the result of the ^ operation on 19 and 13:

```
  00010011 = 19
^ 00001101 = 13
  -------------
  00011110 = 30
```

In this case, ^ produces 30.

Unlike the previous three operators, ~ is a unary operator, so it only works on one operand. It simply flips the bits in each position: A 1 becomes a 0 and a 0 becomes a 1. Consider the result of ~ on 19:

```
 00010011 = 19
~00010011 = 11101100 = 236
```

The result of ~19 evaluates to 236.

As with arithmetic operators, C provides counterparts for the bitwise operators that do the operation and assignment in one step: &=, |=, and ^=.

Bitshift Operators

C also includes a two operators for shifting a data type's underlying bit pattern: <<, the left-shift operator, and >>, the right-shift operator. Both these operators shift a variable's bit pattern left or right by a given number of places. Consider again the bit pattern for the value 19:

```
00010011 = 19
```

Let's say you shift 19 left by 2 places:

```
int x = 19 << 2;
```

All the bits move left by 2 places (zeroes are filled in from the left), resulting in this bit pattern:

```
01001100 = 76
```

Similarly, you can shift 19 right by 3 places:

```
int x = 19 >> 3;
```

Again, zeroes are used to fill the now-missing places on the right, resulting in this bit pattern:

```
00000010 = 2;
```

There are many reasons you may find the bitshift operators useful, but in C programming, they are often used in conjunction with the bitwise operators (discussed in the previous section) to store *flags* in a single variable. In these cases, they are most often used with the bitshift operators. For example, the NSAttributedString header file defines the following enum:

```
typedef enum {
    NSAttributedStringEnumerationReverse = (1UL << 1),
    NSAttributedStringEnumerationLongestEffectiveRangeNotRequired = (1UL << 20)
} NSAttributedStringEnumerationOptions;
```

These flags are composable, meaning that you can combine them. To check if a flag is set, you can then use the & operator. For example, you could declare a variable like the following:

```
NSAttributedStringEnumerationOptions options =
    NSAttributedStringEnumerationReverse;
```

and then check to see if it is set:

```
if ((options & NSAttributedStringEnumerationReverse) ==
    NSAttributedStringEnumerationReverse) {
    NSLog(@"reverse option is selected");
}
```

Referencing Data with Pointers

Pointers are one of the most confusing and misunderstood aspects of C programming, but as an Objective-C programmer, you should already be familiar with them. While initially they can be a bit difficult to comprehend, a basic understand of C's memory model gives great insight to the nature of pointers in the language.

Consider what a variable is: a region of memory that holds a variable. Much like a house address, the computer references this region of memory with a number (specifically, a positive integer). Often times, you do not need to know the actual memory location of a variable; the compiler will take care of those specifics for you. However, sometimes it can be useful to have a variable that points to another variable in memory. You can do that with two operators: * and & (not to be confused with the same operators described in previous sections).

First, to declare that a variable is a pointer, you use the type name followed by an asterisk:

```
int *ptr;
```

Here, ptr is a *pointer to an* int, not an int. You can then set it to the address of another variable by prefixing that variable name with &:

```
int actual_value = 10;
int *ptr = &actual_value;
```

You can read the & operator as "address of."

It is important to note that the value of ptr is a memory address. If you print it (use the %p formatter to printf), you can see the address of the variable it is pointing to:

```
printf("%p\n", ptr);
```

In pointer contexts, the * operator is overloaded; it is also used to get the *value* (rather than the address) to which a pointer points.

```
int actual_value = 10;
int *ptr = &actual_value;
int another_actual_value = *ptr;
```

This is called *dereferencing* the pointer.

It's also important to note that if you change the value of the variable referenced by a pointer, that pointer will dereference to the new value:

```
int actual_pointer = 10;
int *ptr = &actual_value;
printf("%d\n", *ptr);
actual_pointer = 12;
printf("%d\n" *ptr);
```

If you run this code, you will see the following printed to the screen:

```
10
12
```

Organizing Data with Structs

While C does not offer classes, it does offer two data types that allow programmers to group several pieces of data. C's basic type for such grouping is a struct. A struct is a collection of variables that can be passed around as a single entity. It may contain integers, floating-point variables, or even other structs (except for instances of themselves, although structs may contain *pointers* to instances of themselves).

Unlike integral and floating-point types, you must define the structure of a struct. There are two ways to declare the structure. The simplest is when declaring a variable:

```
struct { int x; int y; } point;
```

However, this is generally not useful, as code outside the function in which the variable is declared will not know the structure of the variable. Instead, the structure is often defined first, outside of a function, so that other code can make use of it. These definitions take a type name after the struct keyword. When declaring values, you can use these type names to reference the structure.

```
struct graph_point { int x; int y; };
struct graph_point point;
```

Generalizing Data with Unions

Like structs, unions also group variables together. They are declared similarly to structs:

```
union { int i; double d; } number;
```

Like structs, you can declare the structure of a union with a type name, which you can then use to later reference the union:

```
union number_t { int x; double d; };
union number_t num;
```

Unlike a struct, the union variable only represents *one* of the variables of which it is composed. In the previous example, num can be an int *or* a double, but not both. Unlike structs, a union is a single value—it just represents a variable that may be one of multiple *types*. You initialize a union variable by setting one of its fields to a value:

```
union number_t num;
num.d = 12.1;
```

You must only access the field that was last set in a union—accessing another field is undefined behavior in C. For example, the following code does *not* print 10 to the screen:

```
union number_t num;
num.i = 10;
printf("%.2f\n", num.d);
```

If a union can only contain one value, how are they useful? Unions are useful because they allow a single variable to be multiple types. For example, if you want to have an array of both ints and doubles, you may find that a union is handy.

Referencing Functions with Function Pointers

Just as you can think of variables such as ints and floats as labels for regions of memory holding a value, you can think of functions as labels for regions of memory holding executable code. Just as you can use pointers to reference numerical values in memory, you can use pointers to reference a function's executable block of code.

There are two ways to create a pointer to a function in C. In Listing A-4, a function called multiply is declared. In the program's main function, two variables are declared, f and g, that refer to this function; each uses a different way to reference the function. The initialization of f uses the syntax &multiply. As with data pointers, the & operator gets the address of the function. The initialization of g, on the other hand, simply references the function by name (without parentheses). These two initializations are identical; the latter is simply some syntactic sugar provided by C.

Once you have a pointer to the function, you can call it as though it *is* a function, by passing parameters in parentheses after the pointer's name. In effect, the pointer is just another name for the function.

LISTING A-4: fnptr.c

```c
#include <stdio.h>

int multiply(int x, int y)
{
    return x * y;
}

int main (int argc, char const *argv[])
{
    int (*f)(int, int) = &multiply;
    int (*g)(int, int) = multiply;

    int f_result = f(2, 5);
    int g_result = g(25, 4);

    printf("%d\n", f_result);
    printf("%d\n", g_result);

    return 0;
}
```

The syntax may look a little odd, and it is worth understanding how to describe the *type* of a C function. Like C's other data types, functions also have a type. Consider the `multiply` function:

```
int multiply(int x, int y)
{
    return x * y;
}
```

In simple English, its type is "a function that takes two `int`s as arguments, and returns an `int`." Therefore, its function pointer is "a pointer to a function that takes two `int`s as parameters, and returns an `int`." Expressed in C, its type is `int (*)(int, int)`. Essentially, you take the name of the function, replace it with `(*)` (to denote that it's a pointer), and then add in the parameter types and return type.

Of course, the pointer needs a name so you can refer to it later, so you put the variable name alongside the `*`, making the full type plus variable name `int (*f)(int, int)`.

You can think of function pointers as the C counterparts of Objective-C selectors. They are also conceptually similar to Swift's function data types, in the sense that they allow functions to be passed to other functions as parameters. They are often used as callback functions to implement specific behavior for a more general function or used as fields in a `struct` to loosely mimic methods in an object-oriented style. Core Foundation, a low-level framework on OS X and iOS that is implemented in C, often makes use of C function pointers for one of these two reasons.

Core Foundation provides analogous data types for the `NSArray`, `NSSet`, and `NSDictionary` classes found in the Foundation framework. These data types are `CFArray`, `CFSet`, and `CFDictionary`, respectively. These Core Foundation data types make extensive use of callback functions. For example, the function that creates a new `CFArray`, the Core Foundation equivalent of `NSArray`, has the following signature:

```
CFArrayRef CFArrayCreate(
    CFAllocatorRef allocator,
    const void **values,
    CFIndex numValues,
    const CFArrayCallBacks *callBacks;
);
```

Note the last parameter, `callBacks`. `callBacks` has the type `CFArrayBallBacks *`, which is a pointer to a struct `CFArrayCallBacks` that is defined as the following:

```
struct CFArrayCallBacks {
    CFIndex version;
    CFArrayRetainCallBack retain;
    CFArrayReleaseCallBack release;
    CFArrayCopyDescriptionCallBack copyDescription;
    CFArrayEqualCallBack;
}
```

An instance of a struct `CFArrayCallBack` is simply a set of function pointers that customize how the `CFArray` retains and releases items placed in the array, as well as telling the `CFArray` how to create a descriptive string for an item (akin to `-[NSObject description]`) and how to determine the equality of two items. `CFArray` is meant to be a general-purpose structure, but because C structures are not nearly as flexible as Swift or Objective-C classes, you can tell your `CFArray` instance exactly how to deal with items placed into it. In essence, it makes `CFArray` nearly as flexible and powerful as its `NSArray` counterpart, but in C rather than Objective-C.

For example, take a look at the first entry in the struct, `retain`, which has the type `CFArrayRetainCallBack`. A `CFArrayRetainCallBack` is simply a typedef for a variable of type `const void *(*)(CFAllocatorRef, const void *)`. That should look familiar—in simpler terms, it is a function pointer, specifically a pointer to a function that takes a `CFAllocatorRef` and `const void` pointer as parameters, and returns a `void pointer`. The `retain` parameter need only be a matching function that you have declared, which would look something like this:

```
const void *MyCallBack(CFAllocatorRef allocator, const void *value);
```

You could then use that function in a struct, `CFArrayCallBack`:

```
struct CFArrayCallBack callBack = /* Create the structure */;
callBack.retain = MyCallBack;
```

Because C by its nature is less flexible than both Swift and Objective-C, Core Foundation makes extensive use of callback functions in order to allow you to customize the behavior of its structures. You can think of it as subclassing in C. Unfortunately, it's not as simple as in Objective-C, but it's nearly as powerful.

> **NOTE** *Of course, C programming is a broad topic with a rich history, and this appendix only scratched the surface. While it should be enough to help you with your Objective-C programming, there are many more thorough resources out there that will teach you how to become an advanced C programmer, if that interests you. In particular, you may be interested in reading* The C Programming Language *by Brian Kernighan and Dennis Ritchie, or* C: A Reference Manual *by Samuel P. Harbison III and Guy L. Steele, for more in-depth coverage of C programming.*

INDEX

INDEX